SPIRITUALITY AND EMPTINESS

The Dynamics of Spiritual Life in Buddhism and Christianity

DONALD W. MITCHELL

PAULIST PRESS
New York/Mahwah, N.J.

Note on Diacritical Marks

We have chosen, along with many other publishers, not to insert diacritical marks. The Sanskrit, Chinese and Japanese words in this book are commonly known to those who are familiar with these languages, and the diacritical marks are not helpful to those who are not familiar with these languages.

Sections of Chapter Four appeared in an essay by Donald W. Mitchell in: Taitetsu Onno and James W. Heisig, eds., *The Religious Philosophy of Tanabe Hajime: The Metanoetical Imperative.* Berkeley: Asian Humanities Press, 1990.

Library of Congress Cataloging-in-Publication Data

Mitchell, Donald W. (Donald William), 1943-
    Spirituality and emptiness: the dynamics of spiritual life in Buddhism and Christianity/ Donald W. Mitchell.
        p. cm.
    Includes bibliographical references.
    ISBN 0-8091-3266-4
    1. Spiritual life. 2. Spiritual life (Buddhism) 3. Incarnation. 4. Christianity and other religions—Buddhism. 5. Buddhism—Relations—Christianity. I. Title.
BV4509.5.M583   1991
248—dc20   91-23663
                                                                          CIP

Published by Paulist Press
997 Macarthur Boulevard
Mahwah, New Jersey 07430

Printed and bound in the
United States of America

Table of Contents

For my wife, Ann

Foreword

When I first read *The Seven Storey Mountain,* I was too young to realize how important was Thomas Merton's interest in Eastern religions. Merton's later writings fleshed out that interest and reaffirmed his desire to seek wisdom in the East. That the monk from Gethsemani in Kentucky died in the Far East is symbolism that would not have been lost on him. Merton prepared many for the call to ecumenism and interfaith dialogue issued by Vatican II. For me the next step on this journey was an invitation by Dr. Egon Gerdes to participate in a Protestant–Catholic dialogue that lasted a decade but which has profoundly affected my vision of spirituality and has convinced me that Catholic spirituality must be in dialogue with other traditions if it is to escape insularity. Work on the Ecumenical and Interfaith Commission of the archdiocese of Milwaukee at the request of Sister Maureen Hopkins and under the leadership of Archbishop Rembert Weakland made it possible for me to be involved in ecumenism and interfaith dialogue at the grassroots. Dialogues must flourish at this level if they are to be anything more than mere fancy talk among theorists.

Now Professor Mitchell's *Spirituality and Emptiness* brings the initiation to dialogical religion, inspired by Merton many years ago, full circle. More than ever this book demonstrates the crucial importance of interreligious and intercultural dialogue. Christian spirituality is doomed to parochialism unless it has the daring to see the goodness, truth and beauty of the spiritualities of world religions. *Spirituality and Emptiness* is everything that one expects of this philosopher of religion with uncommon intellectual and religious integrity. Don Mitchell has studied the archetypal theme of emptiness from the perspectives of deeply held commitments inside the Buddhist and Christian traditions. His knowledge and respect for these traditions provide sure guidance to a reader moving back and forth with him in a dialectical effort to bring Buddhist and Christian spiritualities into creative tension over the theme of emptiness. The excursion led by Don Mitchell into unknown spheres of Buddhism helps one to understand and value in a new way Buddhist spirituality and sends one back to Christian spirituality with a renewed sense of the latter's riches. A Buddhist reading these pages will, I am sure, have a like experience. Don Mitchell does in this book what John S. Dunne, C.S.C. describes as passing over and coming back, but Professor Mitchell's lived experience in these two traditions enables him to pass over from both sides, a rare asset in one who writes about interreligious dialogue. The passing over into Buddhism awakens delight at the beauty and integrity of religious traditions that are seen clearly with the help of this able mentor; the passing back to Christianity adds freshness to teaching and practice that have been too familiar to have been fully appreciated. Once again I am certain that the same will be true for the Buddhist sojourner in this book.

The exploration of emptiness is, indeed, a daunting challenge that has been too little engaged in by the Christian tradition. Have Christians not all too often rushed to fill in every emptiness? Do they not still avoid the advice of Simone Weil who wanted readers to let the void be the void. Have Christians not allowed the virtue of humility to become a caricature of truthfulness? And has not the beautiful hymn of Philippians that through the years has been seen as singing of the self-emptying of Christ too often been neglected for a less demanding view of the Christian redeemer? Don Mitchell's book does not let the Christian off so easily. I would not be surprised to discover that he makes similar demands on a Buddhist. With Don Mitchell as a guide one hears the call to look again at the meaning of the kenotic themes of religious experience. He even offers the reader an exploration of neglected Christian themes such as creation as the kenosis of the Father and the kenosis of the Holy Spirit.

Finally, every authentic spirituality must, if human experience is not to be ignored, seek meaning in the emptying of the human person and the human community that occurs through suffering. This book, in its movement between the Buddhist and Christian experience, challenges one to look into the emptiness where differing traditions meet. There Buddhism offers much wisdom for unlocking Christian treasures long held hostage by timidity. However, gurus and spiritual directors are needed when one faces the abyss with its uncharted ways. One is well served by the even-handed guidance of Don Mitchell who takes one into an emptiness where there is an absence of familiar landmarks. This journey with Professor Mitchell is an intellectual as well as a religious journey, elements that ensure a sound spirituality much enlarged by dialogue.

No spiritual journey is without a cultural context since all experience of the divine is human and occurs at a particular time and place. The author not only acquaints one with a philosophy of Buddhist Emptiness and a theology of Christian kenosis, he also grounds one in the particular experiences of persons who have lived the ways about which he writes. In this book I found many parallels to the emptiness of John of the Cross, some of which Professor Mitchell specifically mentions. He is helped also by the writings of John of the Cross' mentor Teresa of Avila. For the Christian not immersed in the Buddhist-Christian dialogue the book is a superb introduction to the many inspiring members of the Kyoto school. Helpful too is a grounding in Shin'ichi Hisamatsu who articulates a communal dimension of kenotic Buddhist philosophy. In Buddhism as in Christianity there is a critical need in the contemporary world for a spirituality that embraces societal transformation. In the West individualism has so invaded every facet of modern life that it is difficult to study spirituality without unconsciously reading into it an individualistic perspective. Individualism is now a habit of the heart that calls for exorcism. Religious traditions everywhere are endangered by the entrenchment in the modern world of pernicious individualism.

In his exploration of a communal kenotic Christian spirituality, Don Mitchell shares with his readers a vignette of Chiara Lubich, the founder and spiritual leader of the Focolare movement. Her doctrine of Jesus forsaken centers one on Jesus of Gethsemani and the cross, paradigmatic experiences that shape Christian discipleship. Don Mitchell knows that a spirituality that is not lived is a hollow and useless shell. Chiara Lubich has lived and taught a corporate spirituality rooted in the kenotic experience of Jesus, a spirituality which she and her followers have expressed in their service of others.

As the twentieth century winds down, one may speculate that there has never been another era in which emptiness has been so pervasive. How shall the emptiness of alienation and of the terrible suffering of this century be redeemed or seen as anything but useless destruction? Where shall we find an emptiness that ennobles rather than destroys, that leads to human fulfillment, not degradation? With a prose that is insightful, clear and sparing, with a heart committed to the dialogue about which he writes, Don Mitchell accompanies his readers on a rewarding exploration of the emptiness that shapes a compassionate heart. Women of compassion, Maya, mother of Gautama Buddha, and Mary, the mother of Jesus, complete this book's sojourn into emptiness, where the emptiness is revealed as enabling Buddhist true life and the resurrected life of the Christian. Maya and Mary open up an horizon from which to venerate the life-giving womb of Buddha and the creative womb in the heart of the God of Abraham, Isaac, Jacob and Jesus.

As I have pondered the wisdom of this exploration of two diverse traditions, I have also been listening to the poetry of John of the Cross. What especially resonated with me as I did so were lines from John's poem *The Spiritual Canticle,* where the absence of God in the life of the God-seeker is simply but starkly stated: "I went out calling you and you were gone." Don Mitchell's book confronts one with a sobering and at the same time comforting interreligious journey to spiritual maturity where emptiness can be embraced as John of the Cross embraced *nada.*

Another friend for the journey during these days of reflection on Don Mitchell's message has been the Carmelite poet Jessica Powers. Her poem "If You Have Nothing," only this morning, spoke words of encouragement against the all too human temptation to eschew the gift of emptiness. I conclude this foreword with the final lines of Jessica Powers' poem where she invites one to celebrate emptiness.

If you have nothing, gather back your sigh,
and with your hands held high, your heart held high,
lift up your emptiness.

Keith J. Egan
Saint Mary's College
Notre Dame, Indiana

Preface

The contemporary world is rapidly shrinking due to the remarkable advancement of technology. East and West are now meeting and exchanging values at all levels of life—in politics, economics, and culture. This, however, does not mean that the world is now being united. For, while mutual understanding is going on in some places, the integration of the world makes the multiplicity of human societies and ideologies more conspicuous, causing unprecedented tensions and antagonisms in all areas of life. The coming global age is producing dissensions as well as a search for a greater unity.

The human societies which, until the present time, have maintained their own cultural and intellectual patterns, are today coming together into one great rushing stream of world history in waves beating and dashing the one against the other. The synchronization of global space by scientific technology forces all people to play their parts on a common stage of world history, and hopefully, to come to some awareness of their roles in the drama. Nevertheless, only after divisions and oppositions have been overcome and a new spiritual horizon for humanity has been opened up shall we have a truly united destiny.

A clear self-consciousness of *one world history* will not be produced simply by forces working from without, but will be the work of the innermost human spirituality. Today, however, we know very little about the inner meaning of spiritual and religious traditions not our own. The discovery of new spiritual foundations upon which "world culture" and "world history" may be built is contingent upon a dialogue between world religions. Without deep mutual understanding among world religions a harmonious global society can never be established. The ongoing dialogue between Buddhism and Christianity is taking place with this need as its background.

Strictly speaking, however, mutual understanding between religions, although always necessary, is not sufficient. In the case of "mutual

ix

understanding," the participating religions assume that their currently established forms will be understood as such by others. However, to cope with the present human predicament every world religion, such as Buddhism and Christianity, must try to reveal the greatest possible depths of its spirituality by breaking through its conventional forms and try to transform itself through mutual learning. Only in this way can we come to a creative mutual understanding. I do not mean by this to say that Buddhism and Christianity should aim at a syncretism. Instead, I mean that through such a serious dialogue both Buddhism and Christianity should purify and deepen themselves respectively; and yet, in this way, come to realize a deeper common ground.

During the past few decades dialogue between Buddhism and Christianity has been increasingly active in the United States, Europe, Japan, Sri Lanka and other Asian countries. But, in most cases dialogue has been theologically oriented, not spiritually oriented. In order to have a vital and creative dialogue and to open up a new spiritual horizon for one united world to come, both Buddhism and Christianity must give more serious attention to their spiritualities and their relation to theology. This book does precisely that in response to this urgent need of our contemporary human situation.

Donald Mitchell attempts to broaden and deepen the current Buddhist-Christian dialogue in order to enrich interreligious and intercultural understanding. In this regard Mitchell, on the Buddhist side, brings in the religious thought of the Kyoto School, focusing on the comparison of Buddhist Emptiness to the kenosis of God. And, on the Christian side, he pays much attention to the tradition of Christian spirituality in order to clarify the real meaning of the kenosis of God and to broaden the Christian response to the Kyoto School.

In this work Mitchell addresses the following two issues. First is the meaning of "kenosis" in Christian spirituality and its relation to Buddhist Emptiness. What is the kenosis of God and how is kenosis lived in Christian spiritual life? How does kenotic Christian spirituality relate to kenotic forms of Buddhist spirituality as discerned in the thought of the Kyoto School?

The second issue pertains to the future of kenotic spirituality in Buddhism and Christianity. What new directions can we discern in Buddhist spirituality, as represented by the Kyoto School, and in Christian spirituality? What is the place of kenosis in these new forms of Buddhist and Christian spirituality? It is especially worthwhile to note that in this regard Mitchell stresses that spirituality today must seek, not only the personal transformation of the individual, but also the social transformation of humankind. Thus he discusses throughout the book the relation, in both Buddhist and Christian spirituality, between personal and social transformation, and between individual and communal forms of spiritual life.

In this form of Buddhist-Christian dialogue attempted by Mitchell he discusses with great clarity the religious thought of a large number of the members of the Kyoto School including not only Zen-oriented members, such as Nishida, Nishitani, Ueda and Abe, but also Pure Land-oriented members, such as Tanabe, Takeuchi and Hase. He also explores the unique thought of Hisamatsu and Tokiwa from the field of Christian spirituality. Therefore, on the Buddhist side, this book serves as a full introduction to the religious thought of the Kyoto School.

On the Christian side, Mitchell beautifully analyzes the Christian notion of kenosis into the creative kenosis of the Father, the negative kenosis of the Fall of humanity, the redemptive kenosis of Christ, the kenosis of the Holy Spirit, the kenosis of individual spirituality, the communal kenosis of collective spirituality and, finally, Mary as a model of kenosis. Thus the comparison of the Buddhist notion of Emptiness to the Christian notion of the Trinity is an underlying theme throughout the book.

On the basis of this trinitarian understanding of the Christian notion of kenosis, Mitchell tries to develop the Buddhist-Christian encounter in a dialogical style. That is to say, each chapter begins with a presentation of a dimension of Emptiness in Buddhist spirituality as discussed in the philosophy of a particular member of the Kyoto School. Then he explores an aspect of kenosis in Christian spirituality as a response to these Buddhist ideas.

For instance, Chapter One deals with Kitaro Nishida's philosophy of Absolute Nothingness in contrast to the Christian notion of the creative kenosis of the Father. Mitchell states that Nishida defines Emptiness as the self-transforming "matrix" (or "place") of the absolute present, and then relates this matrix of Emptiness to the kenosis of creation; that is, to the self-negation of God in creation by a kenotic God of love. Although Mitchell stresses the notion of God-Being, i.e., the experience of being and fullness in Christian spirituality, to him the mystical Void in Eckhart is similar to Buddhist Emptiness. However, Mitchell still goes on even further to discuss whether or not the mystical Void is prior to the trinitarian experience of God as Word and person. This discussion in the second half of Chapter One is one of the most provocative and suggestive sections in the book, and deserves serious consideration by persons seeking to understand the relationship of God to Emptiness.

In Chapter Two, Mitchell presents Keiji Nishitani and relates his view of human estrangement from the essence of Emptiness to the Christian notion of the Fall as the "negative kenosis of humankind." Applying the term "negative kenosis" to Nishitani's view of the "despiritualization" of life and the "demystification" of experience based on the secularization of human existence supported by scientism, Mitchell suggests with Nishitani that true religion, by overturning the field of self-consciousness, offers humanity an emptying out of this negative kenosis into a field of deeper unity with all beings, that is the "home-ground" of our existence. Right here the "gathering of self and world into a unity" is possible by overcoming estrangement. This gathering into one in the field of Emptiness in Nishitani is entirely parallel with a trinitarian dynamic of love and unity in which persons can be fully themselves and fully united with others at the same time. Quoting Thomas Merton, Mitchell also stresses that the overturning from self-consciousness and the kenotic transformation is experienced not as an act of the human will but as the work of God at the ground of our being. By this transformation humanity can discover that the collective original identity of humankind is to be one humanity reflecting the oneness of the Trinity.

In Chapter Three, entitled "Redemption:The Kenosis of the Son," Mitchell discusses Abe's view of kenosis and Emptiness, and presents his own response to it from the viewpoint of Christian spirituality. He appreciates Abe's view that the kenotic love seen in Christ is revelatory of the kenosis of God-Love in creation. But he criticizes Abe's position by saying that Abe ignores the trinitarian spiritual experience of Christian mystics by limiting God to the kenosis of creation. To mystics the kenosis of "the Father" as creation is only one dimension of the kenosis of God. There is also the redemptive kenosis of the Son and the sanctifying kenosis of the Holy Spirit. Further, Mitchell emphasizes that even though God is seen as immanent in creation the far-side reality of God is essentially maintained in Christianity, unlike Nishitani-Abe's understanding of the kenosis of God. These issues are crucial points of Buddhist-Christian dialogue which need a careful and lengthy response from the Buddhist side.

In Chapter Four, Mitchell shifts his attention from the Zen tradition in the Kyoto School to the Pure Land side of the School. He makes Hajime Tanabe's "process of metanoetics" encounter the "kenosis of the Holy Spirit" as God's action of sanctification. For Tanabe, Mitchell states, Absolute Nothingness is understood as the absolute subject of Other-power, and the transformation of the self through death-and-resurrection is an absolute transformation because it is the dynamic functioning of Absolute Nothingness. And this Absolute Nothingness as Other-power is the absolute mediatory activity of beings in mutual transformation.

For Tanabe, the God of Christian theism is a transcendent absolute that is experienced directly without any mediation. He feels that in Christianity, God is seen as a personal "Other," so that submission to his will makes freedom impossible. The Christian God is outside the transformation process and so cannot be the absolute grounding of the spontaneous freedom of *jinen*, i.e., primordial naturalness. Against Tanabe's interpretation, Mitchell emphasizes that for Christian spirituality, while the Holy Spirit of God is experienced within the transformation process, it is also important that the far side of God's reality be maintained as the source of true freedom. For true freedom to be lived by humanity, it must be a living of the resurrection life of the risen one. This involves participation in the life of the Trinity.

Mitchell never fails to point out a social and communal dimension of the experience of death-and-resurrection for Tanabe and Christian spirituality. For Tanabe, Mitchell states, the salvific work of Amida Buddha is actualized in the context of the community of many divine Buddhas. The unity of compassion pervades the relationship between the divine Buddhas. And the communion between human beings can be the context of social realization of this unity between Buddhas. The solidarity between the human and divine communities provides the context for social transformation. Tanabe's "logic of species" is a philosophical formulation of this communal dimension of metanoetics.

In Christian sanctification one is aware of the mediation of the absolute as being a trinitarian mediation of God-Love that is an activity of the Trinity itself. This mediating trinitarian structure reflects what Christians call "Abba, Father." Through the kenosis of the Holy Spirit one possesses the most intimate mystery of divine love and life. The spiritual transformation results from a self-determination of Christ within the person through the mediation of the Holy Spirit. Mitchell also argues that in Christian spirituality, while individual participation in God at the Center of our being can transform one in personal sanctification, so communal participation in God at the Center of the community can transform both the individual members as well as the community as a whole. Here is the basis of communal sanctification in Christianity, where the dynamics of human community reflect the love and unity of the Trinity.

In Chapter Five, Mitchell continues his examination of the Pure Land side of the Kyoto School, particularly Yoshinori Takeuchi's views on Buddhist spirituality. However, toward the end of the chapter, Mitchell refers also to the Zen ideas of Shizuteru Ueda in order to clarify the similarities and differences between the Christian process of spiritual growth and the process of spiritual development realized in both Zen and Pure Land Buddhism.

In Takeuchi's view, salvation takes place at the point where a person's "noble quest" for enlightenment as *jiriki* meets the "compassionate action" of Amida Buddha understood as *tariki*. (However, Takeuchi does not use the expression *jiriki-qua-tariki* and *tariki-qua-jiriki* as Tanabe does.) Referring to this, Mitchell states that, in Christian spirituality, it is also claimed that genuine spiritual experience and growth takes place at the meeting point of the ascetic and the mystical, of the religious quest and the action of grace. In order to explore this parallel between Buddhist and Christian spirituality, Mitchell quotes Takeuchi's explication of the threefold learning of original Buddhism, that is, morality (*sila*), meditation (*samadhi*) and wisdom (*prajna*) in contrast to Christian mystical practice represented by Ignatius of Loyola and Meister Eckhart. Mitchell also confirms that in both Pure Land Buddhism and the Christian mystical tradition the ascetic noble quest meets the grace of the compassionate action of Other-power somewhat in a parallel manner through a spiritual struggle for self-denial.

Further, quoting Ueda's study in the Ten Oxherding Pictures, Mitchell argues the affinity found between Pure Land Buddhism and Zen in terms of spiritual transformation from the kenosis of the self to the fullness in I-Thou relation—although the final freedom is understood in Pure Land Buddhism to be based on the dynamic of Other-power, whereas in Zen it is on the spontaneity of Absolute Nothingness. As for Christian spirituality, referring to Teresa of Avila and John of the Cross, Mitchell compares its ascetic/mystical kenotic purification and conversion into new life to spiritual transformation in Pure Land Buddhism. This portion of the discussion shines out throughout the book.

As Mitchell himself states, Chapter Six is in many ways a crucial chapter. The basic intention of this book is, (1) a dialogical study of Buddhist Emptiness and the kenosis of God in the spiritualities of Buddhism and Christianity, (2) a clarification of the inseparability of individual spiritual growth and the social, communal transformation of humankind, and (3) the future of kenotic spirituality in the two religions. These three issues are intensively discussed in this chapter. For this purpose Mitchell takes up Shin'ichi Hisamatsu, founder of the F.A.S. Society on the Buddhist side, and Chiara Lubich, founder of the Focolare Movement on the Christian side. Mitchell presents the life of Hisamatsu, his philosophy and spirituality, including his idea of post-modern Zen, with deep sympathy and penetrating understanding. So it would be an unnecessary addition to summarize his explanation here. He also describes the life and spiritual struggle of Chiara Lubich and the Focolare Movement that she initiated so vividly that the reader will be moved by his description. And one cannot but be impressed by the amazing parallelism between Hisamatsu and Lubich in their spirituality.

In the final chapter, Mitchell explores models for collective kenotic spirituality in Buddhism and Christianity. He looks at one of Hisamatsu's disciple's, Gishin Tokiwa's, idea of Maya, the mother of Gautama Buddha, and Maximilian Kolbe's and Chiara Lubich's ideas of Mary, the mother of Jesus Christ. Mitchell states that in certain forms of Buddhism, and for Tokiwa, Maya is regarded as the *tathagata-garbha,* or the "womb of the Buddha," and represents the essential nature and existential potential of individual persons and of all humankind as well. Maya proclaims herself to be the mother of all the *tathagatas* of the past, present, and future. Thus Tokiwa, according to Mitchell, sees the image of Buddha's womb (*tathagata-garbha*) in Mary. In Christian spirituality, for instance, Maximilian Kolbe, a Franciscan saint, regards the Holy Spirit as an eternal and divine Immaculate Conception of Love and the personification of the mercy of God. Mitchell suggests that, like Maya, Mary is the Great Womb of Compassion. But he calls to the attention of readers that, from the Christian perspective, Mary was *made* the Immaculate Conception and the mother of God by the grace of the Holy Spirit within her. Mitchell's discussion of Maya and Mary as Buddhist and Christian models for living kenotic spirituality, based on Tokiwa's and Lubich-Kolbe's understanding, is quite unique and insightful and is one of the highlights of the book.

Throughout the above seven chapters Mitchell has tried, in a remarkable scale and clarity, to develop a dialogical study of the Christian notion of kenosis as a response to the ideas about Emptiness and kenosis presented by the Kyoto School. To me, his discussion shows the following three issues to be the unneglectable problems that future Buddhist-Christian dialogue must address.

First, the Buddhist notion of Emptiness as Absolute Nothingness that is not negative but positive and creative indicating absolute being and fullness, must be more clearly and persuasively clarified in relation to the Christian notion of God, especially the trinitarian God.

Second, Christianity affirms God's transcendent dimension, while the inner-trinitarian kenosis of God indicates a mutual kenosis of love uniting the three persons of Trinity on the far side of human existence.

Christianity must clarify why it is that the kenosis of God is transcendent in relation to the near side if this kenosis of the triune God is really a self-opening, a self-giving, a self-donation on the far side. In a complete kenosis of God there can be no distinction between the far side and the near side in love.

Third, through close and vital dialogue between Buddhism and Christianity, including exploration of the above two issues, the future spirituality of humankind must be opened up. This spirituality must be able to contribute to the social and communal transformation of humankind as well as personal transformation. It is a post-modern spirituality which establishes a new spiritual foundation for the one unified world to come. Donald Mitchell's book is clearly an important contribution to this future spirituality.

Masao Abe
Pacific School of Religion
Berkeley, California

Introduction

The first time I met Masao Abe was in 1969 at the Fifth East-West Philosopher's Conference in Honolulu, Hawaii. At that time, I was a graduate student at the University of Hawaii studying comparative philosophy. I remember hearing lectures by both Abe and Keiji Nishitani and being quite impressed. This sparked my interest in the Kyoto School of Buddhist philosophy to which both Abe and Nishitani belong. The next time I met Abe was in 1984, again in Hawaii but this time at a Buddhist-Christian conference. There had been certain changes since our first meeting. In 1969 I was a Zen Buddhist with an interest in Christian spirituality and mysticism. In 1984 I had been studying and practicing Christian spirituality for about eight years. That was about the same amount of time I had previously practiced Zen. So, at this Buddhist-Christian conference, I found myself listening to Abe's presentation from a different point of view than before.

As it turned out, Abe's presentation was on "Kenotic God and Dynamic Sunyata."[1] It was a comparison of the Buddhist concept of Emptiness with the Christian concept of God. The basis of Abe's comparison was his interpretation of Philippians 2.5–8:

> Your attitude should be that of Christ: though he was in the form of God, he did not deem equality with God something to be grasped at. Rather, he emptied himself and took the form of a slave, being born in the likeness of men. He was known to be of human estate, and it was thus that he humbled himself, obediently accepting even death, death on a cross!

This panegyric hymn presents the "emptying" (kenosis) of Christ and calls for it to be the attitude of Christians. Abe sees in this kenosis of Christ a self-communication of God. The kenosis of Christ tells us something about the nature of God, especially in terms of God's self-giving love. In his presentation, Abe explored this kenotic notion of God from his Zen perspective, and then compared it to the Buddhist notion of Emptiness as the Ultimate Reality.

Again, I was quite taken by Abe's remarks. In fact, my own presentation at that meeting was on a topic similar to what Abe was discussing.[2] And I felt that I wanted to pursue more fully this topic of kenosis, especially from the Christian side of the dialogue. At that Buddhist-Christian conference in Hawaii, I was invited by John B. Cobb, Jr. to join a theological encounter group he and Abe had organized.[3] At the next meeting of the group, which was held in Vancouver in 1985, I gave one of the two Christian responses to Abe's presentation on spiritual transformation in Buddhism.[4] From my discussions with Abe about this topic, especially as it relates to his comparison of a kenotic God to Emptiness, I decided to write a book on kenosis in Christian spirituality as a Christian response to Abe and other members of the Kyoto School. Others were giving, and continue to give, responses to Abe's ideas from theological perspectives. And as I talked to Abe, I became convinced that what he was discussing, and what was discussed in the comparison of God to Emptiness by other members of the Kyoto School, also needed a response from the point of view of Christian spirituality. This decision has been reconfirmed in my many conversations with Abe down to the present.[5]

With this project in mind, I traveled to Japan in 1986. There, I spoke with a number of Christian scholars in the field of the Buddhist-Christian dialogue. I met with Heinrich Dumoulin and Enomiya Lassalle at Sophia University in Tokyo, James Heisig at the Nanzan Institute in Nagoya, Hakan Eilert and Fredrik Spier at the NCC Center for the Study of Japanese Religions in Kyoto, and Masaaki Honda in Fukuoka. I was also able to dialogue with a number of Buddhists in Kyoto. I had conversations with Nishitani and Nanrei Sohaku Kobori.[6] I met with Gishin Tokiwa and he invited me to speak and discuss my ideas at the Rinzai Zen affiliated Hanazono University where I also met with Eshin Nishimura.[7] Tokiwa also invited me to talk at a weekly F.A.S. Zen Society meeting.[8] Finally, I met with Ryusei Takeda who invited me to speak at the Shin-affiliated Ryukoku University.[9]

From Japan, I traveled to Rome where I lived with my family for almost five months. There, I met with Marcello Zago and John Shirieda at the Vatican's Pontifical Council for Interreligious Dialogue. During my stay in Rome, I developed my ideas concerning kenosis in Buddhist and Christian spirituality with Giuseppe Zanghi, an international consultor for the Pontifical Council and a specialist on Christian and comparative spirituality. Finally, I was also able to discuss Christian spirituality and dialogue with Natalia Dallapiccola and Enzo Fondi, co-directors of the Focolare Movement's Center for Interreligious Dialogue. Based on these discussions and dialogues in Japan and Rome, and on my own study of the Kyoto School and Christian spirituality, I began writing this book upon my return to the United States in 1986.

I would like to thank all the persons mentioned above for their help in forming this work. I would also like to thank Paul Knitter, David Chappel, John Berthrong and Seiichi Yagi, who helped me to better understand the methodology of dialogue; Taitetsu Unno, who helped me to appreciate the depth dimension of Pure Land spirituality and thought; and Shoto Hase, who presently holds the Chair of Philosophy of Religion at Kyoto University. Hase's suggestions concerning my interpretation of the Buddhist philosophy of the Kyoto School have been critical to the completion of my work. I would also like to thank my wife, Ann, and my children (Jim, David, Kristy and Paul) for their support, love and unity during these past four years.

◆   ◆   ◆

Now a few words of introduction about the content and structure of this book. The paper that Abe read at the 1984 conference in Hawaii has been revised, expanded and published with Christian and Jewish theological responses in *The Emptying God: A Buddhist-Jewish-Christian Conversation*.[10] *The Emptying God* has been hailed as a major milestone in the Buddhist-Christian dialogue in particular and as an extremely important contribution to East-West thought in general. And, from the Christian responses included in the book, one can clearly see that Abe's work is proving to be a primary source for creative theological reflection. However, as Hans Kung notes in his review, those Christian responses are not the last word, "but a first attempt to dialogue."[11]

My own book is a more extended attempt to broaden and deepen this dialogue in order to enrich interreligious and intercultural understanding. I have broadened the conversation in two ways. First, on the Buddhist side, I bring in other voices from the Kyoto School that more fully inform us about their Buddhist comparison of Emptiness to the kenosis of God. So, this book is a good introduction to the religious thought of the Kyoto School as it relates to Christian spirituality. Second, on the Christian side, my focus is on spirituality rather than theology. So, I also add to the conversation certain voices from the tradition of Christian spirituality to better explain what I take to be the real meaning of the kenosis of God. As David Tracy points out in his own response, since Abe's work brings together both thought and practice, Christians can only enter fully into "the demands and promise of Buddhist-Christian dialogue" by giving new attention to spirituality and its relation to theology.[12] So, my own work will broaden the Christian response to the Kyoto School by speaking from the field of spirituality. And in the context of this broader exploration of the comparison of kenosis and Emptiness in terms of Christian and Buddhist spirituality, I try to take the dialogue to a deeper level in a way that presents new ideas, comparisons and challenges to both sides of the conversation.

What exactly is meant by "kenosis" in Christian spirituality? What is the kenosis of God and how is kenosis lived in Christian spiritual life? How does the kenosis of God relate to Buddhist Emptiness, and how does kenotic Christian spirituality relate to kenotic forms of Buddhist spirituality as discerned in the thought of the Kyoto School? These are central issues addressed in this book. However, another important issue that I address relates to the future of kenotic spirituality in Buddhism and Christianity. What new directions can we discern in Buddhist spirituality, as represented by the Kyoto School, and in Christian spirituality? What is the place of kenosis in these new forms of Buddhist and Christian spirituality? As we shall see, my answer to these questions has to do with the relation, in both Buddhist and Christian spirituality, between personal and social transformation, and between individual and communal forms of spiritual life.

In terms of the structure of the text itself, I try to answer these questions in a dialogical style that first looks at the Buddhist side, and then gives a Christian response that is both critical and constructive. That is, I criticize some Buddhist ideas, but go on to utilize others in exploring the Christian understanding of the issues under consideration. I use this dialogical style to explore the notion of kenosis, as I understand it, in Christian spirituality and spiritual theology. Therefore, each chapter begins with a presentation of a dimension of Emptiness in Buddhist spirituality as discussed in the philosophy of a particular member of the Kyoto School. I then explore an aspect of kenosis in Christian spirituality as a response to these Buddhist ideas. The following is an outline of how this is done in the seven chapters of the book.

Chapter One presents Kitaro Nishida's philosophy of Emptiness as it relates to spirituality. Nishida is the founder of the Kyoto School and the primary source of the kenotic thought of the School. I also explain how some of Nishida's ideas have been developed by his disciple, Keiji Nishitani. Then, I go on to explore the concept of creation as the kenosis of God in Christian mysticism. In so doing, I try to show the similarities and differences between this Christian notion and Nishida's views concerning kenosis and Emptiness. I also discuss the ideas of Shizuteru Ueda and Shoto Hase on this issue. What I develop through this dialogical analysis is a relational, incarnational and trinitarian notion of the creative kenosis of God. While I do not devote one particular chapter to a comparison of the Buddhist notion of Emptiness to the Christian notion of the Trinity, that comparison is an underlying theme in the whole book. This comparison is first made in the context of this chapter, which focuses on the Father, and then is pursued in the third and fourth chapters on the Son and the Holy Spirit.

Chapter Two begins with a presentation of the thought of Keiji Nishitani, a leading figure in the Kyoto School today. While Nishida begins with "a study of the good," which is also the title of his first important philosophical work, Nishitani is more interested in "the problem of evil." Nishitani is less concerned with the logic and essence of Emptiness and more concerned with humankind's estrangement from it as our true "home-ground." I relate Nishitani's view of human alienation to the Christian notion of the Fall as the "negative kenosis of humankind." Again, I emphasize the insights concerning this human condition given in the spiritual writings of the Christian tradition. But, I also relate these insights to the modern world marked by the nihilism and secularism that so concern Nishitani.

Chapter Three turns directly to Abe's philosophy. In the first part of the chapter, I examine Abe's seminal essay, "Kenotic God and Dynamic Sunyata." In the second part of the chapter, I explore what I call the redemptive kenosis of Christ in light of Abe's ideas. The creative kenosis of the Father establishes humankind and nature in a certain trinitarian interrelatedness that is emptied out in the Fall. This original nature of humanity must be recovered. And this is the purpose of the second kenosis of God, the redemptive kenosis of Christ. The kenotic christology presented in this chapter leads to an exploration of the existential meaning of the cross in Christian spirituality.

Chapter Four moves our attention from the Zen tradition in the Kyoto School to the Pure Land side of the School. I begin by looking at the "metanoetical" philosophy of Hajime Tanabe. Focusing on what he says about Buddhist spirituality, I examine his notion of Emptiness as it relates to "Other-power" in the process of personal and social transformation. In the second part of the chapter, I explore the trinitarian process of sanctification as the action of the third kenosis of God, namely, the kenosis of the Holy Spirit. In this exploration, I present the traditional views of Christian mystics on the process of personal transformation. And, I also present some recent notions in Christian spirituality concerning communal sanctification and social transformation. In this regard, I also present the idea of the church as the result of, and instrument of, the social dynamic of the kenosis of the Holy Spirit.

Chapter Five continues the examination of the Pure Land side of the Kyoto School. The chapter turns from a study of Emptiness and the kenosis of God, to a study of Emptiness and kenosis as lived in Buddhist and Christian spirituality. I begin the Buddhist section with a study of Yoshinori Takeuchi's views on Buddhist spirituality, especially concerning its kenotic dimension. However, for the sake of balance, after looking at the Pure Land ideas on spirituality I conclude the Buddhist section with the Zen ideas of Ueda. In the famous kenosis passage in his letter to the Philippians, Paul says that the Christian should be in his or her own attitude like Christ in his kenosis. Therefore, kenosis has always played an important role in Christian spirituality. So, in the Christian section, I examine its mystical tradition as it presents us with kenotic spirituality. Again, I try to define the similarities and differences between the Christian process of spiritual growth and the process of spiritual development found in both Zen and Pure Land Buddhism.

Chapter Six is in many ways a crucial chapter. Chapter Five is on kenosis in individual spirituality that seeks personal transformation. However, an important theme in all of the previous chapters is that humankind is created as a collective "imaging" of the interrelatedness of Emptiness or the Trinity. So, Buddhist and Christian spirituality should also have a communal dimension that seeks the social transformation of all humankind. In the first part of this chapter, I examine this possibility in the writings of Shin'ichi Hisamatsu and in the spiritual community he established, namely, the F.A.S. Society. In the second part of the chapter, I examine the same possibility in the writings of Chiara Lubich and in the spiritual community she established, namely, the Focolare Movement. In both cases, I explore the idea of a communal kenosis in spirituality that seeks a transformation of not just the individual, but humankind as a whole. So this chapter looks at the future of spirituality East and West. Indeed, Hisamatsu taught that the transformation of humankind should be the project of Buddhist spirituality in what he calls the "post-modern age." And I agree that if there is to be something called "post-modern" spirituality, Buddhist or Christian, social transformation must be one of its central tasks.

Chapter Seven continues the theme of collective spirituality and social transformation in the thought of Hisamatsu and Lubich. I present two models for kenotic spirituality. On the Buddhist side, I look at the ideas of one of Hisamatsu's disciples, Gishin Tokiwa, concerning the kenotic model of Maya, the mother of the Buddha. On the Christian side,

I look at the ideas of Maximilian Kolbe and Chiara Lubich concerning the existential meaning of Mary and the "Way of Mary." In both cases, these models of kenosis are seen in light of the ideal of the ultimate transformation of humankind.

The title of this final chapter is "Mary: A Model of Kenosis." I mention the chapter title here because it is obviously a Christian title. This is also true of all the other chapter titles. The reason for this is that in this book I am trying to make a dialogical study of the Christian notion of kenosis as a response to the ideas about Emptiness and kenosis that have been stimulated by the Kyoto School and are now current in the Buddhist-Christian dialogue. So, the project of this book is to explain, in a dialogical fashion, what I see as the true nature of kenosis in Christian spirituality. I hope that to some degree I have reached this goal and have thereby contributed to furthering today's historical encounter between Buddhism and Christianity.

Chapter One

Creation: The Kenosis of the Father

Masao Abe and other members of the Kyoto School of Buddhist philosophy have argued that if, as Christians believe, Jesus Christ is the self-communication of God to the world, then something about God's very nature is being communicated to us in the kenosis, or self-emptying, of Christ described by Paul in his letter to the Philippians.[1] If this is true, these Buddhist philosophers conclude, then the nature and action of God must involve the dynamic of self-emptying that is seen in Jesus Christ. In fact, some Christian theologians have also argued this point. In kenotic christology, it is stated that there is a kenosis within the Godhead, a kenosis of enabling love that allows a triune nature: "The begetting of the Son and the Spirit is a kenosis, a process of self-giving to the other."[2] And this kenosis of love is understood to be mutual in establishing the unity of the Trinity. Therefore, the particular kenotic love establishing unity seen in Jesus, is a self-communication of this kenosis of love and unity in the nature of God. And Jesus communicates this trinitarian life of divinity to humanity. In the words of Keiji Nishitani of the Kyoto School: "With Christ we speak of a deed that has been accomplished; with God, of an original nature."[3]

In kenotic christology, kenosis not only is of the nature of God, but, as I said above, also defines his creative activity. That is, God as triune is not self-enclosed, but is creative out of himself: "Creation is never from nothing but out of God himself. Creation . . . is an act in which God communicates his own reality. In creation, God gives of himself."[4] Understood in this way, creation, as the product of kenotic love poured out through the creative Word of God, contains God immanent in all things. God is present in everything that exists as the fundamental ground of existence. This ground of creation is the kenotic love of God whose action constitutes the deepest nature of all things.

9

The Buddhist philosophers of the Kyoto School appreciate this Christian notion of kenosis. And they have compared it to their own notion of Emptiness (Sunyata). What I would like to do in this chapter is to examine the notion of Emptiness as understood by some of the leading members of the Kyoto School and look briefly at how they have compared it to the four dimensions of God's kenosis mentioned above in reference to kenotic christology, namely: (1) creation as the kenosis of God, (2) the kenosis of God's creative love, (3) the creative kenosis of God through the Word, and (4) the trinitarian structure of this kenosis of love in creation. Then in light of this analysis, I will go on to present these dimensions of God's kenosis as I understand them in Christian spirituality.

Kitaro Nishida (1870–1945) was the founder of the Kyoto School of Buddhist philosophy in Japan. So if we are going to examine the Kyoto School's notion of Emptiness and its relation to the kenotic nature and action of God, then it seems proper to begin with his philosophy. Also Nishida's concepts of "pure experience" and especially his "logic of place" can help us understand the later Kyoto School notions of Emptiness in relation to the Christian notion of God.

In Nishida's early works, which were influenced by William James, he speaks of "pure experience" as a fundamental unity of experience prior to the distinction between subject and object.[5] In the absolute selflessness of pure experience, one finds the ultimate reality that grounds our derivative experience of subjective selfhood and the objective world. This reality of pure pre-reflective consciousness is characterized by spontaneity, unity and presentness.[6] And all subjective and objective realities of conscious experience are forms of this unified state of pure experience. The self is the "place" where this dynamic of expression and unification happens. At its deepest level, the self just is the "unification" of pure experience.[7] That is, at the foundation of the intellect and will of conscious selfhood lies a profound unity. This dynamic and original unity underlies all experience of selfhood and otherness and can be discovered in a religious experience that transcends the duality of self and other. Nishida's early philosophical work sought to understand and explicate this unity of pure experience wherein Buddhism finds the oneness of reality as the True or Original Self of all things. And in this framework, any notion of a God that is an "object" of the faith experience (or even of a mystical experience) of a "subject" must be a derivative form of the more ultimate reality of pure experience. This God would be an object, albeit a supreme object, of an experiencing subject both of which derive from the more fundamental reality of pure experience.

In his later works, Nishida speaks of fundamental reality in the less psychological language of his logic of "place" (Gk. *topos*, Jap. *basho*).[8] For Nishida, "logic" refers to the form of our thinking. And "place" refers to the "locus" or "field" in the context of which knowing takes place. The various loci of human experience are understood by Nishida to be like Hegel's concrete universals. That is, they are not abstract, but concrete in that they contain individual instances as specifications or self-determinations of the fields themselves. The fields become articulated in their instantiations as, for example, the universal of color is articulated by particular colors. The highest intelligible loci of experience, according to Nishida, are truth, beauty and goodness. These intelligible fields are the "places" of our conscious experiences of knowing, feeling and willing, of reflective consciousness, aesthetic consciousness and ethical consciousness.

Nishida believes that God is understood in Christianity as the unity of truth, beauty and goodness.[9] But he feels that this unity does not go deep enough. These loci are really within another locus, a locus of absolute freedom that gives one the freedom to think, feel and choose. This leads to the ultimate unification of experience which is the place of "religious consciousness" that is in turn the horizon of reflective, aesthetic and moral consciousness.[10] Nishida refers to this "place" as "Absolute Nothingness." And in Zen, religious consciousness as a self-determination of Absolute Nothingness is a place where there is neither self nor God as other, but a place wherein all things are just what they are (mountains are mountains, and water is water).[11] Therefore, this place is the ultimate "locus" in which all existences, subjective and objective, are "located." But this place as the horizon of all things is itself not a thing. Nor is it a negation of things, a relative no-thingness. Rather, here he presents us directly with Buddhist Emptiness. And just as pure experience was seen by Nishida to express itself as subjective and objective experiences, this Absolute Nothingness is the place, as it were, wherein all existences reside as interrelated determinations of the place itself. And since all things are the self-determinations of this Absolute Nothingness, this place is where one finds the ultimate unity or coincidence of opposites, namely, the identity of the one Absolute Nothingness and the many forms of existence.

God can be understood in this paradigm in different ways. First, God can be conceived of as a "being," as one of the forms of existence, as an object of faith. Or, God can be understood as the unity of the universals of truth, beauty and goodness. But in both of these cases, God would be a derivative self-determination of the more ultimate Emptiness. At times Nishida seems to think of God in these ways. But he was also inspired by the Christian mystical tradition to understand God more as the mystical Godhead which seemed to him to be similar to his notion of Absolute Nothingness. This enabled him to appreciate the kenotic dimensions of God mentioned above. This appreciation is perhaps best seen in one of Nishida's last writings, *The Logic of the Place of Nothingness and the Religious Worldview*.[12] In this essay, he most clearly relates his notion of Emptiness to his own Buddhist heritage as well as to the heritage of Christianity. So it will be worth examining in some depth what he has to say about Emptiness and God in this important essay.

Nishida begins by defining Emptiness as the self-transforming "matrix" (or "place") of the absolute present. And he says that all things including ourselves are "self-determinations of the matrix through the contradictory identity of the many and the one."[13] The many things of the world are grounded in a matrix of unity. And it is in this matrix that the self and the world, the self and other, are not only unified but are mutually revealed and come to be what they are. The self and the world, in this matrix, exist in a "dynamic transaction" of co-determination. Nishida goes on to compare this matrix to Nicolas of Cusa's image of an "infinite circle of God."[14] This circle of God is like an infinite sphere with no circumference so that everything in existence, which is all contained within it, is a center point radiating in infinity. In this way, Nishida relates God to the matrix of Emptiness.

What is important here is that for Nishida the absolute, be it Emptiness or God, cannot be a particular being opposed to other beings: "Yet when related to that which is objective to it, it is not the absolute, but merely relative as well."[15] What is truly absolute for Nishida is what is not merely transcendent to everything else. Emptiness can be such an absolute because it expresses itself through a self-determination that negates itself as other. So given this kenosis, or self-emptying, Emptiness is identified with all of the things of the world, including ourselves, which it contains paradoxically within itself. It contains within its own self-negation, within its own kenosis, all things as self-determinations of that dynamic kenosis. Emptiness is therefore not a being, but as absolute non-being empties itself out as "wondrous being," as the multiplicity of beings so that the forms of existence are just Emptiness and Emptiness just is the forms of existence.

In this kenosis, according to Nishida, the true absolute does not oppose the relative, the true Emptiness as formless does not oppose its forms, and the true God does not oppose the world. In describing such a kenotic God, Nishida says that: "A God merely transcendent and self-sufficient would not be a true God. God must always, in St. Paul's words, empty himself. That God is transcendent and at the same time immanent is the paradox of God. This is the true absolute."[16] Nishida feels that Christianity often stresses the transcendence of God so that we hear God's commandments as coming from a supreme being over the world who will punish those who disobey. On the other hand, Buddhism sees the absolute as always unopposed to us in an immanence that embraces us in its infinite compassion even when we disobey.

However, Nishida does point out that Christianity also "teaches that God has created the world out of love. And this entails the self-negation of the absolute—that *God is love*."[17] This insight provides a connection between the first dimension of kenosis, the kenosis of creation, and the second dimension we want to explore, namely, the kenosis of God's love. God seen in this way contains within himself a kenotic self-negation which is an absolute love that establishes our being in freedom and embraces us always in that love. This kind of kenotic God of love is found immanent in creation, in ourselves as the dynamic, creative act of our life. And this creative dynamic that makes us who we are is the kenosis of God as love. Here we see how Nishida's Buddhist notion of Emptiness enables him to appreciate the Christian notion of a kenotic God of love, a God immanent in a creation that is the self-determination of that kenosis of love. In fact, Nishida says that all exists as "the absolute affirmation through self-negation of God, and this is the true meaning of creation."[18]

For Nishida, our ordinary selves come to be what they are from an affirmation through negation, from the kenosis of God that affirms us in being. This self-giving love not only affirms us, but "lives" us so that we reflect that love and grace in our everyday concreteness. It is in this sense, according to Nishida, that each self in its concrete individuality "mirrors" God as a self-expression of God through the self-negation of God which is love. Thus, each self is "mirroring the absolute." And for Nishida, the source of this mirroring or imaging is not "objectively transcendent," but "immanently transcendent." It is not a God that is apart from or opposing the self, but is rather an "immanent horizon of religious transcendence found in the bottomless depths of the self."[19] Yet this transcendence is not a "thing" but a "freedom" that is discovered in this depth. It is an Absolute Nothingness that is identified with what Zen calls the commonplace and everyday, with things freely existing just as they are. It is a horizon of absolute freedom and love in which we all are what we truly are while reflecting that freedom and love in unique and particular ways.

Nishida is careful to point out that in this horizon of freedom, we are not Nietzsche's supermen, but "servants of the Lord."[20] That is, when we live the ideal of spiritual freedom, we "serve" or reflect God's love. However, this is not the case in our ordinary life. So to live out this true religious freedom, we must pass through the "vanishing point" of the ego-self. In other words, while our *original* nature mirrors freedom and love, in our *ordinary* life, our ego distorts this mirroring of the absolute. But if we do make the spiritual passage through the kenosis of the ego, we can live freely and effortlessly mirroring or imaging the absolute, and not our ego-self. This life of absolute freedom, or better the self-determination of the freedom of the absolute, is understood in Buddhism as a life of compassion. Again, this is because this life is a functioning of love. In Christian terms, as Nishida perceives, it is a life of serving God-Love, it is a mirroring self-determination of God-Love in everyday life. So religious experience for Nishida is not a special "mystical" experience of some transcendent world, but it is the penetration of the depth of our everyday experience and finding therein a religious dimension. Therefore, religious experience is everyday experience lived from an inner horizon of freedom, or place of Absolute Nothingness, issuing in compassion.

For Nishida, Absolute Nothingness is the ground of a life of true compassion. This Emptiness is a matrix of unification in which one finds a religious compassion for, and unity with, others and all creation. Even in his earlier work, Nishida refers to living with others in this deeper unity as a "merging" in love through the negation or kenosis of the ego: "Our loving . . . means casting aside the self and merging with the other. . . ."[21] This kenosis of self "merging" into compassionate unity means concretely for Nishida the sharing of lives. He gives the example of a child merged with his or her parent: "Each joy and sadness of the parent is felt as if it were the joy and sadness of the [child]."[22] This is true compassion lived in the field of the unity of Absolute Nothingness. In this way the compassion of Emptiness is not just to be contemplated but lived. Just as Emptiness empties itself in compassion, a person grounded in the unity of Emptiness can be emptied in compassionate concern for, and identification with, others. This becomes a unifying love between I and thou that arises from the mutual kenosis of both the I and the thou on the field of Absolute Nothingness. This is expressed in an empathetic merging where, as Nishida puts it, "we feel in the self directly what the other person feels . . . and at this time we are loving the other person. . . ."[23]

In terms of the attainment of the fullness of this true life of compassion, Nishida also speaks of the third dimension of kenosis that I want to examine, namely, the role of the "Word of God." In an earlier work, Nishida says that:

True life exists by recognizing that which, being "absolute nothingness," is self-determining, i.e. by hearing the Word of God within the self-determining world, as something which "lives through dying," i.e. something which is a contradiction in itself. *Agape* lies therein. It is not that *agape* is man's looking up in the direction of God, but God's coming down to man. We truly live through *agape*. The love which compelled St. Stephen to pray for those who stoned him to death was not so-called humanitarian love, but this kind of love of God.[24]

The Word of God is found, according to Nishida, within the world as a kenotic reality ("lives through dying") wherein one finds the love of God. And Nishida says that we can live a true life of compassion through this love. This love is not something that results from human will or sentiment. Rather it stems from the absolute source of our existence through the Word of God.

In *The Logic of the Place of Nothingness and the Religious Worldview*, Nishida explains in more detail how he understands the Word of God. He says that the absolute sees itself within itself at the point where the "self-expressive" (the absolute) and the "expressed and expressive" (the human self) relate, namely, in the Word. This "point" in the Word "is the expressive medium between God and mankind."[25] God sees all in the Word and creates all out of this Word through a kenosis of love. And Nishida concludes that "God and self face each other because God, in his absolute identity and will, expresses himself as the creative Word."[26]

While Nishida here demonstrates a profound grasp of the Christian notion of the Word of God, as a Buddhist philosopher influenced mainly by Zen, his own view presents an unmediated identity between the one absolute and the many particulars. However, he recognizes a parallel to the idea of the Word of God in the Pure Land Buddhist tradition. He says that in Pure Land Buddhism this Word of God reality is expressed "by the *Name of Buddha*."[27] And he points out that in Buddhism the Buddha's name is identified with the Buddha. So, too, in Christianity, the Word is identified with God. However, Nishida also sees a difference between the Word of God and the name of Buddha. He feels that in Christianity the Word is most often understood as transcendent, personal and carries a sense of judgment, while in Pure Land Buddhism the name of Buddha always expresses an immanent embracement that is infinite compassion.

Later, we will look at the philosophy of Hijime Tanabe whose notion of absolute mediation develops this comparison in a different direction that is more influenced by Pure Land Buddhism than by Zen. But for now I want to conclude this analysis of the aspects of Nishida's thought which I will compare to Christian spirituality. The last of the four ideas to be considered is Nishida's conception of the kenotic trinitarian structure of the world. For example, he says that:

> . . . each self is a unique monad that mirrors the Father, the absolute One. Conversely, each self is the Word of the Father, as the self-expression of the absolute One; and each self forms the creative world as a spirit vector of the world. In this way the personal self is grounded in the world's own trinitarian structure.[28]

In reading this statement, we should remember that for Nishida, Emptiness is "a self-transforming matrix that exists in and through its own dynamic centers of expression."[29] So, too, the Trinity viewed in this way would be one God dynamically determined or expressed as three persons, that is, having three "dynamic centers of expression." Therefore, Nishida could see this trinitarian structure in the world where all selves and other forms of existence are expressions or self-determinations of one matrix. And again, this determination is the result of a kenosis expressed or "mirrored" in the life of each person. Each self is unified in Absolute Nothingness in a relation of trinitarian-like interrelatedness with all other selves and forms of the world. This interrelatedness is a hidden unity found at the depth of the self through the kenosis of the ego. And this discovery opens the self to a freedom in the field of Absolute Nothingness where one also finds a "merging" of the I with the thou in a relatedness of compassionate interdependence that mirrors in daily life the underlying trinitarian structure of existence.

It was left to the followers of Nishida in the Kyoto School to carry these comparative insights forward in dialogue with Christianity. In so doing, they have developed their own philosophies in new and creative directions. We will explore their ideas in later chapters. For now, let me just mention a few points that may clarify what I have discussed so far concerning Emptiness and the four dimensions of God's kenosis, namely: (1) its relation to creation, (2) its dynamic of love, (3) its relation to the Word of God, and (4) its trinitarian structure.

Keiji Nishitani, another leading figure in the Kyoto School, refers to what Nishida calls "place," or "matrix" as our "home-ground."[30] However, it is not only the home-ground of ourselves but of all beings. As we shall see in the next chapter, Nishitani is concerned not so much with the logic of this matrix as he is that we discover it as our home-ground. For since we and everything else are a self-determination of this home-ground, when we discover it we will discover our True Self which is the True Self of all things. This True Self is our "Buddha-nature." In the radical terms of the great Zen Master, Dogen (1200–1253), "All sentient beings *are* Buddha-nature."[31] Here we have the identity of Emptiness and the multiple forms of existence as found in the earlier Indian Buddhist tradition and developed in the logic of Nishida.[32] But again Nishitani's emphasis is not so much on this logic as it is on the need to discover this home-ground and to live in and from it in daily life.

The discovery of this home-ground is a discovery of Emptiness or what Nishitani prefers to call Absolute Nothingness. As with Nishida, this Absolute Nothingness is not apart from all the forms that constitute the totality of existence. Following the custom of Mahayana Buddhism, Nishitani states that Emptiness just is the interrelatedness of all things (*pratitya-samutpada*). In this interrelatedness, all things interpenetrate with one another in their "spontaneous activity of being just as they are" (*jinen*). And each thing reflects in its own unique way the interrelated totality of the horizon of Absolute Nothingness. Things are absolutely unique exactly in their self-identity with Absolute Nothingness. So in the matrix of Absolute Nothingness, in one's home-ground, one finds a coincidence of opposites, namely that of identity and difference. In this place of paradox, there is a reciprocal interpenetration in which each being is both selflessly in unity with all other beings and yet exactly in that self-lessness is also uniquely itself. Nishitani terms this reciprocal interpenetration of identity and difference *egoteki*. And this has been translated into English as "circuminsessional," which is actually a term used to describe inter-trinitarian relationships where the persons of the Trinity are one and three at the same time.[33]

It is this trinitarian structure that Nishitani, like Nishida before him, sees reflected in the world. Masao Abe also speaks of this type of dynamism as "Dynamic Sunyata."[34] He explains that in this dynamic, in the locus or place of Sunyata (Emptiness), all things are realized in their "suchness" (*tathata*), as they truly are, in a "boundless openness" of "spontaneous" (*jinen*) interrelatedness and interpenetration. This is what Abe calls the "positive meaning of Sunyata."[35] And since the world is identified with Emptiness, then we must conclude that this circuminsessional dynamic seen in the world *is* the dynamic of Emptiness itself.

For Nishitani, this dynamic of Emptiness is kenotic, self-emptying. It empties out any absolute otherness in a manner that allows all things to be what they are in an identity with Emptiness itself. This is called "wondrous being."[36] Because of its identity with Emptiness, being is wondrous. Given this view of kenosis which he shares with Nishida, Nishitani calls Buddhism "the religion of the absolute near side."[37] Here he is taking the notion of "near side" from the Mahayana identity of the "near shore" of this world (*samsara*) with the "far shore" of Nirvana. In other words, any nirvanic reality must be found in this ordinary world in which we live. It cannot be a transcendent or "far-side" reality like Plato's world of ideas or a personal God. For Nishitani, any far side must be emptied out into the near side, that is, as the "immanent center" of the everyday world. So, Emptiness does not exist apart from or behind or beyond ourselves and our everyday world. Here, he rejects the notion of Emptiness as a type of transcendent objective reality. For example, Nishitani says that when Eckhart refers to the Godhead as the ground of a personal God, then he is referring to the far side, the background of God. But if this reality is realized as my own ground, then it is on the near side as the background of the world. And this latter notion of the Godhead would be similar to the absolute near side of Buddhist Emptiness.[38]

Nishitani claims that this near side of Emptiness emptying out as the wondrous being of creation reveals not only a circuminsessional or trinitarian structure, but also a kenosis of compassion. To explain this kenosis of love, Nishitani like Nishida refers to the Christian notion of *agape*. He says that this non-differentiating love, that allows one to love even one's enemies, is a matter of "making oneself empty (*ekkenosis*)."[39] God's love is shown in Christ making himself empty to embrace all persons, the evil as well as the good, in forgiveness. In Christ, this was a deed that was accomplished, but in God, this is his original nature of love: "What is *ekkenosis* for the Son is *kenosis* for the Father."[40] This self-emptying activity is perfect love or *agape* and is the nature of God; God is love. So too in Buddhism, the self-emptying of Emptiness that is wondrous being is the Great Compassion which is also seen in Gautama Buddha. The Buddha, as the selfless and compassionate one, shows us that the self-determination of Emptiness is compassion. And the Buddha as the enlightened one shows that the ground of the compassion is Emptiness itself. Emptiness is itself, as Nishitani says, "a field of love."[41]

Finally, Nishitani also says that the "point" through which all things are self-determinations of the kenosis of Emptiness is named "Buddha" in Buddhism.[42] This is a parallel to the Christian notion of the Word of God through which God's kenosis creates the world. However, again Nishitani is not so interested in the logic of this matter or its name. Rather he is more interested in the attainment of the necessary perspective through which one can find new life in that point, however it is named. For Nishitani, this "True Life," as Nishida called it, is a life of "unity."[43] This is because of the circuminsessional and compassionate dynamic of the kenosis of Emptiness. And for Nishitani, this unity is found in the kenotic "making oneself empty," that unites, or "merges" to use Nishida's term, the self and other in the trinitarian dynamic, the circuminsessional interpenetration of *agape*, of kenotic love. Through such a kenotic Buddhist spirituality, one finds joy, freedom and the fulfillment of life.

◆   ◆   ◆

In weaving together a presentation of the kenotic dimensions of creation, love, the Word and the Trinity in Christian terms, it is important to keep in mind that Christian theologians have most often given a metaphysical priority to being over non-being. Non-being, understood in Christian theology, is typically held to be an absence of, or a privation of, being. God is believed to be Being itself, and creation is believed to be an effect of this Being. Apart from this, there is nothing, non-being. In Christian spirituality, these beliefs are substantiated in the experience that insofar as we exist, we participate in Being or God, for it is "in him that we live, and move, and have our being" (Acts 17.28). God-Being is also experienced as a fullness that fills all things: "I fill heaven and earth" (Jeremiah 23.24). God-Being is understood to be that creative source of all beings which creates, fills and sustains them in being. So, in giving a Christian response to the ideas of the Kyoto School concerning Emptiness and the world, we must begin with the notion of being rather than non-being. Then as we explore the experience of being and fullness in Christian spirituality, we can discover its link with the experience of non-being, of Emptiness or kenosis.

A Christian mystical understanding of God and creation need not entail that God creates things at a certain point in time and then remains transcendent from them. Rather, his creativity is most often mystically perceived as an immanent sustaining presence. So it is through our participation in Being at the foundation or Center of our being that we continue to be. Thomas Aquinas says, for example, that God as Being creates beings like fire burns.[44] In other words, creation is an ongoing process grounded on divine immanence. Or as Aquinas puts it: "Now God causes this effect in things not only when they first begin to be, but as long as they are preserved in being. . . . Therefore, as long as a thing has being, God must be present to it. . . . God is innermost in each thing and most deeply inherent in all things."[45] So one can say, "Lord . . . Thou has wrought all our works in us" (Isaiah 26.12).

This perpetually creative Being, which is the fundamental ground within all beings, allows us to see God reflected in nature: "Ever since God created the world his everlasting power and deity, however invisible, have been there for the mind to see in the things he has made" (Romans 1.20). To use Nishida's terms, God is the "place" of nature, he "underlines" nature like the lining of a dress.[46] And all things "mirror" or reflect in a multitude of ways the Being of their being. Bonaventure says that all forms of life reflect God in their origin, magnitude, multitude, beauty, fullness, activity and order.[47] Therefore, we can glimpse in the dynamic interrelatedness of nature, a fullness with a trinitarian structure stemming from the movement of God's self-giving and uniting love. This interrelated structure is the originating and ordering activity of God that seeks a unity through love where all beings express their full beauty. And it is precisely in this activity that we can also begin to glimpse the link between God, his kenosis of love and creation. That is, God is not seen as a self-enclosed transcendent reality but, through a dynamic kenosis of love, God brings all creation to be reflections of his glory. And it is because of this kenosis of love that we are able to behold his love as well as his fullness of Being through nature. Indeed, the activity and Being of God are not two separate things. The activity of Being is love, creative love, and in essence "God is love" (1 John 4.8). The creativity of Being is love and the effect of this kenosis of love is creation.

Bonaventure says that we not only behold God "through" nature, but also "in" nature.[48] Here he agrees with Aquinas that this is because God is actually "in" all things by his "essence, power, and presence." For Bonaventure, the realization of God's presence *in* all things is a higher form of contemplation than the beholding of God *through* all things. For example, we can behold the love and light of God through the warmth and brightness of the sun. But we can also experience, like Francis of Assisi, the sun as our brother. Our being and the being of the sun are effects, or "children," of the same Being. So in the deep unification of Being, we are united in God's love that radiates from a kenotic presence within us all, a kenosis that makes us to be and to be unified in a fullness of love as brothers and sisters of the same Father. And in this mystical vision, we begin to see the trinitarian structure of the world. This is especially the case when we remember what Nishida correctly says about this creative kenosis. That is, the Father sees everything in the Word, the Son, and creates them through the Word by a kenosis of his love, namely the Holy Spirit. We will look at how this is so later when we discuss the sanctifying dynamic of the Holy Spirit.

The contemplation of God's kenotic and creative immanence can also lead us to seek the fullness of God not only in nature around us, but also within ourselves. When we realize that God is, as Aquinas says, to be found "innermost in each thing and most deeply inherent in all things," then we realize that our own relationship with God is not something externally added onto our existence, but is its very inner foundation.[49] Here we find what has been called a "natural union" with God, or a "natural participation" in God. In order to avoid the distinction between the natural and the supernatural, I prefer to call this an "original union" or an "original participation." It is an original and fundamental participation in a reality that fills all the universe including our very selves. It is the innermost origin and principle of life, the source of our own "aliveness" and the full and dynamic life of the entire universe.

Thomas Merton refers to this original presence as "an immediate existential union with [God] residing in our soul as the source of our physical life."[50] This is an original presence that unites us through our natural participation in it with all forms of life. So we are not the center of ourselves or of the universe. Rather, there is a single Center of all beings including ourselves. This single Center is God and is discovered as Being itself at the depth of all beings. This Center that we find within us is not something that we contain. Rather, it contains us. It is something in which we participate along with everything else in creation.

John of the Cross explains this paradox in an Aristotelian way. He says that a thing's "deepest center" is "the farthest point attainable by that object's being and power and force of operation and movement."[51] This farthest point, this Still Point toward which we all restlessly tend, is not contained in ourselves. Rather it is found at a place *in* ourselves that is the place *of* ourselves. This is because the place at which we find this Still Point within ourselves is where our being opens into Being, it is a mystical horizon where the immanent is identified with the transcendent. Therefore, as Nishida notes, it is a place of absolute freedom. It is a spiritual point referred to in Christian spirituality as the "divine spark" of our soul because it is where we emerge from the "divine fire" of God. Or in other terms, this point is the Word of God in which God sees our original beauty in original union with him. It is the point through which he creates us by a kenosis of love (the Holy Spirit) that is likened to "speaking" words out of Silence through the Word. As Nishida and Nishitani affirm, it is the place or point where we can discover our "home-ground" in order to find joy, freedom and the fullness of True Life.

In discussing this movement of the person into God, John of the Cross gives the example of a rock in the earth.[52] The rock is in its center, the earth, but not in its deepest center which for it would be the middle of the earth. So, too, when we experience God within us, we find that like a rock in the earth we are really in that Center or home-ground along with all other things. God is the single Center that is found in all things and yet contains all things within itself. But like the rock, we can always dwell more and more deeply in our Center. This is possible through the development of the spiritual life. And the paradox of this development is that as we find God more deeply within us, we find ourselves more deeply within God. The immanent leads us into the transcendent, or, in Nishida's terms, there is an "immanent transcendence."[53] And to find God immanent within us is to find a reality of absolute freedom and transcendent openness that is single and all-encompassing. In God at the Center of our being, we find ourselves in a trinitarian structure united in love together in a fullness that embraces all creation. At the depths of our being we transcend our limited selves in Being through the "vanishing point of the ego" and find our unity with all beings in a trinitarian structure of love and unity. Since the act of this Being is love, our original participation in Being is discovered to be a participation in God's love that "merges" us, to use Nishida's term, so that we live compassionately as brothers and sisters in God.

God is love, he knows us perfectly, and sustains us freely through his grace. This is true of all creatures. But human life has a unique potential in that we have the degree of consciousness necessary to realize this fact.[54] The awareness of God's original presence within us makes us aware of our original potential. That is, it is God's presence within us that establishes our transcendental potential for freedom, knowledge and love. Freedom, knowledge and love take us beyond our limited self-enclosure, they are self-transcendence. And insofar as we are free, know the truth, and are able to love at all, it is because of God's original presence. We are created in the image of God. That is, we are created images because we "mirror" God and also because we have the potential to reflect back to God this freedom, knowledge and love. We can freely choose him, know him and love him as he has freely given us being, knows us, and loves us.

In Christian spirituality, as we choose, know, and love God to a greater degree, we move in a greater degree toward the Center of our being. Teresa of Avila tells us that in the center mansion in the interior castle of our soul, we find the Lord of the castle.[55] We find Christ. We find in him the love and healing touch of our Father. And we find the life-giving and life-transforming Holy Spirit. In this trinitarian reality, since our Center is the single Center of all existence, we find a deep compassionate unification with everyone and all things. The Center is Being, but not the pure universal being of the philosopher. It is the personal God of the pious. It is the triune God of love and unity. God's personal healing, guiding and consoling touch moves us more deeply into a more spiritual participation in Being, in God as immanent Center and as fullness of being.

Now we come to a very important turning point in our analysis of God's creative kenosis. It should be clear that I understand the act of creation as the trinitarian kenosis of the Father through the Son by the Holy Spirit.[56] Yet until now I have spoken about the experience of God in terms of Being, the fullness of being seen in nature, and the immanent Center of our being. I have also spoken of this experience as involving a personal relationship with God. But as the spiritual participation in God that I have been describing deepens, our soul, our "house," as John of the Cross puts it, is sometimes stilled, darkened, and left quiet in the mystical silence of its "home-ground."[57] Just as our being opens to the immanent-transcendent Being at our Center, so too this Being-as-fullness, present to us in an intimate, trinitarian and *personal* way, seems to disappear into an emptiness, a Void, an *impersonal* infinite mystery. On the mountain peak of mystical experience, a Christian mystic is silenced in front of the Silence. The personal, trinitarian God-Being seems to disappear into an impersonal Godhead that grounds all in a formless Silence or Void.

This Void is experienced in Christian spirituality as the ground of Being and beings. It is an absolute non-being that *seems* to give form to all things including the personal trinitarian forms of God in one's religious experience. It could be considered a final Darkness beyond the light, a final Silence beyond all words, a final Godhead beyond the Trinity. If this were true, as Eckhart may have believed, then this mystical Void may also be similar to Buddhist Emptiness, especially if the Void were to be understood as a kenotic reality that is *not* an absolute transcendent reality apart from the world. We should remember here that Buddhists understand Absolute Nothingness as a dynamic reality that is not separate from creation. They see a dynamic identity between Absolute Nothingness and the forms of creation.[58] The kenosis of Emptiness, seen from the near side by Buddhists, is an emptying out of Emptiness as the fullness of the world in an absolute sense that leaves nothing transcendent from this world.

What we are beginning to explore here is the relation of the experience of Emptiness and non-being to the experience of fullness and Being. In the way I have presented the Christian approach, one first experiences fullness and then Emptiness. This, I believe, is because of the focus on God as Being in Christian spiritual life. One is therefore led first to a sense of the fullness of God throughout being. It is only later that one may find the ground of that fullness in Emptiness, in the kenosis of God. On the other hand, with the Buddhist focus on Emptiness, one is led in their traditional practice first to Absolute Nothingness with no attachment to the forms of life. Only then, with that horizon of experience, with that locus of selflessness, is one returned back to multiplicity seen anew as a dynamic fullness, as wondrous being.[59]

In discussing this relation between fullness and Emptiness in Zen Buddhism, Shizuteru Ueda, another important figure in the Kyoto School, refers to them as "correlatives."[60] Ueda says that in Zen practice, one leaps into the Great Death and finds Absolute Nothingness. Yet one is at the very same time moved back into the world through a type of "resurrection" out of nothingness. This results in the Grand Affirmation of the fullness of life, the simplicity of nature just as it is (*jinen*) in its "suchness" (*tathata*). We will examine this process later on. But the important thing here is that Emptiness is the locus for the experience of fullness: "The blooming of flowers are nothingness, nothingness is the blooming of flowers."[61] Ueda says that fullness and Emptiness are like two sides of a piece of paper. The Emptiness side turns one to the fullness side, and vice versa. To use Nishitani's terms, the near side is the far side, *samsara* is Nirvana, Emptiness is forms and forms are Emptiness. In this way, Emptiness experienced in Buddhism moves one back to the world of forms to find it anew as a fullness of wondrous being.

But is this true of Christian mystical experience? How exactly can Christians understand the mystical Void? And what is its relation to Buddhist Emptiness? Is the Void something that is "prior" to God? Is it an Absolute Nothingness out of which even God arises? And does the Christian experience of this Void only turn us back to the world leaving the Void as the ultimate horizon of its being? This is certainly a possible conclusion that one can draw from the above aspect of the Christian experience of the Void looked at through the lens of Buddhist philosophy. Indeed, in a recent book on Christian spirituality as seen "through Taoist-Buddhist eyes," the authors suggest that Christian spiritual growth involves a movement into "formlessness."[62] They argue that Jesus' kenosis provides us with a model for moving beyond all subject-object dualism. In that movement, Jesus and the personal God are interpreted as dissolving "in the Void."[63] It is not that the authors deny the existence of a personal God, but rather they claim that such a personal God is a personification of an "infinite principle" which is ultimately a formless mystical Void.[64]

It seems to me that as some Christians are experiencing Emptiness through Zen practice today, they are prone to use Buddhist categories to interpret that experience in ways similar to what these authors suggest. However, I believe that this is not the only interpretation that one can make of this experience. And I also believe that it is not the correct way to understand the Christian mystical experience of the Void. Simply put, the particular mystical experience of the Void into which the personal

God seems to disappear is only a *partial* experience of that Void. There is another dimension to the mystical experience that must be added for it to be a *full* Christian experience. So, I would propose that while the Buddhist experience of Emptiness perceives no far side apart from the near side, a Christian mystic finds that through the grace of Christ indwelling within, he or she is given a "spiritual eye," as it were, to see into the mystery of the Void. And he or she finds therein a far-side dimension that is *not* absolutely identified with the near side of creation, and is *not* formless and impersonal.

Now this is a very crucial point and I want to make it as clearly as I can. In fact, it should be clear that I am not just responding to Buddhist thinkers, but to other Christian thinkers who are also using Buddhist concepts in a dialogical approach to spiritual theology. The point I want to make is that Absolute Nothingness for Buddhism is not an onto-theological category of experience. It is not a reality that can be an object of experience. It is rather a field on and from which we can experience the objects of this world. When one experiences from the place of Absolute Nothingness, which is in itself nothing, one experiences the concrete beings of daily life. Absolute Nothingness is not a "something" that attracts our attention. Rather, it is a transparent "nothing" that directs our attention to the forms of life in a new and compassionate way. Because of this, it is an Emptiness of the absolute near side.[65]

So, if the Christian mystic discovers the Void, and with it as a horizon of experience turns his or her attention to the forms of his or her experience of the world and of God as a person, then the Void does seem to be prior to Being and its Word and Spirit that seem to disappear into its silent darkness. However, this is to consider the Void *only* from the near side of mystical experience. If, on the other hand, one turns one's attention into the heart of the Void, then that Void becomes, unlike Buddhist Absolute Nothingness, an onto-theological category of experience. And if that attention is graced in a particular way by God, one can discover therein that the Void has a personal trinitarian far-side dimension. Therefore, the Void may seem to be formless and prior to a personal God if that Void is viewed as a mystical horizon of the world. But if one sees through the Void itself, one finds that it is not prior to a personal God. It is this possibility that I want to explore in the rest of this chapter, and in later chapters as well.

In Christian spirituality, Christ as the Word is that point or "eye" through which God knows us and through which we know God. And that Word can lift the mystical veil enough to reveal the mystery of the Trinity in the very heart of the mystical Void. So for the Christian, the mystery of the Void on the near side opens into the mystery of the Trinity on the far side. And what a Christian mystic beholds through this eye is that the Trinity is not a derivative reality or something less than the mystical Void. Rather, he or she sees that what is experienced by many Christians as a triune personal presence within them is a presence of the ultimate mystery of the Trinity. A Christian could think that the Trinity is a triune form derived from a prior formless Godhead if he or she were to experience only the triune presence in his or her life and the Void that is the mystical kenotic horizon of that inner presence. But from a more complete trinitarian vision, the Void is the kenotic dynamic of the Trinity, the kenosis of the Trinity, experienced from the near side as the ground of our existence and indeed of the fullness of all creation. In other words, the Trinity *is not* derivative from the kenosis of the Godhead. Rather, the Godhead *is* the kenosis of the Trinity. It *is not* that a formless Godhead generates the divine forms of the Trinity. Rather, the Godhead just *is* the dynamic kenosis of the Trinity. The Godhead is the pure non-being of the kenosis of God as Trinity, a kenosis that on the near side creates beings through Being. It is a kenosis that when realized is a dynamic non-being whose force directs one back to the world in a new way, namely, with a new perception of things and their value, and a new love for all things in their suchness.

Therefore I would venture to suggest that the circuminsessional dynamic of Buddhist Emptiness experienced as unification and compassion on the absolute near side is, for a Christian mystic, the kenotic, circuminsessional dynamic of the love and unity of the Trinity that can *also* be experienced on the far side. That is, the Void is a field of love and unity out of which Being creates beings. From the near side, this field of trinitarian love and unity gives a trinitarian structure to the world that Buddhists experience as circuminsessional unification and compassion. From the far side, this same field of trinitarian love and unity gives a trinitarian structure to paradise. So the Buddhist experience of Absolute Nothingness is an experience of God, of God as the kenotic ground of existence. But this Emptiness is not prior to God, it is the depth of the kenotic dynamic of the triune and personal God that is the other side, as Ueda puts it, of the fullness of God in creation and ourselves.

Masao Abe says that "the pure activity of absolute emptying is true Sunyata."[66] The Christian parallel to this Buddhist notion of the pure activity of absolute and compassionate emptying is the pure activity of the kenosis of God as the non-being grounding Being and its creation of beings on the near side. This non-being just is the pure activity of the love and unity of the Trinity on the far side emptied out to "line" the near side. So again, Emptiness is not prior to God. As the "pure activity of absolute emptying," Emptiness is best identified with the kenosis of God at the ground of creation. The Christian mystic finds that this kenosis of God pours forth at the near side of our experience a fullness of the love and unity of the Trinity from the far side.

Buddhists may feel uncomfortable with this notion of the "far side of the Void," or the transcendent far side of the creative kenosis of God, in relation to their notion of Emptiness. Indeed, it may seem that the notion of the Void that I am suggesting is both dualistic and relative, that the kenosis I am suggesting is not radical enough. And I can appreciate that criticism in light of the Buddhist ideal of selfless compassion and unattached freedom in the world. Yet the Christian ideal involves something else that in turn necessitates the positing of a transcendent dimension to God. To explain what this something else is, I want to look at Shoto Hase's comparison of the Buddhist view of "Absolute Nothing-ness-qua-Love" to Simone Weil's view of creation as the kenosis of God.[67] Hase quotes Weil where she says that:

> On God's part creation is not an act of self-expansion but of restraint and renunciation. God and all his creatures are less than God alone. God accepted this diminution. He emptied a part of his being from himself. He had already emptied himself in this act of his divinity; that is why Saint John says that the Lamb had been slain from the beginning of the world. God permitted the existence of things distinct from himself and worth infinitely less than himself. By this creative act he negated himself, as Christ has told us to negate ourselves. God negated himself for our sakes in order to give us the possibility of negating ourselves for him. This response, this echo, which it is in our power to refuse, is the only possible justification for the folly of love of the creative act.[68]

Hase emphasizes that the negation of God in creation can be lived by us in our own self-negation, or kenosis, and that at the point "where these two self-negations come together, penetrate one another and turn into one another, the working of 'Nothingness-qua-Love' material-izes."[69] Indeed, Weil herself sees God, the creative principle of the world, as the "absolute model" of the kenosis that passes beyond self. In one's own self-negation, one imitates the creative self-negation of God: "We imitate the divine love which created this universe of which we are a part."[70] Yet it is *also* the case that Weil recognizes the trinitarian far side of God as well: "But, before all things, God is love. Before all things God loves himself. This love, this friendship of God, is the Trinity."[71] And I might add that for Weil, this love is one that produces a trinitarian unity within God as well as within creation: "God is so essentially love that the unity, which in a sense is his actual definition, is the pure effect of love."[72]

Hence, in the Buddhist experience of Absolute Nothingness, when mind and body drop away and one's ego is no more, there is a "pure experience," as Nishida calls it, of the "pure activity of absolute emptying." But if there is an opening-up of the far side of this phenomenon, Christian mystics like Weil believe that one will also find the Trinity that gives a trinitarian structure or unity to the near side *and* to paradise on the far side. So when the Christian mystic penetrates the Void, he or she sees therein all the saints united and yet paradoxically unique. Each in their selfless compassion contains the others in deep unification and yet maintains his or her own personhood in the context of this mutual in-dwelling. This condition is within God where the Father is like a vast horizon of kenotic love illumined by the light of the Son (like the sun) and filled with the atmosphere of the Holy Spirit.

Given this vision of the ideal life in God, we can see why Christians *must* affirm God's transcendent dimension even if it leads to the above-mentioned Buddhist critique that the ultimate in Christianity is only dualistic and relative. Christians must distinguish between (1) the inner-trinitarian kenosis of God that is a mutual kenosis of love uniting the three persons of the Trinity on the far side, and (2) the free creative act of kenosis by which God creates the world on the near side. One cannot, as a Christian, make a simple identity between these two that collapses them into one another and misses their uniqueness.[73] A Buddhist can speak of an absolute near side in which any far-side reality is emptied out, but a Christian cannot. The kenosis of God as a near-side reality does not fully empty out the far side since it would thereby empty out its own foundation as well as the foundation of Christian hope. However, it does empty out any self-enclosure of the Trinity. So the love and unity that binds the persons of the Trinity are emptied in a kenosis that gives the causative power on the basis of which Being creates beings. And since this kenosis is trinitarian, it also accounts for why we can experience this trinitarian structure of unification and compassion as a fullness within our deepest Center and within nature.

In summary, in terms of the near side of the Void, the kenosis of God is a self-opening, a self-giving, a self-donation that is the dynamic source of God's creativity. It is the dynamic activity of kenosis that makes God to be the Being. And the effect of this Being is beings or the creation of the world. For Christians, the nature of this fundamental kenosis is seen then in the Being of God as the presence and activity of creative trinitarian love. And all beings are seen as the effects or creatures of this love embraced in fullness. We find God's presence and love through and in all beings. We see that God is not a static Godhead, but a dynamic kenotic Godhead of self-emptying love. And we see in that love the fundamental kenosis of God that makes of Being a divine trinitarian presence of an infinite mystery in and through all things.

In terms of the far side of the Void, the vision of a Christian mystic not only sees God's love in Being effecting beings, but also in non-being. In non-being, he or she sees the kenosis of the Father emptying his creative love into the Son, his divine creative Word in whom the Father sees in this love the pattern of all creation. The Son does not hold that love for himself but, being completely transparent, empties it through the Holy Spirit who is love itself. And in this triune kenosis of divine love, each person is unique not in distinction from the others but in unity with the others. In loosing themselves into each other, they are fully themselves as dynamic self-determinations of love. They live one another in unity and yet in so doing are truly themselves. It is also the case that this trinitarian life is emptied out through the Son and by the Holy Spirit so that we are formed in God's image and sanctified in God's grace. Therefore, we can, as Weil and Hase point out, live this kenotic love and unity. The Christian hope is that in this way we can also return as gifts of the Son for the Father. Thus, in the very heart of the Void, we can experience the dynamic kenosis of trinitarian love which is the "place" of our created life on the near side and the "place" of our eternal life on the far side.

So finally, a Christian mystic is able to cry into the Void "Abba, Father" (Romans 8.2) because it is not the person that cries but the Son. It is the Son returning the sanctified heart of a son or daughter to their Father. The Void as the pure dynamic of emptying also flows in the other direction and opens into paradise, a paradise in a love that is found in a mystic's vision to be a hidden treasure in all his or her brothers and sisters. The fullness of all of creation, nature and humanity, is linked or unified by a "golden thread" of love. This is the love of God who emptied himself that we might be, and who calls us to be one with each other united in him by his kenotic presence of love in us. And, as Nishitani says, what is important is to live this True Life of love and unity for the good of all humanity and creation. In Christian spirituality, too, kenosis is not to be contemplated only, but lived. We are to live the Trinity, to live its love and unity with one another. Or better, we are to live such that our love and unity is a self-determination of the love and unity of the Trinity. By "making oneself empty" in order to "merge" into a deeper I-thou relationship on the field of love is, as we shall see in detail later, an important goal of Christian spiritual life.

In the end, the vision of the Trinity at the ground of the near and far sides of human existence gives a Christian mystic his or her corresponding vision of a new and united world on the near side made possible by the kenosis of God's love from the far side. This kenosis does not empty out God-Love absolutely, but enables us to live on earth what we will live forever in heaven. But for this ideal to become a reality, to be lived, a transformation of our human condition must take place. And it is to an analysis of this condition and its need for transformation that we can now turn.

Chapter Two

The Fall: The Negative Kenosis of Humanity

Keiji Nishitani, another leading figure in the Kyoto School, is less concerned about the logic of Absolute Nothingness and more about humanity's estrangement from that "home-ground." It is this estrangement from the true ground of our being, understood in Buddhism as Emptiness and in Christianity as God, that I am referring to as the negative kenosis of humanity in the title of this chapter. Humanity has emptied itself out from this "original" ground in its "ordinary" way of life. So in this chapter, I will first look at Nishitani's analysis of this situation from a Buddhist point of view. Then, I will go on to present an analysis of this negative kenosis from the point of view of Christian spirituality.

The philosophical treatment of this topic by Nishitani reflects his evaluation of the contemporary world. While he is a disciple of Nishida, Nishitani is more directly concerned in his work with the relationship between religion and modern culture. Following Nishida, he believes that our historical situation is grounded in an ultimate reality which the Christian mystics proclaim and which Zen refers to as Emptiness. His own contribution to the philosophy of the Kyoto School includes an analysis of our modern estrangement from this reality. Following a Buddhist methodology, he describes the dissatisfactory nature (*dukkha*) of this alienation, its cause and how it can be brought to an end. But in developing his analysis of this situation, he is influenced not only by Buddhism but by Western philosophy, as well as Christian theology and mysticism.[1] So, this means that Nishitani's work is a rich source for comparisons to Christian spirituality.

In describing the modern dissatisfactory condition (*dukkha*) of life, Nishitani begins with an analysis of contemporary scientism. Our modern world is really a result of the success of modern science and the

31

techniques of science. What concerns Nishitani is not this success itself, but the scientific way of knowing that externalizes, objectifies and analyzes everything in our experience including ourselves. Scientism holds that this mode of knowing is the *only* way that we can understand ourselves and the world around us. Therefore, scientism defines not only the nature of existence but also the proper manner of knowing existence. The world, known in this scientific manner, is a material world ruled by laws of mechanical necessity. And if humanity is also known in this manner, there is a reduction of humankind to the mechanics of nature. Nishitani calls this reduction the "dehumanization" of humanity.[2] The true nature of humanity is emptied out and lost if it is known only in this scientific manner.

Viewed in this way, humanity is not derived from God or Emptiness but is a product of matter through the conditioning of natural and social forces that can be studied by science. Therefore, from this point of view persons are "mechanically manipulatable and controllable."[3] And if this is the case, then persons can be evaluated in terms of their physical energy or power. A person is valued as a source of labor, or for their earning power or combat potential. In this way, people are dehumanized into being mere things. They become "its" rather than "thous." And by using this same paradigm, people not only seek to exercise power over each other, they also attempt to exercise power over nature. In the materialistic and mechanistic view of the world, nature is also emptied of its naturalness, its inherent value as nature. Rather, it is seen only as a source of energy for human use. Nishitani says that in this reductive kenosis, nature is "denaturalized."[4] And through this negative kenosis of the dehumanization of humanity and the denaturalization of nature, the spiritual dimension of life is also lost. The spiritual life is emptied out of humanity and nature leaving only material and secular existence. This is not a "positive kenosis" of Emptiness or God at the ground of all forms of life, but it is a kind of "negative kenosis" that denies the reality of anything spiritual beyond the secular and material world. This denial leads to the "despiritualization" of life and the "demystification" of experience based on the secularization of human existence supported by scientism.

In this secularization of modern life, everything is exteriorized in a material universe devoid of spirit, devoid of any spiritual ground beyond the brute material facts of perceptual experience. And for Nishitani, this secularization deprives the world of its character as "home." It is no longer a place wherein we can find our "home-ground." And this for Nishitani is the basis for modern nihilism. The world known by science is meaningless in itself because there is no larger context, no "place," in which it can have a meaning. It has no greater purpose for its being and no inherent value can be found in it.[5] Things are just what they are and that is all we can say about them. Scientism shows us that whatever value, meaning and purpose we create are always on what Nishitani calls an "abyss of nihility."[6] According to scientism, these values and structures of purpose and meaning are not grounded in reality, but in the subjective will of the experiencing individual. And it is here that Nishitani locates the alienation of the person. That is, modern scientific secularism denies the possibility of knowing the "ground" of our existence. For scientism, there is no empirical method by which one can find any "place" or "Center" in which we are located as persons in a "circuminsessional unity." Rather, each individual is understood to be an autonomous center grasping experience with his or her own reason and projecting meaning onto it from his or her own "self-will."[7] In this restless projection of the aims of the self-will out of boundless possibilities (since there are no objective values to set limits), all meaning and purpose is ego-centered, not reality-centered. Therefore, scientism exposes a self-centered mode of being in the world that sits alone on a sea of nihility.

It is here that Nishitani's analysis gets to the heart of modern estrangement. Using Nishida's notion of "place" or "field" (*basho*) as a matrix of experience, Nishitani says that our "subjective self-consciousness" is the "field of consciousness" from which we ordinarily experience the world.[8] It is from this "field" of self-centered awareness that one experiences the world in the externalizing fashion mentioned above. One looks at things as objects of one's own consciousness where the independent self is the center of experience. In this way, we put ourselves at the center of everything "and weigh the significance of everything as the contents of our lives. . . ."[9] This creates a separation of the self from the world of that experience. On this field of self-consciousness, there is no possibility for the "gathering" of self and world into a unity that can overcome estrangement. It is only by finding a deeper field of unity that this alienation can be negated. But the scientism of the modern world denies that such a field is possible. Through the despiritualization of secularization, religions that promise such a field are rejected.

In fact, Nishitani insightfully points out that on the field of subjective self-consciousness, religion is of no purpose just because its real purpose is to "overturn" that very field.[10] For Nishitani, in this very overturning, religion offers a cure for the modern condition of *dukkha*. It overturns the cause of this situation of modern alienation by moving the person beyond the field of self-consciousness. It reverses the negative kenosis by presenting the real ground of true selfhood, namely, the field of Absolute Nothingness which is our true home-ground where the unification of self, other and nature is found. True religion offers humanity an emptying out of this negative kenosis into a field of deeper unity with all beings. True religion enables this original field to open up at the foundation of experience in a salvific manner that overturns the self-centered field on which alienation is experienced: "The field on which all others ought to find salvation (rather, the field on which they are at bottom saved but do not know it, and where their salvation is actualized when they do come to take notice of it) is one that opens up in Dasein."[11]

Nishitani uses an image of circles to clarify this movement from one field to another deeper field.[12] To simplify his diagram, one can draw a circle with a center "A." Then on the circumference of this first circle, one can put a point "a." This point "a" can then become the center of a much smaller circle. Moving from point "A" to point "a," is like a person leaving his or her true Center or home-ground and establishing an alternative center. This second center, "a," is an ego-center on the circumference of his or her true existence. This "a" is like the center of the field of self-consciousness on which one's ordinary experience takes place and is evaluated. The experience of oneself and the world is quite different from the circumference than from the Center. One constructs, as it were, one's self-identity and one's world on the field within this circle of self-consciousness. It is also an identity that distinguishes oneself from the other points on the circumference. One appears, in this small circular field of experience, to be a distinct individual separate from others. And others present themselves in one's field of self-consciousness as "individual, multiple, and self-enclosed" objects of sensation and reason.[13]

Given this derivative experience of self and things, there seems to be no possibility of overcoming the distance between oneself, others and nature. On the circumference of the large circle, all the other little circles have separate centers: "b," "c," "d," etc. There is no place on the circumference where one can draw their common center that can provide a unification for all the small circles. At this level of ordinary experience, there seems to be no possibility to escape the alienation of persons from each other and from nature. In fact, Nishitani says that a true unification of persons and nature, of all forms of life, can only take place at their true and common Center, "A." So there must be a spiritual overcoming of the field of self-consciousness on the circumference and a "return" to this Center. Through spiritual centering, one can find this "place" of unification wherein the self, others and nature can find their "oneness."

This Center is a point that opens into an infinite field with no circumference. It is the field of Absolute Nothingness wherein all things are selfless. The Center "A" is not the ego-center "a," but a True Self that embraces all existence. Therefore, the centering that leads to this condition involves a kenosis of self, of ego-centeredness, so that people are selfless and can be "gathered into one."[14] So while the centers on the circumference of the circle are separate from one another, the Center of the circle is the one Center of all beings. This is what Nishitani means when he says that on the field of Absolute Nothingness "the center is everywhere."[15] It is here in this Center that all things are embraced in a fundamental unity.

However, Nishitani is concerned that modern scientism refuses to recognize this possibility of spiritual centering. In this refusal, scientism unknowingly supports what Nishitani calls "an orientation toward infinite tangential dispersion."[16] One's attention, indeed one's life, is directed along tangential lines on the circumference in a way that disperses one's consciousness toward the possession and control of other things at the circumference. This movement of the person goes in the opposite direction of centering. It leaves one dispersed among the things of the world instead of centered in one's home-ground in unity with others and nature. On the other hand, while uncentered, one can create interpretive theoretical structures by which one can project meaning onto the world one encounters in this tangential movement. But such meaning is a subjective creation of the will and not an inherent meaningfulness discovered in the world itself. If one can come to realize this nihilism implied by scientism, the abyss or sea of nihility opens before one. One finds that each of the small circles of "self-enclosed" consciousnesses floats on this sea of nihility. That is, they float aimlessly with no objective purpose or direction, only giving themselves purposes which are grounded in nothing more than their own subjectivity. There is, from this point of view, no solid ground of our existence, there is only the sea of nihility in which each particular and isolated field of self-consciousness floats. Nishitani refers to this isolation of persons as an "abyss of solitariness."[17]

According to Nishitani, the only solution to this existential problem is found "in the return from the circumference (namely, from the fields of sensation and reason) to the center (the home-ground of things themselves). . . ."[18] This center "A" is a place of gathering, a place in which all the points like "a" can find a common ground to overcome their isolation and be unified into one. Nishitani repeats over and over that at this center, there is "a gathering into one," or "a gathering of things together."[19] Therefore, he believes that the unity needed to overcome the isolation and conflict between peoples and cultures can only be found in

such a spiritual gathering: "The possibility of all things gathering together and constituting one world, and the possibility of existence where
each thing can 'be' itself by gathering itself into itself, can only be constituted on the field of sunyata."[20] This gathering into one is a "circuminsessional" dynamic, according to Nishitani. Only in a trinitarian dynamic
of love and unity can persons be fully themselves and fully united with
others at the same time. So in the end, what one may call one's "circumferential isolation" is emptied out on the field of Absolute Nothingness
into a "circuminsessional unity." This unity is discovered in the Center
"A" where one finds one's True Self which is the True Self of others and
nature in this universal common Center of all being.

What is the Zen process for emptying the circumferential center "a"
in order to discover the circuminsessional Center "A"? How can one
find the field of Emptiness wherein there is an overcoming of alienation
and realization of unity? First, one must turn from tangential living on
the circumference and begin to be aware of the sea of nihility below.
Nishitani believes that we can eventually discover this field if we start to
pay attention to this sea of nihility on which our secular mode of being in
the world is floating. In a sense, this nihility can itself be a "field of
radical negation," or the radical deconstruction of the constructed aims
and values of the self-will. To make his point, Nishitani presents another
image, that of "greenhouses."[21]

On the field of self-consciousness, we construct worldviews that
provide structures of teleological orientation by which we give meaning
to our lives. These constructs are like greenhouses because in them we
are "planted," as it were, in something artificial, something of human
making. We are not planted in the real earth or true ground. Now the
view of scientism clearly shows the artificial nature of these meaning
structures in which we normally live. Scientism shows us that whatever
meaning we give to life is merely a subjective projection onto objective
facts. By understanding this claim of scientism, one can be opened to
nihilism as the fundamental meaninglessness of existence. And on this
"field of nihility," the objective meaninglessness of these artificial greenhouses becomes evident. There is, according to Nishitani, an existential
"destruction of the house and demolition of the hearth."[22]

Nishitani says that this emptying on the field of nihility that decon-
structs the meaning structures constructed on the field of self-consciousness, exposes a radical nihility that is like an "abyssal death." The problem is that scientism has no way to enable a person to pass beyond this
condition of nihility. But Nishitani believes that through Zen, the nihility
can be "transmuted" into what is called the "Great Death."[23] In the
Great Death of Zen, there is a final emptying out of the negative kenosis

that led to nihility. The nihility is taken to its extreme in the negation of not only the meaning structures constructed on the field of self-consciousness, but also of that very field itself. All is emptied out in a radical kenosis of the entire scope of ordinary experience. However, this Great Death as the radical completion of the negation of scientism is not an end in itself. Rather it provides a passage or a "conversion" to the absolute field of Emptiness. This is the passage into the "True Life" to which Nishida referred. It is a "reversal," a negation of the previous negation, in which the whole universe is experienced as new. On the field of Emptiness, one realizes the true "suchness" (*tathata*) of existence because here one is rooted in the true ground of existence, our home-ground, that is the real and singular "ground of the self and all things. It is the true reality of the self and all things, in which everything is present just as it is, in its *suchness*."[24]

The link between the "abyssal death" and the "Great Death" in Zen spirituality is what is called the "Great Doubt."[25] In Zen practice, the Great Doubt takes the nihility of the abyssal death to the radical and all-encompassing degree needed for the conversion of the Great Death. The doubt is "great" because it negates everything inside and outside of oneself. All distinctions disappear between doubter, doubting, and the object doubted. One becomes what is known in Zen as a "doubt-mass" along with everything else in existence. This kenotic condition is the great *samadhi* meditation where one experiences "being doubted," as it were, by the Great Doubt. Nishitani calls this the "self-presentation of the Great Doubt."[26] He explains that this is like a "purgative fire" in which the self and everything else is consumed into a single Great Doubt. The important thing here is that since the self-will is consumed in this fire, the doubt is not produced by the self. It is experienced as something happening to oneself (like being doubted) or as arising from beyond oneself because it does not arise on the field of self-consciousness. It is a function of the real ground of the self, the home-ground that reveals itself through the Great Death.

In this way of Zen, the limited greenhouses, the paradigms of orientation created on the basis of our negative kenosis, are completely destroyed. And the sea of nihility that caused this destruction is also emptied out in the Great Death. One is thereby planted, as it were, in one's true home-ground. This reality is called in Buddhism the "unborn" because it is not "born" or created by persons on the fields of perception, reason and will. Through the Great Death, the negative kenosis of one's humanness is emptied out into that place where all phenomena including humanity "emerge manifesting themselves as they really are."[27] Here one is not willfully "making" oneself on the field of self-consciousness.

Rather, it is "the field of emptiness (Sunyata) or absolute nothingness . . . which enables the myriad phenomena to attain their true being and realize their real truth."[28]

It is in this ultimate field, Nishitani believes, that modern alienation can be overcome. This alienation is a function of humankind's attempt, on the field of self-consciousness and self-will, to seek knowledge of the world through scientific technique and to control the world through scientific technology. This has produced a scientism that has dehumanized humanity and denaturalized nature, and has led to the alienation of the self from others, nature and its own being by denying their common spiritual ground. What is needed to overcome this condition according to Nishitani is the discovery of this spiritual ground through the Great Doubt and the Great Death. In this discovery, one finds oneself gathered together with others and nature in a unity that overcomes alienation. In this way, there is an emptying out of the negative kenosis of the human condition into a new and united encounter at a depth where persons and nature find a common ground and are truly themselves in unity with each other.

Now the question arises as to what kind of unity we are talking about. Nishitani says that on the field of nihility, the theoretical and teleological structures that give meaning and purpose to life are destroyed. And in this destruction "all nexus and unity is broken down."[29] That is, on the field of self-consciousness, one can create a certain unity of experience within a particular theoretical framework. One can also build a unity with others, and people can create a unified social fabric. But in the field of nihility, these forms of unity are seen to be only human constructions and they are then burned in the Great Doubt of Zen practice. However, the Great Death leads to a discovery of the field of Absolute Nothingness as the "absolute single Center." This singleness indicates an original unity that is different from the previous unities that have "broken down." That is, it is not a unity "made" by persons from a previous disunity. It is not a built unification of separate parts achieved by human willfulness. Rather, for Nishitani it is something quite different. It is a self-determination in one's experience of the original unity on the field of Emptiness itself. This original unity, that we can find in our experience of others and of nature, is a self-determination of the original unity of that home-ground itself.[30]

This unity is also a "force."[31] It is not by the force of our will that this unity exists. Rather, it is by the force of the home-ground of unification that we in fact exist. We originally exist united together in this home-ground by its force of unification. However, having lost an awareness of that home-ground, we must be reunified by its force with one another in our Center. This is the basis of the gathering of things to-gether about which Nishitani so often speaks. The emptying out of the negative kenosis of humanity on this field of Emptiness is an emptying by a force that also gathers humankind into unity. By the death of one's alienated ego-self, one is gathered into a new relationship of unity with others in the home-ground of all existence. So, in this field on the abso-lute "near side" of the self, one is united with others through a force that produces the kenosis of the field of self-consciousness with its self-attachments and self-centeredness. One is therefore in a selfless unity with others. One is not self-centered but other-centered and defines oneself in the context of this relational unity. One is not oneself separate from the other, but one is oneself for and together with the other. This living for the other through the kenosis of self enables the circuminses-sional interpenetration of the absolute to be lived in unity with others. So this unity is not something to be reflected upon but to be lived.[32] When it is lived, it is not something one lives by the force of one's will, but one is lived by the force of this unity that gathers one together with others and all of creation into a self-determination of the circuminsessional inter-penetration of our common home-ground.

Another characteristic of true unity, according to Nishitani, is that it is a compassionate unification in Emptiness. Living Emptiness, rather than just reflecting on it, is living what Nishida calls "True Life." And the hallmark of this True Life is compassion. Emptiness empties itself out as compassion. Abe, as we shall see later in some detail, characterizes the dynamic of Emptiness as compassion. The dynamic functioning of Emp-tiness in its unifying circuminsessional interpenetration is compassion. I find two aspects to the living of this compassion in Nishitani's thought. First is the kenotic aspect of "making oneself empty":

> What is it like, this non-differentiating love, this *agape*, that loves even enemies? In a word, it is "making oneself empty." In the case of Christ, it meant taking the form of man and becom-ing a servant, in accordance with the will of God, who is the origin of the *ekkenosis* or "making himself empty" of Christ.[33]

By living in this compassionate manner, a person is, according to Nishi-tani, also a "servant" to everyone. Here, Nishitani affirms Nishida's claim, mentioned above, that in the matrix of freedom, one is a "servant of the Lord." Such a person is empty of self and is other-directed. This is the True Life of pure compassion.

Now the second aspect of the life of compassion takes place when this compassionate kenosis becomes mutual. Here, where two or more persons live in this selfless way, there can be a bonding self-determination of the unity, or "absolute harmony" of their home-ground: "Where the other is at the center of the individual, and where the existence of each one is 'other-centered,' absolute harmony reigns. This might be called 'love' in the religious sense."[34] Again, Nishitani seems to be affirming Nishida's notion of the "merging" of persons in true compassion that we discussed above. And both Nishitani and Nishida agree that this merging in absolute harmony can only take place on the home-ground of Absolute Nothingness through the kenosis of self by each person in the encounter. When lived in interpersonal relations, this kenosis makes the True Life of compassion and unity a social reality. It becomes the basis of social transformation as well as personal transformation.

To live this True Life of compassion is, according to Nishitani, to be "utterly real." If, on the other hand, one lives a self-centered mode of being, then one's existence is "utterly illusory and shadowlike."[35] This shadowlike life is our "ordinary mode of being" based on our self-centered prehension of ourselves as independent beings on the field of self-consciousness. This mode of living is a result of what I have called the negative kenosis of our "original mode of being" on the field of Emptiness. And so when this negative kenosis is itself emptied out, that original ground of our life, our true original life is rediscovered. What is found is the "very aliveness" of Absolute Nothingness.[36] On this field of Emptiness, there is a bursting forth of real selfhood united in the context of a circuminsessional interpenetration of kenotic compassion with all creation. When this is "realized" in social relations, the harmony of the absolute "reigns" in all its realness and aliveness.

In this way, the basis of real and alive I-thou relationships can be found. This is because authentic I-thou relations assume the encounter of real persons, whose true identities are established in unity *with* others, and not just individuals, whose shadowlike identities are determined in self-enclosed isolation *from* others. This discovery of unity, of "merging" to use Nishida's term again, is not only important for personal I-thou relations, but for the social fabric of humankind as well. And Nishitani warns that "unless the relations between individual and individual, between nation and nation, between all factions, all groups, return to this condition, there remains only the battle between wolves in the wild."[37] War, imperialism, poverty, racism, etc., are created on the field of self-consciousness where the shadowlike self-centered ego is supreme. Modern revolutionary ideology preaches that through violence, people can regain their humanity that has been exploited by other systems and structures. But Nishitani claims that such a revolutionary destruction of structures on the field of self-consciousness only creates new systems and structures of exploitation.[38] It is the field itself that must be overturned. Unless the negative kenosis of self-centeredness is emptied out into the real ground of our humanness, true peace and harmony will not be possible; and for Nishitani, "The field of circuminsessional interpenetration is the field of just such harmony."[39]

Finally, absolute harmony or unity on the field of Emptiness is lived in self-emptying service, in kenotic love that is the dynamic of True Life with a trinitarian structure. A Christian can easily see in this True Life the mirroring of the divine Trinity here on the near side. For Nishitani, this lived unity is the realization in social form of the identity of the near and far sides, of Nirvana and *samsara*. It empties out the samsaric dehumanization of humanity and denaturalization of nature created by modern scientism and secularization as part of the negative kenosis of humankind. In this way, religion overturns the field of this estrangement so that all living, all doing, has the character of "religious observance."[40] Work is done from a deeper Center so it is no longer a "burden" but a "vocation." Free from self-centeredness, one is no longer burdened by, and alienated from, one's tasks. These tasks and all actions are seen as the self-determination of the worker at the service of, and for the benefit of, others. Labor as other-directed and other-centered is a service of religious love shouldered as "debt" to others and to all beings. This is the Buddhist Bodhisattva Ideal of compassion. It is an Ideal presented philosophically by Nishitani as a "cure" for the modern negative kenosis of humanity. And if it is lived, he believes that it will overcome modern alienation and promote both personal and social transformation of individuals and society toward the goal of a more united world.

◆   ◆   ◆

In Christian spirituality, one also seeks to overturn a certain mode of being in the world that is seen as dissatisfactory (*dukkha*).[41] And this negative mode of being is caused by what I have called a negative kenosis understood as involving the emptying out of an original and true nature. This negative kenosis produces an estrangement from the ground of our being, namely God, as well as from other persons and nature. This "Fall" of humankind not only affects human beings in the world, but all of creation. Given the trinitarian structure of creation as the kenosis of the Father, the interrelatedness of all creation is affected by a change in each part of creation. All creation is affected by the negative kenosis of humanity. Therefore, Christians also seek in their spirituality to regenerate their union with God for themselves and all creation: "creation itself also shall be delivered from bondage. . . . the whole of creation groaneth and travaileth in pain until now" (Romans 8.20–23). In Christian spirituality, God is understood to be not only the original source of our being, but also the transcendent potential of our being: our potential for freedom, knowledge and love in union with God and in unity with humanity and all creation. Therefore, this movement into union with God and unity with others is not a move backward, but it is a movement forward toward the re-creation of authentic personhood, as well as a New Humanity, in the building of the Reign of God.

Thomas Merton, in his own dialogue with the ideas of the Kyoto School, recognizes that the realization of this potential is a function of the discovery of our original source in God. And like Nishida and Nishitani, he believes that this realization and discovery entail a change of consciousness.[42] In his analysis of the modern influence of secular, activist and anti-mystical influences on modern Christianity, he claims that the consciousness to be changed is the modern consciousness of the "Cartesian *cogito*." In a way that echoes Nishitani, Merton says:

Modern man, in so far as he is still Cartesian . . . is a subject for whom his own self-awareness as a thinking, observing, measuring and estimating "self" is absolutely primary. It is for him the one indubitable "reality" and all truth starts here. The more he is able to develop his consciousness as a subject over against objects, the more he can understand things in their relations to him and one another, the more he can manipulate these objects for his own interests, but also, at the same time, the more he tends to isolate himself in his own subjective prison, to become a detached observer cut off from everything else in a kind of impenetrable alienated and transparent bubble which contains all reality in the form of purely subjective experience. Modern consciousness then tends to create this solipsistic bubble of awareness—an ego-self imprisoned in its own consciousness, isolated and out of touch with other such selves in so far as they are all "things" rather than persons.[43]

This "bubble" of self-awareness that alienates the person from others and nature is like the "field of self-consciousness" in Nishitani's philosophy. It grounds the manner in which one knows the world and oneself and estranges one from both one's True Self and the real world grounded in God. Based on this mode of consciousness, Merton believes that even in Christianity, God can become a "God-object" sustained by self-will and manipulated for self-centered ends. That is, God becomes simply an object of faith to be called upon for aid in times of need. But

Merton also reminds his readers that there is another form of conscious-ness available to modern humanity:

> It starts not from the thinking and self-aware subject but from Being, ontologically seen to be beyond and prior to the subject-object division. . . .This is totally different from an experience of self-consciousness. . . . It has in it none of the split and alien-ation that occurs when the subject becomes aware of itself as a quasi-object.[44]

And following Nishida, Merton calls this consciousness that can overturn modern estrangement, "pure consciousness."[45]

Merton believes that for the overturning of our ordinary mode of self-consciousness to take place, a person must become aware of himself or herself as "a self-to-be-dissolved in self-giving, in love, in 'letting-go,' in ecstasy, in God. . . ."[46] Through this kenosis in Christian spirituality, one regains one's ground "in God," the fallenness of one's ordinary mode of being in the world is overcome and one's transcendent potential mentioned above is realized. That is, freedom, knowledge and love are realized in a field of openness once lost and then recovered. In this recovery, one also realizes that this grounding in God was always there at the root or Center of our created nature in the creative kenosis of the Father. That Center is the "place" in which the Christian finds union with God as well as true selfhood in unity, given the Center's trinitarian and all-embracing structure, with others and nature. As Merton says, in a way that reminds one of Nishitani's circle image:

> The self is not its own center and does not orbit around itself; it is centered on God, the one center of all, which is "everywhere and nowhere," in whom all are encountered, from whom all proceed. Thus from the very start this consciousness is disposed to encounter "the other" with whom it is already united anyway "in God."[47]

This original union with God and unity with others in God is some-times referred to by the Christian mystical tradition as "innocence" or, in more classical terms, as "original justice."[48] This is a condition of dynamic interrelatedness. In this circuminsessional interrelatedness, one is *integrated* in creation with an *integrity* of self and an *intimacy* with God. The story of the Fall points to a loss of this condition of true selfhood in union with God and unity with others. In discussing this Fall, Merton says that the knowledge of good and evil makes the self conscious *of* itself and conscious of what is good or bad *for* itself.[49] And this involves what he calls a "complete change in perspective." There is a movement of the self into a field of self-centeredness that results in an alienation from others and from God. In this movement of fallenness, the negative kenosis, as I have called it, one empties out his or her original imaging of God and creates, in this new perspective, a false self, a "disfigured image" of what one really is. This false self relates to the world through attachment and grasping and in the end creates a mode of being in the world that is ultimately dissatisfactory (*dukkha*).

Merton follows the tradition of the Fathers of Christian spirituality who, like the Buddhists, call for an overturning of this perspective. Augustine says that this condition of "original sin" is informed by ignorance and concupiscence.[50] For Merton, it seems to me, this means that one is living in a "bubble" of self-awareness that is ignorant of one's original union with God and caught in the self-centered desires of the heart. One should note that the Buddha taught that *dukkha* is caused by ignorance (*avidya*) and selfish desires (*tanha*). How the conditions of original sin and *dukkha*, as well as the dual factors that cause them, are understood in the two traditions certainly involve some differences. However, the point is that there exists a dissatisfactory human situation conditioned by ignorance and self-centered desires that must be overturned. And this overturning entails a change in one's consciousness of self, God, others and nature.

Merton says that this overcoming in Christian spirituality is a recovery of the pure consciousness or innocence mentioned above. He calls this the "purity of heart" referred to by Jesus in his sermon on the mount.[51] It is a condition of purity in which one can see God: "Blessed are the pure in heart: they shall see God" (Matthew 5.8). This purification involves not only a change of perspective but an upheaval of one's entire being. And this is not something one can make happen by his or her own will, for it is the will that must itself be transformed. It is interesting to note that the Zen tradition agrees with this position. For example, Abe calls the root of human bondage "blind will."[52] This is a blind will "to be" and "to have" that functions at a pre-conscious level and determines the condition of our being in the world. And Abe points out, as does Merton, that this can not be changed by conscious volition. There must be a radical transformation of the very root of one's being, and this can only take place at its deeper ground, at its Center. Merton too says: "this cannot be the work of our own 'self.' It is useless for the 'self' to try to 'purify itself,' or for the 'self' to 'make a place in itself' for God."[53] For the Christian, this kenotic transformation is experienced as the work of God at the ground of our being. And also for the Christian, this purity is not the final goal. It is an overturning that is itself an enablement for something else: "Purity of heart established man in a state of unity and emptiness in which he is one with God. But this is the necessary preparation . . . for the real work of God which is revealed in the Bible: the work of the *new creation*"[54]

Nishitani would also certainly agree with Merton and Abe that one cannot make oneself enter the home-ground by an act of the will. Such an entrance into what Merton calls "a state of unity and emptiness" is itself due to the force of that new life in the person. It is achieved by a self-determination of the unity and emptiness of new life itself. And Nishitani would also agree that this new condition is a "necessary preparation" to give social form to this unity that will effect a new creation. It also seems to me that from a Christian viewpoint, it is in fact one's blind willfulness, or ignorant concupiscence, that conceals in a type of negative kenosis one's original union or participation in God. This dissatisfactory condition of original sin is like a darkness in which one is unable to see his or her original nature in God at the Center of one's being.

Humanity stands in need of an overturning of this condition, an emptying out of this negative kenosis, so that people can both see and live that fundamental reality of God's presence, and his kenotic love, as the creative source of new life. Humankind needs to discover the creative trinitarian structure of reality in which every person and all creatures are united together as brothers and sisters. The blind willfulness to be and to possess darkens human life so that people cannot recognize the true nature, value, meaning, and indeed the very sacredness of all things. We fail to see within ourselves and the world around us the presence, beauty, and compassionate and loving activity of God. So humanity needs an overturning to see and live the truth of its original union with God, a union that has been distorted by blind will. To do this is to overturn or empty out the negative kenosis of humankind into a New Humanity. If we do not return to this condition as a basis for working for a "new creation," then as Nishitani says, "there remains only the battle between wolves in the wild."

At this point, the patristic distinction between the "image" of God and the "likeness" of God may be helpful.[55] The passage in Genesis which states that the human person is created in the "image and likeness" of God is an example of Hebrew repetitive style (Genesis 1.26). However, some of the Greek Christian Fathers made a distinction between the "image" as the real essence of the person, the ontological dimension of true personhood, and the "likeness" as the existential character of the person. What is distorted by our blind will is the likeness of God in the imaging. Merton refers to this as a "disfigured image." Image here should not be seen as a static substance but as a dynamic activity. Given the trinitarian structure of reality, our original nature as image of God is a dynamic identity. We are an act, an event of the creative kenosis of the Father such that we image more or less the love and unity of God in our own unique way. However, although this imaging is always going on, it can be distorted or disfigured in our existential condition through blind self-centered willfulness. Thus, we do not image the likeness of God but only our own ego-self.

On the other hand, the imaging of God by the pure of heart is dynamically self-emptying and other-centered. It reflects purely the self-giving love of God. And since God is Trinity, this imaging has the potential to become mutual. In that case, there is an imaging of the very unity of the Trinity. Persons living in this unity make themselves one with each other in religious love or *agape*. This is perhaps similar to Nishida's notion of "merging" or Nishitani's idea of the "gathering into one" of I and thou when the I "takes the Thou to itself."[56] For Nishitani, this is possible because there is a mutual breakthrough "to the ground of the encounter."[57] And because of this breakthrough into the place of true unity, "the reality of the encounter between one man and another may be transformed *as it is* into a superreality. That is to say, here reality manifests itself in its original aspect of superreality."[58] In Christian spirituality, too, we find something similar to Nishitani's notion of unity. The true unity between persons for which Paul is pleading in the kenosis section of his letter to the Philippians is possible not through the power of human willfulness but through the power of God. It is possible because the Trinity is not only a far-side reality, but enters our lives on the near side as well. So as Merton says, unity can be found in the ground of human encounter, that is, in God. And here, too, the encounter is transformed in a way that images or manifests a likeness of the Trinity. Or better, there is in this encounter a self-determination of the very love and unity of the Trinity such that this dynamic trinitarian life of love and unity can be lived in I-thou relations. In this way, persons can image together a trinitarian structure that reflects existentially and dynamically God's kenotic unity of self-giving love. And in this self-determination of unity, the "superreality" of love is a force that can overcome alienation in the modern world.

In summary, the collective original identity of humankind is to be one humanity reflecting the oneness of the Trinity. Humankind is created to image, or "manifest," the self-giving and uniting love of God in unity together and with the rest of creation. This unity can be achieved by being in union with its trinitarian source at our common Center. In that way, there can be a self-determination of the love and unity of that trinitarian Center in humanity's communal imaging of God-Love. And to find our original identity is to find ourselves being imaged together in the collective act of unity's self-determination. Here, in this trinitarian field lived in human relations, we can not only find the solution to modern alienation, but also the foundation for the creation of a new and more united humanity. This is the goal of kenosis in Christian spirituality. But before discussing in later chapters how that positive kenosis leads to this goal of unity, I want to conclude this chapter on the negative kenosis of humankind by looking more closely at the existential condition of modern humanity in light of Nishitani's critique. That is, I want to examine from a Christian point of view the negative kenosis of our modern world as an emptying out of fundamental interrelatedness into a condition of estrangement, disunity and violence.

This negative kenosis involves a loss of a unity based in God that establishes one's true personal identity and the true collective identity of humankind. The Russian Orthodox writer, Pavel Florensky, explains this change in an almost Buddhist fashion.[59] He develops a "metaphysics of participation" in which each person is understood to be a part of an organic whole. It is the interrelatedness of that whole, its trinitarian structure, that makes each person what he or she truly is. Therefore, one's true identity cannot be defined by oneself. Florensky says that "A" cannot define "A," rather "A" is defined by "non-A." "A" is what it is in its participation in a larger trinitarian field of interrelatedness. Florensky calls this true participatory identity one's "dynamic identity." This dynamic identity exists in a "primeval unity" and is a creative "living act" both of and in that unity. One's dynamic identity in this unity involves one in a dynamic relatedness with all creation in its participation in God.

Florensky says that in the condition of original sin, one is not aware of one's identity in this participatory nexus and proceeds on the basis of self-interest to "create" an identity for oneself. This self-made identity is called by Florensky a "static identity." It arises when we assert ourselves as self-identical beings independent of God, others and all creation. "A" is "A" with no regard to its participation in "non-A." In this condition of original sin, one "dis-integrates" oneself by rejecting the dynamic nexus, or home-ground, that gives one his or her true form or identity in dynamic relatedness to others. This disintegration of a real selfhood that is united to God and others in God, is a negative kenosis of self from the "place" of its integration and primal unity. It creates an alienation from its true nature, others and God. That is, one looses one's real Center and in an uncentered, distorted and disintegrated mode of being, one generates "evil" as a "privation" of true being, of true selfhood. The static self is a privation, through a negative kenosis, of the true dynamic self so that its actions are often not what they should be because the self is not what it should be. Florensky writes: "The self-affirmation of personality in its contraposition to God is the source of dismemberment and decay of personality and the impoverishment of its internal life."[60] There is thereby a dismemberment of the wholeness of humankind's life in God. And the decay of the disunified parts of humankind is the tragic story of human history.

In today's chapter of that history, our secular world presents us with the view that one is not created to image anything more than oneself. From this viewpoint, there is no fundamental unity to be discovered. One is not imaged into the world by God-Love, one is "thrown" into the world by chance. In this secular existentialist view, there is no inherent meaning to life. Meaning and value are created by imagination and projected onto the events that make up one's life. Today, scientism, as Nishitani notes, supports this view by denying the existence of any teleology in these events. The world is made of brute facts to be understood by science and manipulated by technology. Any attempt to posit religious ideals to guide science and technology is itself a subjective act of the will. These ideals are created to give purpose to life; they regulate and structure life with meaning and value. But in the end, by creating its ideals, humanity creates itself. If one believes that there is no original nature to be discovered, then one is left with only a secular existential character to be created and formed by these ideals.

On the other hand, if we reflect on these ideas it becomes clear that most of us in today's secular world do not think in such radical existentialist terms. We do not see ourselves as consciously creating our personal identity with self-created ideals. Rather, the ideals that structure our ordinary secular lives with meaning and purpose are most often unconsciously adopted through simple socialization. Our contemporary societies, under both liberal democracy and real socialism, have created secular ideals that operate as formative powers molding the character of modern humanity, East and West. The result is a global secular socialization whereby religious life is pushed to the periphery of modern consciousness. Or to use Nishitani's image, our consciousness is pushed to a periphery alienated from its Center. In any case, the spiritual dimension is no longer experienced in ourselves, in others, or in nature. It becomes more and more remote so that it is no longer considered to have any formative importance in the interpretation and evaluation of contemporary experience.

This secularization does not always involve a direct attack on religion, but often involves a disinterest in religion or permits a modest participation in religion that does not allow it to have any real formative effect on one's daily life. In this latter case, the actual lives of many persons who participate in religious communities are molded by secular ideals such as pleasure, wealth, power and fame. In this way, spiritual life is compromised by the secular ideals of society. In both Buddhist and Christian societies today, the existential character of the identity of both religious and non-religious persons is constituted by common secular ideals. And it is these people who are truly poor because of their spiritual impoverishment, even in the midst of secular wealth in the East and in the West. Through the creation of a secular identity guided by secular ideals, these persons lose touch with their real treasure. They empty out their real identity as images of God, their original participation in God. This is a negative kenosis whereby one empties one's real identity, one's own unique and dynamic imaging of God, into a static and socialized secular identity.

Of course, this kenosis is never successful because it is impossible to fully empty the sacred into the profane. Therefore, one's secular identity never seems to "fit," as it were. There is often an existential sense that one is not really being oneself. This existential anxiety stems from an alienation or estrangement of the secular and static self from its ground in God. As Abe points out, the loss of spiritual grounding, of one's True Self, or real identity, is a fallen condition shared by modern humanity East and West.[61] From the perspective of a secular identity that has been created through the guidance of secular ideals, the notion of a spiritual identity that is discovered through the guidance of a spiritual Ideal seems like something alien. The more that one establishes one's secular identity, the more alien one's spiritual Center seems to become. This secular estrangement from God, this "despiritualization" of one's life, is a modern "spiritual homelessness." When one does not behold God through nature or within oneself, God seems to be a stranger. And since God is one's true home-ground, one feels himself or herself to be a stranger, a homeless person in a world of alien objects.

In order to escape this existential homelessness, many people create "homes" by joining religious or non-religious groups or organizations. They avoid facing the sea of nihility by entering "greenhouses," to use Nishitani's image, in order to find a sense of belonging, a being at home in the world. Since it is a person's grounding in God as the real home-ground that connects one to others as brothers and sisters, when that grounding is emptied out through the negative kenosis of secularization, one naturally feels a need to "merge" or "gather together" with others in groups that provide this sense of belonging. And a person feels more at home with others who share his or her ideals and have formed their identities in a similar fashion. Yet in the end, these homes cannot provide the boundless connectedness that humanity desires and that its real home-ground provides. Therefore, until this home-ground is discovered, there will always remain a certain feeling that one is still not really at home. As Augustine points out, the human heart will always be restless until it rests in God, its true home. So these groups in all parts of the social spectrum, religious or non-religious, cannot provide a real remedy for modern alienation. One can only be fully at home in a place that does not divide one from others but unites one in God with all humanity and nature as well. This home-ground does not, I should add, negate social belonging and ethnic identity. True unity is not just uniformity. Rather, real unity puts them into a larger whole in which all persons can be united with one another in a way that maintains their social and ethnic uniqueness.

This larger unity of peoples in the modern world is of utmost importance. All one has to do is to look at the ethnic and religious strife around the world to be convinced of this fact. And if one looks at social divisions, this need is also clearly seen. For example, the rich who prosper in secular life often use their wealth to create a "home" of luxury, security and comfort that even physically alienates them from the rest of humanity. The rich become "different," like alien beings similar to the ancient gods who enjoyed pleasures in a manner that ignored the cares and needs of other creatures. In order to maintain this life-style, the insensitivity of the rich sometimes leads them to violent capitalistic or dictatorial exploitation of other persons and of nature. At the other end of the social spectrum, the poor are so oppressed and exploited that they become alienated and marginalized from the secular economic, political and social system in which they live. In their alienation on the margins of society, some realize that the ideals of this society are false and need to be changed. They are often aware that the identity that society has given them is false. It robs them of their dignity as human beings and their sacredness as children of God. It is easy to understand their desire to destroy the structure of a secular society that has unjustly marginalized them against their will and in so doing has alienated them as well. When such an alienated person is not aware of his or her dynamic identity with others in God, it is a short step to the violence of revolutionary terrorism.

Both the violence of capitalistic or dictatorial exploitation on the right and the violence of socialist repression or revolutionary terrorism on the left are symptoms of the spiritual poverty of modern society. And this judgment applies to the violence of the religious right and left as well. For even in the case of religious fanaticism, there is a spiritual poverty that is dehumanizing in that such fanatics do not recognize all human beings as images of God-Love and as ultimately united in that love as brothers and sisters with all creation. They remain in their created "homes" fighting with each other unconscious of their mutual home-ground in God-Love. It is in the discovery of this deeper spiritual ground of existence that a person can find a true formative Ideal for his or her life. For in God, one finds an Ideal of love and unity that can empty out the negative kenosis of our often violently divided modern world into a more united humankind characterized by peace and harmony.

In the light of this Ideal, one can discover one's true and original self and the value, meaning and purpose of life. This is a discovery not based on a humanly created ideal but on the Ideal of God-Love. Only such a ground and Ideal has the universal formative power that can provide humanity with the true basis for a just and united society. Even the Communist attempt to establish an equal and united humanity under real socialism led to totalitarian violence and human alienation because, in part, it has failed to recognize the spiritual dimension of life. Communism, as structured by purely secular ideals, failed to acknowledge the human need to discover the spiritual identity of humankind that is the necessary basis of a real and lasting unity of humankind. Because of this, it may have proclaimed the ideal of unity, but we can now see in recent events that this was a forced unification, not a real unity. Once the force was removed, the old divisions reappeared with the eruption of even more violence on the unconverted field of self-centeredness.

It should be clear at this point that the negative kenosis of humanity is not only an individual phenomenon. It is a collective one as well. God is Trinity, a communal reality. Therefore, humankind as a whole stands before God created to be a communal image of the Trinity. Humankind is created to image together, to be a dynamic communal imaging of the love and unity of the Trinity. This is the real identity of humanity based on its original communal participation in God. So, not only is the human person created in the image of God and therefore capable of being a dynamic image of love, but humanity is also created as a whole with the capacity to dynamically image trinitarian love and unity. To realize this capacity in society is the concretization of the Ideal we can find in God-Love. The result, like the result to which Nishitani refers, is a New Humanity living together in peace and harmony on the field of other-centeredness reflecting the trinitarian structure of the near side.

The concrete emptying out of the negative kenosis of self-centered secular life into the True Life is indeed the "vocation" of humanity and the "cure" for its ills. Abe says that the unity of love, to be united in selfless and self-giving love, is the essential nature of a "single humanity."[62] In Christian spirituality, the realization of this oneness is the goal of human solidarity. But as I have said, using Nishitani's notion of the self-determination of the absolute, this goal of unity for which Paul was pleading in his letter to the Philippians can only be achieved by the grace of God, by the grace of God's own self-determination of trinitarian love and unity in human interrelations. So true unity may require a kenosis of self-centeredness, but that is ultimately beyond the ability of ordinary human willfulness. What is needed is a redemptive power, a force of grace, that can transform humanity and "gather" it together into a self-determination of the love and unity of the Trinity. This redemption can change the salvific condition of humanity, by emptying the negative kenosis of humankind into a new unity with God that restores and reintegrates creation. So, we can now turn to an examination of this redemptive kenosis of God that empties out the negative kenosis of humanity and forms a New Humanity united in peace and love.

Chapter Three

Redemption: The Kenosis of the Son

Perhaps the member of the Kyoto School who is most actively involved in the Buddhist-Christian dialogue today is Masao Abe. His comparison of the kenotic notion of God in Christianity with the Buddhist notion of Emptiness has been published in two recent books.[1] I first heard Abe discuss his insightful comparison at the Second Conference on East-West Encounter in Honolulu, Hawaii in 1984. That discussion has been extremely formative for my own thought concerning the kenotic nature of divine reality and its relation to Emptiness as understood by Buddhism. So in this chapter, I would like to present a summary of Abe's view, some reflections on the broader Buddhist philosophy that underlies that viewpoint and how it has been appropriated by some Christian theologians, and finally my own response to it from the viewpoint of Christian spirituality.

Because of his engagement in the Buddhist-Christian dialogue throughout the world, Abe has developed an awareness of the wider socio-historical context in which the encounter is taking place. He has discovered that while those involved in the dialogue assume the value of religion, modern secularization has made most people quite skeptical about, or indifferent to, religion:

> While interfaith dialogue presupposes the validity and significance of religion, many people in our present secularized world do not. Such people ask, "Why is religion necessary?" and "What meaning does religion have for us today?" They think they can live without religion and thus are quite skeptical about or indifferent to religion. Moreover, ideologies that negate religion prevail in our society. Scientism, Marxism, traditional

Freudian psychoanalytic thought, and nihilism in the Nietz-
schean sense all deny the *raison d'etre* of religion, not merely on
emotional grounds but, on various rational or theoretical
grounds.[2]

This modern problem for religions today is the same one that Nishitani
analyzed in depth in his philosophy. However, Abe is not so interested in
analyzing the problem as he is in addressing the problem by reinterpreting the teachings of his Buddhist tradition in a way that answers the
above types of questions in a manner that overcomes the theoretical
criticisms of secular ideologies.

Abe has kept this task in mind in his engagement in the Buddhist-
Christian dialogue. In that dialogical engagement, he has realized that
both sides of the encounter are facing the same problem of secular
irreligion East and West, and that neither side can really ignore the other
in addressing this problem. Both religions, indeed all religions, must
reinterpret their traditions in the face of irreligion and in the context of
religious and cultural pluralism:

> It is precisely at the meeting point of the two problems, namely,
> the interreligious problem of Buddhism and Christianity on the
> one hand, and the problem of religion and irreligion on the
> other, that the most serious question for modern man, the ques-
> tion of his self-estrangement should be asked: and it is precisely
> there that we may expect to find an answer to it.[3]

Gone are the days when Christian or Buddhist thinkers could carry out
their work oblivious to the views of other religious traditions. Today,
Christian theological discussions about the contemporary relevance of
the notion of God impact modern Buddhist philosophers. And when
Buddhist philosophers discuss the relevance of their notion of Emptiness, that too is having an impact on Christian thinkers. Given this situation, Abe emphasizes the importance of addressing the common problem of irreligion from a dialogical approach that can suggest more
comprehensive and coherent answers, and that can develop a more universal theoretical paradigm to explain religious experience in all of its
various forms.

Ultimately, it is this project that is behind Abe's own work on the
notions of Emptiness in Buddhism and kenosis in Christianity. That is, he
reinterprets Buddhist Emptiness in dialogue with Christianity and, in so
doing, he also gives a reinterpretation of the Christian notion of kenosis.
In this enterprise, he is trying to address the problems of interreligion on

the one hand and irreligion on the other by reinterpreting Emptiness and kenosis in ways that are not opposed to each other, and that are able to meet the objections of the various forms of secular idealism and scientism. In this way, he hopes to provide a practical way of spiritual life that will be appropriate to our modern and pluralistic world. The place where this project is most fully worked out is in his long essay on "Kenotic God and Dynamic Sunyata" published in *The Emptying God* mentioned above. So, in looking at this essay, I want first to show how Abe understands Emptiness and God in a way that respects the importance given to empiricism in our modern world. That is, Abe reinterprets Emptiness and God in ways that reject a leap of faith in a transcendent ultimate reality and instead posits this world as the locus of ultimate reality. In this way, he hopes to offset the critiques of secular idealism and scientism. Second, I want to show that for Abe, both Emptiness and God are realities that have existential meaning. That is, they provide an existential basis for living in a manner that overcomes modern alienation and gives new meaning to one's life. The first of these two tasks has to do with ontology, and the second with spirituality. In the second part of this chapter, I will also give a response to Abe's view, both in terms of its ontology and its spirituality, but with emphasis on the latter.

Abe says that if Emptiness (Sunyata) "is conceived as *something outside of* or *beyond* one's self-existence, it is not true Sunyata. . . ."[4] Emptiness is not Being as distinguished from beings, nor is it a transcendent God distinguished from this world, nor is it a nothingness distinguished from the "somethingness" of ordinary life. It is not to be found outside oneself, nor is it to be found inside oneself. If it were any of these things, or if it were found in any particular place, it would be a relative emptiness, that is, it would be relative to something it is not. Instead, Abe says that Sunyata is an Absolute Nothingness that absolutely empties itself of anything that would make it a thing apart from the things of our ordinary experience. Therefore, Abe concludes that "the pure activity of absolute emptying is true Sunyata."[5]

This dynamic activity of emptying that is identified with the things of the world ("Form is emptiness and the very emptiness is form.") is what Abe calls "dynamic Sunyata." In this dynamic of emptying, the things of the world are emptied of substantiality and thus cease to be objects of attachment for those who are aware of the emptying. As the Zen saying goes: "first mountains are mountains and rivers are rivers, then mountains are not mountains and rivers are not rivers." However, since Emptiness empties itself and so cannot itself be an object of attachment, dynamic Sunyata empties itself out as just the things themselves. So in the end, mountains are again "mountains and rivers are again rivers."

For Abe, in the realization of Emptiness, "form is ceaselessly emptied, turning into formless emptiness, and formless emptiness is ceaselessly emptied and forever freely taking form."[6]

To realize this dynamic fact of existence is the goal of Zen Buddhism. Abe makes it clear that this is not a realization of something beyond this world but of the true nature of the very things of this world, including ourselves. In the absolute present, we are "*in* Sunyata. . . . We *are* Sunyata at each and every moment of our lives."[7] This is what Buddhists mean by the identity of Sunyata and our True Self. Sunyata is what we truly are so that the realization of Sunyata is a realization of our True Self and vice versa. And since all things have this Sunyata as their True Self, or their "suchness," then "When you realize your own suchness, you realize the suchness of everything at once."[8]

With this realization of one's True Self as Sunyata, as the very suchness of all things, one is led from an ontological understanding of the true nature of things to an existential transformation of one's being in the world. That is, since Emptiness empties itself out as the things of the world, Abe says that:

> Once we return to that point of suchness, everything is realized in its distinctiveness. The distinctions between self and other, good and evil, life and death, are *regrasped* in the new light of suchness. Accordingly, it becomes the real point of departure for our lives and for our activity.[9]

Here we can see that Abe is true to his hermeneutical project, he has interpreted Emptiness in a way that does not deny scientific truth or posit a transcendent reality apart from the world of our ordinary experience. He simply explains how it is that the things of the world exist from a Zen Buddhist point of view. And then he says that the realization of this mode of empty being has a soteriological meaning, it is transformative of one's life in the world in a real and concrete sense.

Before looking at the nature of this transformation, I want to say something more about its cause, or rather about Abe's conception of its cause. Abe says that for Buddhism, the "*basis* of salvation [is] the transpersonal, universal dimension common to human beings and nature."[10] This universal basis of salvation is Sunyata as the True Self of all forms of life. Abe points out that this is very different from Christianity which posits a personal divine-human relationship as the basis of salvation. I think Abe is correct in this particular comparison. What I call the particular redemptive kenosis of Christ is a personal and historical reality that is not to be reduced to the universal creative kenosis of God. However, a crucial question is the following: If the creative kenosis of God is what Buddhists experience as the dynamic of Emptiness, then does the Buddhist *experience* of Emptiness assume the unseen influence of the redemptive kenosis of Christ? I think that if the Buddhist experience is in fact salvific, then the kenosis of Christ must be present over and above the creative dynamic of Sunyata or God's creative kenosis.

On the other hand, for Abe, this dynamic of Sunyata is transformative in the fullest sense in and of itself. There is no other dynamic needed for salvation. And Sunyata is not anthropocentric nor is it theocentric. It is a "boundless openness" that includes each and every thing in a spontaneity called *jinen*.[11] *Jinen* is the primordial naturalness underlying humanity and nature in a unity of interdependence and interpenetration. Sunyata is the dynamic of this interpenetration in which all things are empty of independent substantiality. When this universal fact is observed, "*Nirvana* is realized right in the midst of *samsara*, and *samsara*, when its nonsubstantiality is realized, immediately transforms into *nirvana*."[12] And for Buddhists, this final result of any true soteriology is realized on the basis of Sunyata itself with no need for any divine historical intervention.

So far then, we have looked at Abe's interpretation of Emptiness as the way in which things really are in their suchness. Now we must move on to look at how this Emptiness can be an existential reality, how it can be lived in an authentic mode of being in the world. For Abe, it can be lived because "Sunyata contains the two characteristics of wisdom (*prajna*) and compassion (*karuna*)."[13] Emptiness empties out in a naturalness that, if realized, can be existentially a clarity of the mind and a compassion of the heart. In this way, Abe concludes, "Sunyata should not be understood as a goal or end to be attained in Buddhist life, but as the ground or the point of departure from which Buddhist life and activity can properly begin."[14] With Emptiness as the ground of one's life, one experiences phenomena "in the light of wisdom" and "in the light of compassion" simultaneously.[15]

What this means is that wisdom shows one the non-substantiality of phenomena and one can thereby be released from self-attaching and self-binding relations. One can then live in the locus of Emptiness so that one *lives Emptiness* in its self-emptying compassion. Being empty of self, one can be free to live for the sake of others, for the sake of all sentient beings. In this way, Emptiness empties itself into compassionate action and this becomes the existential basis for True Life. In this regard, Abe says that Emptiness "should not be understood in its noun form but in its verbal form for it is a dynamic and creative function of emptying everything and making alive everything."[16] So too, by living Emptiness, one can empty himself or herself of every attachment in order to make everything else as alive as possible. And, paradoxically, in the very living of this kenosis of self, one just is fully alive as well. In dying to self, one finds the fullness of True Life.

It is important to note that this kenosis is not an achievement of the will but is itself the self-emptying action of Emptiness itself: "True Sunyata is not Sunyata thought by us, but Sunyata lived by us. In this living realization of true Sunyata, self and Sunyata are dynamically identical."[17] Abe says that before the "living realization" of Emptiness, this identity is a universal existential potential. With its realization, "the Dharma is realized as the Dharma in its universality . . . through a particular realizer."[18] And this realization of Emptiness is in fact nothing but the self-realization of that Emptiness itself. By the total negation of the ego-self, by the kenosis of self-centeredness, this original nature awakens in the realizer. And since Emptiness empties out as compassion, this awakening is a realization of lived compassion, of the compassion of Emptiness lived in the realizer.

For the Buddhist, the first person in our era to realize this truth of Emptiness, the Dharma, was Gautama Buddha. Indeed, the Buddha said: "Who sees the Dharma, he sees me. Who sees me, he sees the Dharma."[19] So, what one sees in the Buddha is the historical self-realization of the eternal Dharma. Therefore, the Buddha is the model for the existential realization of Emptiness. He is the realization of Emptiness in the pure clarity of his wisdom, and he is the functioning of Emptiness in his great compassion. Therefore, the Truth of the Dharma was realized in the wisdom of the Buddha and given to humanity in his teachings. And the Great Compassion of this ultimate Truth (*Dharmakaya*) was realized in the compassionate actions of the Buddha. The Buddha actualized this wisdom-compassion dynamic and thereby revealed the True Self as the essence of all sentient beings. He showed the world that the dynamic of clarity and compassion that characterizes the functioning of the Dharma as our original nature can be realized and function as our own enlightened nature. Therefore, this realization of Buddhahood is a potential for all persons. By following the Buddha's Path one can realize one's True Self and manifest the Dharma so that one can also say "Who sees me, he sees the Dharma." Abe points out that actually everything in the universe manifests the Dharma in its original nature: "Mountains and rivers and the great earth: everything reveals the Body of the Dharma."[20] But one needs to realize this in one's own existence, to make it a reality for oneself.

In Christianity, one can also say that we all have an original union with God, given the creative kenosis of God at the ground of our being, and that we can obtain a realization of this fact through a redemptive union with God. But there is a major difference here between Buddhism and Christianity. In Buddhism, one can become a Buddha in the realization of Emptiness. But in Christianity, one cannot say that one becomes a Christ in the realization of the redemption. Rather, this Christian realization is a participation in Christ's redemptive kenosis. As Abe correctly observes about traditional christology, "To become one with the Christ means to participate in Him. Therefore, one does not become a Christ in the same way as one can become a Buddha."[21] In living the kenosis of Christ, or rather through the kenosis of Christ living in us, we are re-formed in the image that God has of us in the Word. But we are not identified with this redemptive Word of God as was Jesus Christ. On the other hand, while Abe makes this distinction between traditional Christianity and Buddhism, he suggests that this Christian understanding of redemption might be changed through dialogue with Buddhism. He even goes so far as to suggest how this could be so in light of his Buddhist understanding of Emptiness. So, this brings us to Abe's notion of a kenotic God.

Abe begins his exploration of the kenotic mystery of God by quoting the following passage of Paul's letter to the Philippians:

> Have this mind in you, which was also in Christ Jesus: who, existing in the form of God, counted not the being on an equality with God a thing to be grasped, but emptied himself, taking the form of a servant, being made in the likeness of man; and being found in fashion as a man, he humbled himself, becoming obedient *even* unto death, yea, the death of the cross.[22]

Abe says that this is for him one of the most "touching" passages in Christian scripture. It is so because it shows the complete abnegation of Christ, an abnegation that

> indicates the self-sacrificial love of Christ for humankind which was disobedient to and rebellious against the Will of God. Through the incarnation (kenosis), death, and resurrection of the Son of God, Christ, God reveals Godself in terms of unconditional love beyond discriminatory justice. The unfathomable depth of God's love is clearly realized when we come to know and believe that Christ as the Son of God emptied himself and became obedient to the point of death, the death on the Cross.[23]

For Abe, this kenosis of the incarnation and cross is an act of Christ that reveals his original nature. It is not the case that Christ was originally the Son of God as a person who only later emptied himself in the incarnation. The very original nature of Christ as the Son of God "is essentially and fundamentally self-emptying or self-negating. . . . The Son of God becomes flesh simply because the Son of God is originally self-emptying."[24] This is the original kenotic nature of Christ. However, Abe goes on to claim that in the kenotic act of the incarnation and cross, Christ *completely* empties out this divine kenotic nature into his humanity. It is a radical *substantial* self-negation. On the other hand, the paradox is that for Abe this does not mean that Christ ceases to be God, rather in being fully a human person he is fully a kenotic, or self-emptying, God.

It is in this way, Abe feels, that one can talk about Christ being fully human and fully God at the same time. This is not a matter of two substances being identified as Western theology has claimed. In this regard, Western theology has been defined by Greek concepts. A Buddhist, according to Abe, would see the identity in terms of Emptiness and form. Christ can be fully a human form and fully a kenotic God because the kenosis is emptied fully as the form, and the form is taken fully by the kenosis. So Jesus, in completely emptying himself of his divinity into human form, is fully human, and is in that very act fully a kenotic God.

In good Zen fashion, Abe claims that to understand this original nature of self-emptying made manifest in Christ, one must make it an existential problem for himself or herself. That is, it must be understood in "our own existential self-denying."[25] Abe points out that Jesus emphasizes that "He who finds his life shall lose it, and he who loses his life for my sake shall find it" (Matthew 10.39). Or in Paul's terms, it is in the death of the "old person" that there is the life of the "new person." It is in our existential self-denying that we become our true selves, we regain our original selfhood in the denial of independent selfhood, in the kenosis of being for others. This is our original nature, a dying that brings True Life. It just is in our full kenosis of self for the good of others, as seen modeled in Jesus, that we are fully our True Self. And this, for Abe, is the living of the paradoxical mystery of kenotic love that gives us an understanding of the mystery of the kenotic God. For Abe, this kenotic love is the original nature of the Son of God that we see in the incarnation and the cross and discover by our own living of kenotic love.

This is Abe's understanding of the Son of God based on his Buddhist analysis of the kenosis of the incarnation and the cross. But he also feels that this kenosis tells us something about God "the Father." Abe asks: "Is it not that the kenosis of Christ, that is, the self-emptying of the Son of God, has its origin in God 'the Father,' the kenosis of God?"[26] What Abe suggests here is that the kenotic love seen in Christ has its origin in the kenotic love of the Godhead. Since Jesus is the self-utterance of God, his kenosis is an *act* that displays the *nature* of the Godhead as being kenotic Love. To make his point, Abe quotes Karl Rahner on the kenotic creativity of God: "Insofar as in his abiding and infinite fullness he empties himself, the other comes to be as God's very own reality. . . . he creates by emptying himself, and therefore, of course, he himself is in the emptying."[27] In fact, this is in line with what I have stated about the creative kenosis of God in Chapter One above.

However, Abe goes on to say that he cannot accept the "traces of dualism" that he finds in Rahner's further explication of this creative kenosis. That is, Rahner maintains the duality between God and the creatures his kenosis creates. Like Nishitani, Abe feels that Absolute Nothingness entails the *total* emptying out of any far-side reality apart from the near side of our world. He cannot accept any dualism between God and creation: "If God is really unconditional love, the self-emptying must be total, not partial. It must not be that God *becomes something else* by partial self-giving, but that in and through total self-emptying God *is* something—or more precisely, God *is* each and every thing."[28] And for Abe, it is through this total kenosis that redemption is achieved. He says that: "Only in God's total kenosis, is everything, including the unjust and sinner, natural and moral evil, forgiven, redeemed, and satisfied, and the love of God completely fulfilled."[29]

One sees in Abe's notion of a totally kenotic God the influence of the Buddhist identity of Emptiness and all forms of existence. Abe feels that with this notion of a totally kenotic God a common ground with Buddhism can be found, and, in this way, Christianity can share with Buddhism the realization of Absolute Nothingness beyond any kind of dualism and monotheism. Further, by so doing, Christianity can also, according to Abe, deepen its spirituality by opening up a "deeper religious dimension in which [we] can collectively share a much greater religiosity."[30] In this way, Abe has focused and sharpened the challenge of the Kyoto School of Buddhist philosophy to both Christian theology and spirituality. This is a challenge to the Christian tradition that rivals, as Hans Urs von Balthasar recently noted, the challenge of Neoplatonism many centuries ago.[31] I will try to present a Christian response to Abe's position, in regards to spirituality, in the second part of this chapter, leaving to the theologians the task of formulating a systematic theological response.[32]

In the meantime, let me say here that I greatly appreciate Abe's study of the Christian notion of kenosis. It does seem to me that the kenotic love seen in Christ is revelatory of the kenosis of God-Love in creation as I have described it in Chapter One. The essence or original nature of God is an eternal dynamic of kenosis, or non-being, that makes

God to be the Being that effects beings. And I think that Abe shows an extraordinary insight into this kenotic dynamic. However, I must register the following reservation with Abe's position. That is, it seems to me that by limiting God to the kenosis of creation, Abe ignores the trinitarian spiritual experience of Christian mystics. From their experience, one must conclude that the kenosis of "the Father" as creation is only one dimension of the kenosis of God. There is also the redemptive kenosis of the Son and the sanctifying kenosis of the Holy Spirit. The second may reveal, as Abe notes, something about the first. And it may result in the third. But ultimately all three of these depend on a more primordial kenosis within the Trinity itself. To reduce the dynamic of the kenotic interrelatedness within the divine and between the divine and creation to a mere identity between the creative kenosis of God and its creation is to lose the richness of the Christian vision of the mystery of God. And to collapse the far-side reality of God into the near side is to empty out Christian hope of eternal life in the heart of this trinitarian mystery. It is this hope that is revealed in the ultimate *result* of the kenosis of Christ, namely his resurrection.

After saying all this, it is important to note that Abe does in fact propose a certain kind of trinitarian understanding of the kenosis of Christ. He examines Jurgen Moltmann's notion of the "crucified God" which presents a trinitarian interpretation of the event of the cross rather than an interpretation in terms of two natures in the person of Christ.[33] For Moltmann, to understand the significance of the cross, one must look at the inner-trinitarian relationships, one must move from the "exterior" of the mystery of God in man to the "interior" of the mystery of the trinitarian God. In the Trinity, Moltmann says, one finds Father and Son united in a mutual kenotic surrender which generates the Spirit of Love. In the abandonment on the cross, one also finds this mutual kenosis between Father and Son. That is, Father and Son are one in their surrender. And what proceeds from the unity of loving surrender is the Spirit "which fills the forsaken with love."[34] Through Jesus crucified and forsaken, the Holy Spirit of love and unity enters all human history and all human history is assumed into the life of the Trinity. So there is no suffering that is not taken up into God by the power of the cross. As Moltmann says: "Even Auschwitz is taken up into the grief of the Father, the surrender of the Son and the power of the Spirit."[35]

Abe criticizes Moltmann for an incomplete penetration into the "interior" of God. For Abe, the "absolute interior" of God transcends the duality between interior and exterior. To fathom that transcendence, Abe looks to the Godhead of the Trinity. The three Persons of the Trinity are three distinct *hypostates* that share a common *essentia*. For this *essentia*

of the Godhead not to be a fourth person, Abe says, it must be understood as the *Nichts* of the mystics. This nothingness is not something to
which the persons of the Trinity can be reduced. It is the deepest interior
of God. It "is the unconditional, self-negating love" that defines the
persons of the Trinity as distinct persons and at the same time is the
kenosis of love that unites them in divine oneness.[36]

Now for Abe, it is this "absolute interior" of the Trinity, this kenosis
of love, that is paradoxically identical with the "exterior" of God,
namely, with the divine-human event of the incarnation. Here again we
see the Buddhist logic at work. What is ultimate (Emptiness, the "interior
of God") is identified with the relative (forms, the "exterior of God").
And by denying all duality, Abe concludes that "only when the sonship of
Jesus is understood to be ultimately rooted in *Nichts* as Godhead, can the
event of the cross of Jesus be understood truly as the event of an uncon-
ditioned and boundless love fully actualized for the Godless and the
loveless in this law-oriented society."[37] And it is in Jesus crucified and
forsaken that this kenotic love of God is most fully revealed.

Here again I am extremely impressed with Abe's insight into the
kenotic essence of God as it is revealed in the kenosis of Christ. However,
Abe goes on to say that not just Jesus but all things reveal the kenosis of
God since, from the Buddhist point of view, God is identified with "each
and every thing." This in turn leads Abe to deny the uniqueness of the
incarnation of Christ. Abe asks: "Why is this total identity of God with
Christ through God's kenosis not applicable to everything in the universe
beyond Christ? Can we not legitimately say that each and every thing in
the universe is also an incarnation of God together with Jesus Christ on
the cross and his glorious resurrection?"[38] It would seem from these
questions that Abe is suggesting that through the universal kenosis of
God "each and every thing" is an "incarnation" of the "absolute interior" of God just like Jesus was. Again this view certainly comes from the
Buddhist identity of Emptiness and *all* the forms of existence.

I would respond to this view of Abe's by pointing out that while the
kenosis within the Trinity, to which Abe is so sensitive, involves a love and
unity that determines the identity of the persons of the Trinity, this
kenotic inner-trinitarian determination is different in kind from the kenotic determination of creation simply because the persons of the Trinity
are different in kind from the forms of creation. The persons of the
Trinity are God by their eternal kenosis, and the created forms of this
world are what they are by God's creative kenosis in space and time.
Further, the kenosis of the incarnation and cross of Jesus Christ is a
unique redemptive kenotic act of the divine *hypostatis* of the Son. We
simply cannot say that of anything else in creation. Again, to reduce all

types of divine kenosis to the one particular kind that we discern in creation is to impoverish the richness of the mystery of God. To show that such a reduction should not be made in the case of the incarnation of Jesus Christ, I would like to turn now to an analysis of the redemptive kenosis of Christ. I hope that this analysis will answer Abe's questions about why the particular identity of God with Jesus Christ is not applicable to everything else in the universe.

♦　　♦　　♦

The Japanese Christian theologian, Katsumi Takizawa (1909–1984), in his own reflections on the experience of realization in Buddhism and Christianity, develops the concepts of "primary contact" and "secondary contact."[39] Primary contact refers to the fact of "God being with us" (Immanuel) at the foundation of every human being. This is humankind's primary contact with God that I have presented above as being within the locus of the creative kenosis of God at the ground of our being. Secondary contact refers to the awakening to the fact of this universal primary contact. It is through this secondary contact that the primary contact is activated and makes itself an existential reality for the realizer. Takizawa's understanding of this secondary contact is influenced by Mahayana Buddhism in general and by one of his teachers, Kitaro Nishida, in particular. That is, he claims that it is on account of the primary contact that one realizes the secondary contact with God. This is similar to the Buddhist claim, voiced by Abe, that Sunyata is the basis of both existence and liberation. And given this understanding, Takizawa concludes that Jesus was a human being who fully realized the secondary contact. In this he is the model and measure for such contact, but he does not bring it about. If the secondary contact does happen in a person's life, it is not because of Jesus Christ but because of the power of the primary contact itself. Therefore, for Takizawa, Jesus Christ stands "alongside" Gautama Buddha who was the first person in the Indian tradition to be fully awakened to the primary contact.

In his brilliant essay, "A Bridge From Buddhist to Christian Thinking: The 'Front-Structure,' " Seiichi Yagi presents the Buddhist notion of Emptiness, the condition of the mere-ego and its need for transcendence, and the ideal of communal integration in ways that parallel my own work.[40] However, he also uncritically accepts Takizawa's understanding of primary and secondary contact with God. For both Takizawa and Yagi, Jesus was just a human being in which the universal primary contact with God was actualized. After Jesus' death, that actualization was realized in his disciples. And using the concepts of their times, they,

Takizawa and Yagi claim, misinterpreted this actualization to be the result of the power of a resurrected Jesus active in them. Therefore, both Takizawa and Yagi would agree with Abe that Jesus Christ is not unique. He is a human being who realized his True Self in a secondary contact with God. And since this experience is accounted for by the primary contact that is universal for all persons, then this realization achieved by Jesus is a potential for all persons.

What I wish to suggest in this section is that the primary contact with God does not in fact account for the secondary contact as Takizawa and Yagi claim. Rather, while the creative kenosis of the Father accounts for the primary contact with God, the redemptive kenosis of the Son accounts for the secondary contact with God. Jesus is not just a model and measure of the secondary contact, but is the very redemptive kenosis of God that accounts for secondary contact. Now in saying this, I am aware that one motivation for positing the primary contact as being the cause of the secondary contact rather than Jesus Christ as being the cause may be that in so doing one can avoid the conclusion that only Christians are saved. Therefore, I want to say that the redemptive kenosis of God is at work in all humankind just as the creative kenosis of God is at the ground of all human existence. What I will present in this section is how that redemptive kenosis is understood in Christian spiritual experience. And it should now be clear that in this presentation I will not only be responding to Abe's ideas, but will be presenting an alternative to the christology of Takeuchi and Yagi.

Turning now to Abe's philosophy, perhaps the main point of his analysis of the kenosis of Christ on the cross is to show that it is revelatory of the innermost nature of God. Here, I agree with Abe. In the kenosis of Christ, God communicates himself. He is not revealing something other than himself. He "speaks" himself in his Word. And the essence of this message is love: "For God so loved the world that he sent his only son" (John 3.16). This love of God for the world that is revealed in the kenosis of the cross, is also found in the kenosis of love at the core of creation that is in turn an expression of the eternal Love that just is God himself. As Lucien Richard points out in his work on kenotic christology: "Jesus' kenosis is a manifestation, a revelation of the kenosis of God. Jesus' self-emptying, his kenotic love in the poverty and humility of his historical existence points to the eternal kenosis of God."[41] The event of the kenosis of Jesus was an action of the kenosis of God, a free act that communicates what Abe calls the "deepest interior" of the life of God, namely, his kenotic love. This life of God the creator is at work in the activity of his creation. Everything that is created, all things that come to life are "enlived" by this life of divine kenotic love. It is this kenotic love that establishes our primary contact, our original unity, with God. This kenosis of love is how "God so loved the world." And the depth of this love is revealed in the kenosis of Christ.

It is this creative kenosis of the Father, revealed in the redemptive kenosis of the Son, that is the near-side reality of God. The essential quality of the kenosis of both the Father and the Son is love. The emptying out of this kenosis as love is a dynamic that underlies the world on the near side of existence and is experienced as a pure emptying by the pure and humble of heart. This emptying is a compassionate dynamic that is discovered at the core of one's being and seems to take form as not only oneself, but also as all things. To the Christian mystic, all things seem to "move" and even "shine" in harmony with this reality within oneself. Everything seems to reflect this dynamic of God's creative love. More than that, each thing seems to give form in its uniqueness to that formative power.

The experience of this near-side reality of God's kenosis could lead one to conclude that the kenosis or emptiness is identified in an absolute sense with the forms of creation; that God empties himself out into and as creation in a total sense. However, this is not the case. It is true that the kenotic love of God is "a pure *agape* that empties itself into the world. . . ."[42] But the radical dependence of creation on God is not matched with a radical dependence of God on creation which would be called for by the Buddhist logic that identifies Emptiness and forms.[43] Even though God is seen as immanent in creation, the far-side reality of God is maintained in Christianity. Creation is not just the effect of pure love, it is the effect of pure will. It expresses the kenotic compassion and sympathy of a self-giving God, as well as the loving choice of God to create the world. In this personal choice of love at the ground of creation, one finds the Christian affirmation of the far side of God. This far side is a trinitarian reality that one finds immanent in all creation accounting for the near-side trinitarian structure of the world discussed by Nishida and Nishitani. But it also maintains its integrity as a triune God. And, I might add, this is precisely what guarantees the uniqueness of Jesus Christ. He is an incarnation of the second person of the Trinity, and not only an effect of the kenosis of the Trinity like the rest of creation. So if we want to look at what the kenosis of Christ reveals about God, we must look at the Trinity.

The first thing to note about the Trinity is that the identities of the persons of the Trinity are not static but dynamic. Their identities are constituted by their relations with one another. And at the heart, or what Abe calls the "interior," of these relations is kenotic love. As Richard puts it, in the Godhead there "is a kenosis, an act of self-emptying that results in a letting-be, in the enabling of another to be. Kenosis in the

Godhead means that there is 'otherness' within God."[44] And as Richard concludes, God's triune personhood cannot be dependent on what is not God, so "he must be his own otherness."[45] The interrelatedness of emptiness and love within the Trinity that is reflected in creation constitutes the I and the Thou of God's triune nature. God is a mystery of reciprocal love with a dynamic of self-denying and self-giving that is reflected in nature; and humanity is created in its image.

It is this mystery of trinitarian love that is revealed in the kenosis of Christ on the cross. Again Richard, following Moltmann, says, "What happens on the cross manifests the relationship of Jesus the Son to the Father, and makes possible the movement of the Spirit from the Father."[46] The inner-trinitarian kenosis of love between the Father and Son generates the dynamic reality of the love and unity which makes them one. This is the Holy Spirit. We see this kenotic mystery of love and unity in Jesus on the cross who, in complete kenosis in relation to the Father, makes possible the pouring of the Holy Spirit out of the Trinity into the life of humankind. So given this trinitarian interpretation, we see in Jesus crucified and forsaken the ultimate in kenotic love that generates unity. We see the kenotic self-determination of trinitarian love and unity itself.

This far-side reality of the Trinity, that is revealed in the kenosis of the cross, is not emptied out, as Abe suggests, in a total sense as the "place of the world," but also remains a "place of hope for the world," a paradise wherein the fullness of the life of love and unity can be lived forever. On the other hand, Abe is correct in saying that this kenosis of love can be lived here on earth. In Buddhism, Emptiness is not to be thought but lived. So, too, the kenosis that Jesus reveals can be lived. Indeed, Paul at the beginning of his passage in Philippians on the kenosis of Christ, says that one must be "united in your love," one must be "self-effacing, always looking to others' interests," and that one's "attitude must be the same as that of Christ." So the kenosis of Christ not only reveals the innermost nature of the triune God, but also reveals how to live, in Christian spirituality, this trinitarian kenosis of love that generates unity. And it is to this existential dimension of kenosis, so important to Abe and the other members of the Kyoto School, that we can now turn our attention.

To explore this existential turn in the interpretation of the kenosis of Christ in Christian spirituality, I want to examine the notion of "Jesus forsaken" in the writings of Chiara Lubich.[47] Lubich, like Abe, refers to "Jesus forsaken" as a model for how to live kenotic love. For Lubich, one important reason for living kenotic love is so that the unity for which Jesus prayed, and which is encouraged by Paul, can become an historical fact in the existence of humanity. The way of the cross, modeled by Jesus, involves a kenosis that leads from self to ground, from the field of self-centeredness to the field of other-centeredness, from the isolation of self-consciousness to compassionate interrelatedness, from aloneness to unity. That is, it is a lived answer to the modern problem of irreligion, to the self-alienation of humanity's negative kenosis that is such a concern for both Nishitani and Abe.

How can this be so? How is Jesus forsaken a model for living kenotic love such that self-alienation is overcome and unity is realized? Lubich points out that as the suffering servant, Jesus forsaken shows that one must be willing to lose everything, to be detached from everything, in caring for one's neighbors. Indeed, the "self-emptying" of Jesus forsaken is, according to Paul, related to non-clinging: "Yet he did not cling to his equality with God" (Philippians 2.6). So Jesus did not cling to anything, even holy things, in order to make himself one with those in need. In his kenotic love for humanity, he was not even attached to the Father. And in this way he is a model for the emptiness needed to be one with others. He shows that the path to the sanctity of unity is the way of the cross where one gains through losing. Also in the cry of the abandoned one, "My God, my God, why have you forsaken me?" (Matthew 27.46), one hears that Jesus felt he had even been emptied of his very relationship to his Father. So in making this attitude one's own, as Paul asks the Christian to do, one must be able to give up everything, even one's spiritual riches to become poor, humble, and empty before one's neighbor who is in need.

Lubich also points out that Jesus forsaken embraced all humanity in his kenosis. The love in that kenosis enwrapped all humanity in its universality. In this, he reveals the universal love of God that includes everyone in its scope, even the most evil of sinners: "For he makes his sun to rise on the evil and on the good, and he sends rain on the just and on the unjust" (Matthew 5.45). In this way, Jesus forsaken shows the scope of love and the unity it produces. He shows that the Great Compassion of God universally serves all humanity, "not to be served, but to serve" (Mark 10.45). And in making this an existential principle, one is called to make himself or herself empty before all people, to be servants of all, in realizing the unity that includes all on earth as it does in heaven.

But according to Lubich there are other lessons to be learned from Jesus forsaken as well. Jesus forsaken was the first to love in his relation to humanity. So, we should be the first to love, to be the first to put love into practice with each neighbor. Also, Jesus forsaken loved to the end and even gave his life for his neighbors. So, too, one should go beyond natural limits in order to love all in giving one's life for one's fellow human beings. Many of the human beings for whom Jesus forsaken died were his enemies. So again, one is called in following the model of Jesus forsaken to die to oneself in the practical things of daily life even for one's enemies. And finally, Jesus forsaken identifies in his death with the victims of injustice, with the oppressed, the poor, the outcasts, the prisoners, the hungry, the homeless; in a word, with the least. So one's kenotic love should especially go out in that direction. Namely, it should reach out to the least and draw them into unity with the rest of humanity and God. And Christians believe that in doing this for the least, one is also doing this for God in them: "Whatever you do to the least of my brothers and sisters, you do unto me" (Matthew 25.40). So by following this model, one can be empty before all people and "live them," as Lubich puts it, by sharing their joys and sufferings. Jesus forsaken lives us all by taking into himself all the sufferings of humankind. So, too, by being empty, one's neighbors can pour their sufferings into one's heart, feel understood and loved, and be drawn into unity.

While one does not love in order to be loved, kenotic love often invites a response. And if the person who is served responds to the care he or she receives, the kenotic love can become mutual and unity can be realized. There is in mutual kenosis what Lubich calls a "co-penetration," a mutual interpenetration of love, a mutual indwelling of unity.[48] So in this spiritual environment of mutual kenotic love, with Jesus forsaken as model, we see how out of emptiness comes fullness, as Ueda puts it. That is, out of self-emptying comes compassion and out of this compassion made mutual unity is realized. Therefore, Jesus forsaken is a model for living emptiness, a kenosis of love that can become mutual and thereby become the "place," the "locus," where we can discover the self-determination of the fullness of unity itself. That is, this unity is not produced just by the will of those who love one another, but it is the self-determination of the very unity of the Trinity. In this way, the kenotic love and unity of the Trinity can not only be a transcendent ultimate reality, but also a "lived reality" that has existential meaning for our being in the world. Let me explore this notion of lived trinitarian unity in a bit more detail.

Traditionally, Buddhists have realized that compassion is the functioning of Emptiness. One's experience of Emptiness as a kind of "secondary contact" with Emptiness in enlightenment makes Emptiness "real" for the experiencer. And the living of this "reality" is compassion. What I am suggesting here is that this lived reality of compassion can be mutual and provide a spiritual environment for true unity, the kenosis of love can lead to a unity that is truly a self-determination of the unity of ultimate reality itself. I think that this is what Nishitani means when he says:

> Where the other is at the center of the individual, and where the existence of each one is "other centered," absolute harmony reigns. This may be called "love" in the religious sense. . . . the encounter between one man and another may be transformed as it is into a super reality. That is to say, here reality manifests itself in its original aspect of super reality.[49]

This super reality of absolute harmony that is manifest in other-centered relations is a product, according to Nishitani, of the death of the ego and its self-centeredness. However, ultimately it is not produced by the will of the individuals, but is a self-determination of Absolute Nothingness itself. So for Nishitani, the Zen environment is not only a place where personal realization of Emptiness can occur, but where its functioning as compassion can be lived so that the absolute harmony of interrelatedness can be existentially realized as well.

In Jesus forsaken, we see the Christian's key to this kind of unity. He is a model for living this reality of kenotic love that leads to a realization of unity. But he is more than just a model for such a realization. Here I am presenting an alternative to Takizawa's and Yagi's view of Jesus. I want to affirm the traditional Christian view that what Jesus *did* on the cross has redemptive meaning. His kenosis is not just a revelation of the kenosis of God, it was and is a redemptive kenotic force. Jesus forsaken is the transformative power that enables a person to be renewed in the image he models. One may choose to follow the way of the cross, modeled by Jesus, and accept the suffering implied in its mode of kenotic self-denial and love for others. But to actually follow this way, not only a revelation but an *enablement* is needed that transforms one's life making it conform to the model of Jesus. This enablement comes through the grace of the redemptive kenosis of Christ. So at this point, let us examine how Christ not only *reveals* the kenotic love of God, but *enables* one to live that love in a manner that fosters the self-determination of unity.

Lucien Richard approaches this redemptive event from an anthropological position.[50] He points out that if one understands the self as a knowing subject which is an independent substance apart from objects known, as is implied in Descartes' *cogito*, then personhood is essentially constituted by the *private* activity of thought. This leads to the aforementioned existential problems discussed by Merton and Nishitani. However, if one understands the self as already in relation to others and as being constituted in its identity by those relations, as is implied in trinitarian thought, then personhood is essentially constituted by the *public* character of interrelatedness. In this interrelatedness, we as finite persons suffer and cause suffering to others. Our own suffering can bring a heightened sense of isolation, and the suffering of others can cause us to isolate ourselves from them in self-defense. Yet, if in a kenosis of love we can accept our own suffering and the suffering of others, we can transcend ourselves into a greater compassionate solidarity with others. Shared suffering in the interrelatedness of life creates human solidarity. In the cross of Jesus forsaken, God shared the suffering of all humanity not just to reveal his kenotic love, but to generate a new solidarity with, a new unity with, all humankind.

When Jesus forsaken cried, "My God, my God, why have you forsaken me?" he embraced the isolation that suffering can cause and filled every void in every painful condition in history. In that solidarity with all humanity, he takes all humankind into his compassionate heart and binds humankind to God in a solidarity of love. And given the trinitarian structure of existence in which our personhood is constituted, this unity can remake our identity. Jesus shares our suffering, and our sin, in a solidarity that generates the Holy Spirit that can renew our lives. This is the redemptive side of the kenosis of Christ: "He was rich, yet for your sakes he became poor, so that through his poverty you might become rich" (2 Corinthians 8.9).

In this way, the kenosis of Christ is more than a revelatory event, it is a redemptive event as well. The word "redemption" means both to "rescue" from a negative situation, and to "recover" something of value that had been lost. In terms of rescuing us from our negative situation in life, or what I have called the negative kenosis of humanity, Jesus as the uncreated Image of God empties himself beyond the life of the Trinity and enters our human condition of alienation and self-centered estrangement from God, others and nature. He identifies himself with this dissatisfactory condition. On the cross, our suffering became his suffering, our darkness became his darkness, our sin became his sin. What we feel and suffer is felt and suffered by Jesus forsaken. The pain we feel in our flesh is his pain. Nothing separates our cross from his cross.[51] In this way, God fills the void of humankind's negative kenosis through his own positive kenosis. The power of this redemptive kenosis rescues us, it overturns our ordinary mode of being in the world and recovers our original mode of being in the world. In so doing, it recovers our original union with God and unity with others and all creation. As the kenosis of the love and unity of the Trinity, it recovers our dynamic circuminsessional interrelatedness that integrates us into creation with an integrity of self and an intimacy with God. And as the kenosis of the Image of God, it recovers our original dynamic imaging of God.

This recovery of our original imaging of God, of our "primary contact" with God, requires its existential realization in a "secondary contact." In Christian spirituality, this means that one must appropriate the redemptive power of the cross as an existential reality. This is similar to what Nishitani calls the realization of the "force" of Absolute Nothingness that draws all into harmony, or to what is called "Other-power" in the Pure Land inspired philosophies of Hajime Tanabe and Yoshinori Takeuchi which we will look at in the next two chapters. In all these cases, Buddhist and Christian, the point is made that the rescue from humankind's dissatisfactory condition entails the realization in human existence of something more than can be produced by human willfulness. In Christian terms, this redemption cannot be accomplished just by the human will's choice to follow Jesus as model. As Abe points out, the "blind will" itself must be overturned by the deeper ground of the will. For Christians, this is understood as being accomplished by the self-determination of the ground of being in the redemptive kenosis of Christ.

In this redemptive kenosis, the negative kenosis of humanity is emptied out in a negation of the negation of True Life and one becomes a "new creation." In existential terms, this is not something one does, but it is done to one such that the creative trinitarian structure of reality, in which we and all creatures are united together, is realized concretely. Humanity is rescued from its blind willfulness and its disfigured image of God and recovers its kenotic love and unity and therein its original and true imaging of God. Again, this is accounted for by the redemptive kenosis of God in Christ. The kenosis of the Father results in creation, God effects beings. The kenosis of the Son results in redemption, God effects new beings. The effect in both cases comes not from the human will, but from its ground in God. The Son as the uncreated Image of God rescues us, through his redemptive kenosis into our human condition, from our existential unlikeness to God and recovers our essential "imaging" of God so that we are enabled by our solidarity with him " . . . to become the image of his Son so that his Son might be the eldest of many brothers" (Romans 8.29).

Becoming what we originally are, making that original nature an existential reality is a process that involves the total reformation of the person. It involves the regeneration of our true identity, or a renewal of the imaging of God in a more perfect likeness to God. This ultimate transformation involves an elevation from fallenness, and elevation of the whole person to a profound reintegration with God, others and nature. So we are not talking about redemption as a "forensic justification," a "legal acquittal," or external "declaring just." We are talking about a formative change in the total condition of the person. It is a "making just" as a new spiritual formation that touches the very core of one's existence. Therefore, this formation cannot be achieved by the human will, but rather is achieved by the religious Ideal itself, by God-Love. This Ideal gives form and purpose to one's life by the formative power of the kenosis of the Son, by the power of the cross.

But it is important to see that this redemption is not just an individual matter. When one speaks of "reintegration" with others, one has to recognize the communal dimension of redemption. The redemption of humanity enables persons to live the kenotic love seen in Christ for the ultimate unity of humankind by realizing the very love and unity of the Trinity as an existential communal reality. Therefore, the reintegration of humankind is the self-determination of the trinitarian structure of Being. And humanity itself must be reintegrated in this structure in a manner that makes the structure's dynamic of kenotic love and unity concrete in social form. The negative kenosis of our world must be emptied out into a more united humankind where "absolute harmony reigns," as Nishitani puts it. In this way, society can recover its capacity to dynamically image together, in a collective fashion, the Trinity. Again this is very different from a collective acquittal. It is a formative change in the nature of society. And here it is clear that such a change is beyond the scope of human volition. It involves the re-creation of a New Humanity in the image of the Trinity through the power of the kenosis of Christ that pours the very life of the Trinity into humankind.

For the Christian, faith is at the basis of the kenotic mode of life by which this regeneration of life is realized within us and among us. This faith is not an intellectual assent to doctrines combined with ethical perfectionism. This would be at the level of the intellect and volition and could never touch the deeper blind will that generates humanity's dissatisfactory condition. Rather, faith involves both trust in and obedience to what is a transformative power within the individual and among the community. In the context of a Christian community, both the individuals and the community as such must entrust themselves to the overwhelming power of Christ's kenosis and live in fidelity to everything that entrustment entails. In this way, the individuals and the community can experience "salvation." That is, salvation implies a "salve," a "healing ointment," that restores life. It rescues from sickness and recovers health. So, too, the kenosis of Christ brings health, aliveness in full measure to persons and to society.

This kind of redeemed condition involves not only faith but also, as the members of the Kyoto School remind us, a day-to-day dying and rising with Christ. This existential participation in the death and resurrection of Christ is, as Abe says, a sharing in his kenosis on the one hand and in the new life that results from that kenosis on the other. In a very deep spiritual sense, one can participate in this kenosis, or in Buddhist terms, this kenosis can realize itself in oneself, such that one is led through the wound of Jesus forsaken in one's own suffering into the True Life, or the resurrection life of God. And this is possible because of the identity of Jesus forsaken with each person. One's cross is *the* cross and therefore one can pass through it into the resurrection life: " . . . joined to him in death, so that as Christ was raised from the dead by the Father's glory, we too might live a new life" (Romans 8.4).

And here we can see the redemptive meaning of suffering, both individual and communal. In one's own suffering, one can find the redemptive presence of Christ. And united with Jesus forsaken, one can by grace die to the old life and be brought into new life: " . . . we carry with us in our body the death of Jesus, so that the life of Jesus, too, may be seen in our body" (2 Corinthians 4.10). So united to Jesus forsaken, one's suffering becomes part of one's redemption, part of the process through which he rescues one from alienation and deepens one's union with God. This does not rescue one from suffering. Rather, it gives it redemptive meaning. It gives suffering redemptive meaning not only for oneself but for others as well. Given the trinitarian structure of reality, one's own sufferings are not isolated from the rest of humanity. Jesus forsaken within one's own suffering humanity is shared by all suffering humanity. So Paul could say that "In my own body, I fill up what is still lacking in the sufferings of Christ for the sake of his body, the Church" (Colossians 1.24).

Here we get to the heart of Christian spirituality. Again as Abe notes, Emptiness must be a lived reality. And this is not just a matter of a belief or a particular experience. It is a matter of living day by day the dying and rising of Christ. It is a matter of participation in the kenosis of Jesus forsaken and passing through that kenosis into a deeper participation in the True Life. We are enabled to do this through the power of the cross. The kenosis of Christ both *reveals* this spiritual passage and *enables* us to make that passage into God. However, we must make the choice each day, indeed in each moment, to make that holy journey with and through our embracement of Jesus forsaken. Later, we will see how this is so in the case of individual spirituality, communal spirituality and in the life of the church as the suffering servant. But now I would like to conclude this section on the redemptive kenosis of Christ with a few more remarks on the existential meaning of the cross in Christian spirituality.

To participate in the redemptive kenosis of Christ, not to just reflect upon it or have faith in it but to live that kenosis, is at the heart of Christian spirituality. Through the embracement of him in our sufferings *and* in the sufferings of others, we can live Jesus forsaken, or better Jesus forsaken can live through us, for the good of humanity. We can participate in the suffering servanthood of Jesus forsaken for the sake of unity. Our own kenotic love can be added to his redemptive kenosis to generate "what is still lacking in the sufferings of Christ." However, after saying this, it is important to add that this does not mean that one should focus on one's sufferings. Rather, in the kenotic spirituality of the cross, one must learn to transcend suffering. What does this mean concretely? It means finding God as the principle of transcendence in whatever wounds us, to say "yes" to that presence, and then to turn beyond ourselves to love others. God as self-transcending Love found in the sorrows of life is the power that enables one to go beyond suffering in this way. This is because in embracing Love within one's suffering, that Love becomes the force of love that enables one to love others beyond one's own suffering condition. Suffering is, in this way of the cross, transformed into love. And we can thereby empty out our negative kenosis into the positive kenosis of Jesus forsaken and find there the power that enables us to live beyond suffering in love for others. This movement beyond suffering is a movement through the cross of Jesus forsaken into his resurrection life. The forsaken one and the risen one are the same Jesus. To embrace the former is to find the latter.

This is really the mystery of death and resurrection. We embrace Christ crucified and forsaken and are led through the power of God-Love incarnate therein into a deeper participation in the resurrection life of unity. The *emptiness* of kenosis is itself emptied out as the *fullness* of True Life. And as Buddhists note, these are not two different realities. The life of kenotic love just *is* True Life. So in losing everything, we gain everything back new and contribute to the renewal of everything because the crucified Christ just *is* the risen one. Now again after saying this, it is important to explain that it is certainly true that Jesus is risen and has no need for our consolation. Yet it is also the case that in his abandonment he identified with all suffering humanity in all times.[52] So, we find the face of the crucified one in every human suffering. And when we embrace him forsaken in suffering, we not only find him risen but we also share more profoundly in that risen life. It is as though he gives us who he truly is, his Godhood, when we discover him and embrace him in his forsakenness in our suffering. In this way, living his kenosis effects our divinization. By our participation in the kenosis of Christ, we find that the emptiness of our suffering humanity is emptied out into a fullness of new life. And by our participation in this new life of the risen one, we live in deeper union with God and unity with others and all creation. Our hearts are filled with light, peace and joy.

This movement from the cross to the resurrection does not mean that one's sufferings are taken away. To live *beyond* suffering in love does not mean to live *without* suffering. Rather, suffering is experienced as having redemptive meaning for oneself and others. For example, sometimes in the spiritual life, especially at the beginning, there is a special grace in the discovery of Jesus forsaken and one finds a joy in the midst of suffering. This consolation is an encouragement in the way of the cross. In the more mature life, one can also find peace in the sufferings one undergoes. This is often true at the time of death. However, I must add that the point here is that all suffering has been *redeemed*. It has been *rescued* from meaninglessness and *recovered* by God into himself. So in the very center of suffering, there is an emptiness that is a sacred place. This is also the experience in Buddhism.[53] For the Christian, this is an experience of God, of his redemptive kenotic presence at the core of suffering.

In this redemptive process, through one's own suffering and one's suffering with others, one's mode of being in the world is purified. One finds the "purity of heart," that Thomas Merton emphasized, and with that purity of heart, one grows in compassion: one loves and lives for the sake of others. This leads to a growth in unity, the kind of "absolute harmony" that comes from kenotic love. This purity of heart that expresses itself as a compassion that tends toward unity is perhaps something like the *Bodhicitta*, or "heart/mind of enlightenment," in Buddhism.[54] With *Bodhicitta*, the Bodhisattva, or person of compassion, lives the holy life not for himself or herself but for the good of all sentient beings. So, too, the kenotic love of the Christian is purified in the crucible of suffering if it is united to the kenosis of Jesus forsaken. The result is a compassionate empathy that moves the person to live for the realization of the unity of all humankind in the glory of God. As ice burns, so too the absolute stillness of Jesus forsaken on the cross is an absolute kenotic activity of love that purifies a person in a "burning" that makes that person into what he or she receives. That person becomes a presence or a form of the redemptive kenosis of God. He or she becomes a self-determination of kenotic love for the unity of humankind. In this way the unity achieved is not a product of human ascetic willfulness, but of a divine mystical union with God. It is a unity realized on the field of divine kenosis that brings into human experience the very life of the Trinity.

While it is true that the kenosis of Christ is discovered within one's own self, it is also true that it can be found in others as well, indeed in all creation. The negative kenosis of humanity affected all of creation so that today "the whole creation groaneth and travaileth in pain together until now" (Romans 8.22). Because of the universality of the redemptive kenosis of Christ, the suffering of all humanity and creation is taken into God. So we can find Jesus forsaken in all of the sufferings around us. And in so doing, we can grasp the deep meaning to Jesus' words: "Whatever you did for the least of your brothers and sisters, you did unto me" (Matthew 25.40). And we see why Jesus described "the least" as those most in need: the hungry, the thirsty, the stranger, the naked, the ill, and the prisoner. It is in these that the face of Jesus crucified and forsaken can be found in a special way. One can discover him and embrace him in all the forms of suffering we encounter around us. In each person who is in need, one can see the countenance of Jesus forsaken to be embraced and loved. While each suffering is willed or allowed by God for the divinization of humanity, for deeper union with God and unity among humanity, each suffering is the cry of the abandoned one urging us to find him there and reach out with ever greater kenotic love to care for that person in need. And through that kenosis of compassion, unity can be established with the person for whom one is caring, a unity established on the field of the kenosis of Jesus forsaken that gives it a divine depth. As we shall see, this is the basis for communal kenotic spirituality as well as for the vocation of the church as the suffering servant.

Finally, in Jesus forsaken, heaven and earth meet. In him we find the redemptive kenosis of God. And in that kenosis we find all of humanity and creation.[55] Here, both the near and the far sides are linked in unity through this kenosis of God-Love. This linking is not a matter of simple identity, but of dynamic solidarity. By this positive kenosis of God, the unity of heaven (the Trinity) is poured through the Holy Spirit into the negative kenosis of humanity and its distortion of nature. We can find the power of this kenosis in the particular crosses that we encounter within our own suffering humanity and in that of others. Through their embracement, we find that *person* of the cross, Jesus forsaken, can become an existential reality. We can participate in and live the redemptive kenosis of Christ for our own sanctification, the transformation of society and for the divinization of the cosmos. In this way, our lives can become the self-determination of the True Life that comes from this kenosis. And alienation from others and lostness from God can be overturned. We can be rescued from our unlikeness to God and recover our true imaging of God-Love for the good of all living beings. And since God is Trinity, this is true for both individuals and the human community. So in Jesus forsaken, we find not only a *model* for kenotic love, but the mystical kenotic *power* of love in which we can participate in a manner that transforms our being in union with God and unity with others and nature. This transformative process of death and resurrection is the work of the Holy Spirit and involves his own kenosis that generates this sanctification of persons and the divinization of creation. So it is to an analysis of this phenomenon of death and resurrection in Buddhist and Christian spirituality that we can now turn.

Chapter Four

Sanctification: The Kenosis of the Holy Spirit

At the same time that Kitaro Nishida was writing his final reflections on religion in *The Logic of the Place of Nothingness and the Religious Worldview* (where he also gives his concluding critique of Kant's philosophy), another great philosopher of the Kyoto School was writing his own views concerning religion. This was Hajime Tanabe (1885–1962). Tanabe had studied philosophy with Husserl and Heidegger and later assumed the chair of philosophy at Kyoto upon Nishida's retirement. However, Tanabe and Nishida had a philosophical parting of the ways some years earlier. So Tanabe's book, entitled *Philosophy as Metanoetics*, also contains criticisms of some of the central ideas in Nishida's philosophy while never actually mentioning Nishida by name.[1] While Nishida proposed a "logic of place," Tanabe proposed a "logic of species." And while Nishida emphasized the unmediated self-determination of Absolute Nothingness, Tanabe stressed a dialectic of absolute mediation. While Nishida was influenced most profoundly by Zen Buddhism, Tanabe's notion of metanoesis was informed to a large extent by Pure Land Buddhism: "My experience of conversion—that is, of transformation and resurrection—in metanoesis corresponds to the experience that led Shinran (1173–1262) to establish the doctrine of the Pure Land Shin sect (*Jodo Shinshu*)."[2] However, it is also the case that Tanabe's philosophy of metanoetics is also influenced to some degree by both Zen Buddhism and Christianity as well as the Western philosophical tradition. Therefore, his work not only provides another Buddhist alternative to Nishida's views, but a rich source for East-West dialogue as well. In this chapter, I will only mention the aspects of Tanabe's thought that touch on the issue of spirituality.

Tanabe defines "metanoesis" (*Jap. zange*) as "the activity of conversion and transformation performed by Other-power (*tariki*)."³ For Tanabe, the advance in his own philosophy toward metanoetics was the result of Other-power acting in and through his personal *zange* as he faced the horrible war situation in Japan in the early forties. In a letter to Yoshinori Takeuchi written on July 7, 1944, Tanabe said: "The national mood is extremely somber, and yet I feel a strange sense of light streaming over me that fills me with indescribable gratitude."⁴ It was certainly this type of experience of spirit and transformation, so characteristic of authentic spirituality, that led him to write:

> Once I have submitted myself to this requirement and devoted myself to the practice of *zange*, I am met by a wondrous Power that relieves the torment of my shameful deeds and fills me with a deep sense of gratitude. *Zange* is a balm for the pain of repentance, and at the same time the source of an absolute light that paradoxically makes the darkness shine without expelling it. The experience of accepting this transforming power of *zange* as a grace from Other-power is ... the very core of metanoetics.⁵

> In the life of the spirit . . . "resurrection" must mean regeneration to a new life. I no longer live of myself, but live because life has been granted to me from the transcendent realm of the absolute which is neither life nor death. Since this absolute is the negation and transformation—that is, conversion—of everything relative, it may be defined as absolute nothingness. I experience this absolute nothingness through which I am reborn to new life as nothingness-qua-love.⁶

For Tanabe, this "life of the spirit" is not achieved by the effort of the will, or what Buddhism calls "self-power" (*jiriki*), but through the mediation of the transformative Other-power (*tariki*). He says that this Other-power "that acts within me exercises its power in a way so overwhelming that it obliges me to perform *zange*."⁷ And the dynamics of this life of metanoetics is the subject of Tanabe's *Philosophy as Metanoetics*. This dynamic life is a process of living, or better, being enabled to live, the "practice of death-and-resurrection." I say being enabled to live this way because such a life is the result of Other-power. So before looking at the spiritual life that Tanabe calls "death-and-resurrection," we should first examine its cause. We need to explore what exactly this Other-power is for Tanabe and what its relation is to Absolute Nothingness in

Buddhism and to God in Christianity. Then we can go on to examine the spiritual life of "death-and-resurrection."

While Pure Land Buddhism conceives Other-power as being the power of Amida Buddha to transform one's existence through his grace, Tanabe takes a middle path between this Pure Land position and the position of Zen Buddhism.[8] While he recognizes that religious faith can conceptualize Other-power in a theistic manner, his approach is from the philosophical point of view that understands this phenomenon in a very different way. For Tanabe, "the absolute subject of Other-power is absolute nothingness."[9] The transformation of the self through death and resurrection is an absolute transformation because it is the dynamic functioning of Absolute Nothingness. This functioning of Absolute Nothingness is Other-power as the absolute transformation of the forms of life. Therefore, all things including ourselves exist through the mediation of Absolute Nothingness, that is, through the absolute transformation of Other-power. This mediation sets up a relationship of mutual transformation between self and world that just is the dynamic of Absolute Nothingness understood as Other-power. In this way, Tanabe sees being as a mediation of Other-power, or as "a mediative moment of absolute nothingness."[10]

It is important to note that for Tanabe, Absolute Nothingness cannot function apart from this dynamic of being. It is similar to what Nishitani calls a near-side reality; Other-power is not something beyond and outside the transforming process of being. So while this process transforms the person through death-and-resurrection by breaking into the person as grace, this grace actually emerges from within the depths of the self. Other-power is not a something that confronts the self from the outside, but it is an inner "action seen as the transformation of the self."[11] It is the "force" of Absolute Nothingness that converts the self and restores it to a new life through death-and-resurrection. While it may be experienced as transcendent, it is at the same time immanent.

So it is clear that Absolute Nothingness for Tanabe is not a reality that can exist apart from beings: "Nothingness cannot function apart from the cooperation of being."[12] There is a Zen-like reciprocal penetration between Absolute Nothingness and being. This penetration in one's self-consciousness is experienced as the grace of Other-power. For example, Tanabe says that "I am graced with a personal experience of emancipation from the eternal darkness of mind, as if a serene light had poured forth from eternity into my mind."[13] Yet for Tanabe, this pouring forth of light that brings new life is not from a personal God, but just is the dynamic of Absolute Nothingness as absolute transformation or Other-power. The God of Christian theism seems to Tanabe to be a transcendent absolute that is experienced directly without any mediation.[14] This, in Tanabe's mind, would make God a relative Other-power, that is, existing apart from the process of transforming action and affecting it directly through his transcendent will. For Tanabe, to place the absolute in opposition to the relative is to make it another relative. On the other hand, Absolute Nothingness as Other-power is the absolute mediatory activity of beings in mutual transformation.

It seems from Tanabe's reluctance to conceive Other-power to be a theistic God that he wants to maintain his notion of absolute mediation in a way that is compatible with the Buddhist notion of Emptiness. That is, Absolute Nothingness is transforming mediation and can only function as the mediation of beings. This means that each person is an "axis of transformation."[15] Each person is a mediator of Absolute Nothingness and thus serves as an axis of transformation for others. And here we find the heart of the matter. Tanabe says that this brings us to the meaning of life:

> The world exists for no other reason than that of *upaya* ('skillful means'): it is the world of mediation through which such a reciprocal transformation enables relative beings to move toward nothingness and to return to the world to serve as a means of enlightenment and salvation for others. Metanoesis is the mediatory activity of transcending being in terms of "being as *upaya*."[16]

It is through our reciprocal mediation of absolute transformation that we are ourselves transformed through death-and-resurrection and are enabled by that process of Other-power to be an expedient means of that death and new life for others. To be "mediative moments" of Absolute Nothingness one must be transformed by Other-power into what one truly is through dying and rising to new life.

One can try to achieve this goal through the exercise of will or "self-power." But if this exercise of the will is pursued to the end, action no longer belongs to the self. Rather a higher action is manifest, what Shinran calls the "Great Action" (*taigyo*). For Tanabe, this is the Other-power action of Absolute Nothingness that transforms the person into an "empty being."[17] This graced kenosis of the self makes the self empty and thus enables it to function as a true mediator of Absolute Nothingness. The action of the self is empty and yet expresses a new life, the life of compassionate transformation. Again this is not based on will or self-power, but on a "faith" (*shin*) "in which the self abandons itself and submits obediently to absolute nothingness, the faith of a self-conscious action based on total self-abandonment."[18] The metanoetic practice of self-abandonment cooperates with Other-power which can then transform the self into a true mediator of Absolute Nothingness.

In this transformation of the self, the mediation of Absolute Nothingness "realizes" itself in a manner that is transformative for others. This is the "returning to the world" (genso) so important in Shin Buddhism. Actually, given the grace of Other-power, one's return to the world is a "being returned" to the world "as a true Bodhisattva cooperating with the Great Compassion of nothingness, the self performs the action of gratitude toward the Great Compassion of nothingness."[19] In fact, Tanabe says that the very movement into nothingness is the action of absolute genso. He quotes Pascal's comment: "Instead of saying: 'If God were not merciful, we should have to make every effort towards virtue,' we should on the contrary say that it is because God is merciful that we must make every effort."[20] Tanabe explains this in Buddhist terms. In Shin Buddhism, it is believed that with the grace of Amida Buddha one can progress in this world toward being reborn in the Pure Land after death. Then after gaining full enlightenment in the Pure Land, one can be reborn back into this world to help others in their progress toward the Pure Land. Oso means "going toward" the Pure Land, and genso means "returning to" this world from the Pure Land in order to help others. Metanoetics is the philosophy of absolute genso. That is, metanoesis is itself a kind of absolute genso of Other-power itself in the world. Metanoesis is Other-power acting within one in such a way as to overwhelm the self obliging it to perform conversion: "The absolute as a 'returning to' this world is the motivating force behind our performance of zange."[21] It is interesting to note that Tanabe contrasts this notion of genso with Christian mysticism which he calls the "path of oso." He states that mysticism is a self-power path that seeks, through methods of contemplation, to achieve sainthood. I will criticize this view of mysticism in detail later in this chapter and in the next as well.

Now that we have seen how Tanabe relates Other-power to Absolute Nothingness and God, we can examine the transformative process that this Other-power effects in human existence. Tanabe calls the transformation by Other-power the "metanoesis of death-and-resurrection." This metanoesis is necessary because of the given condition of humanity. His description of this condition has obvious parallels to Christian thought. In a way that is similar to what I have described above as the "negative kenosis" of humanity, Tanabe argues that our being is constituted by a "radical evil" that is the consequence of our freedom.[22] Here he means that our identity is established by our free self-assertion. One has the freedom to determine one's identity and this can lead one to forget one's relativity and presume to be absolute. The natural emergence of the individual self entails a displacement of one's primordial center, and in its place there develops a position of self-centeredness.

Tanabe terms this innate human tendency toward arrogance "original sin." And he points out that this tendency is grounded on a misuse of freedom. The freedom we enjoy "is rooted solely in the grace of the absolute."[23] On the other hand, the grace of the absolute can also negate this freedom, and the identity one creates through it, in order that one may find "true freedom" in the resurrection of new life. This is the dynamic Tanabe calls "death-and-resurrection." It is in entrusting oneself to this process that one acquires true freedom and true identity. Metanoesis is the self-negation of one's rebellious being in self-surrender to grace. And through that negation one's being is affirmed and rediscovered in what Tanabe calls "new life." The negation of death is transformed into the affirmation of new life. This is the dynamic of metanoesis that is a continuous process of spiritual growth.

Again this negation-affirmation is not something one does, but is done to one by Other-power. This activity of negation-affirmation by Absolute Nothingness is called by Tanabe "Great Nay-qua-Great Compassion."[24] The kenosis of the self is not an activity of the self only, but it is an emptying of the self that just is the self-determination of the Great Nay. Real kenosis is accomplished by the power of the Great Nay of absolute transformation. And since that Great Nay is the Great Compassion, the kenosis is not left in negation, but empties out through a negation of the negation into new life. However, Tanabe also feels that this does not free the person from the inclination to evil. The disposition to isolate oneself from the absolute, and others in the absolute, is grounded in the principle of our freedom to differentiate ourselves. Given this situation, one must constantly practice metanoesis in the continuous entrustment of self to this ongoing process of kenotic negation and Grand Affirmation. In this regard, Tanabe quotes Buddhist and Christian sources: "to be restored to life again once and for all immediately after dying the Great Death" and "to come to life by dying with Christ on the cross."[25] Finally, it is important to note that this coming to new life is not an end in itself. Rather, given absolute *genso*, one becomes the true axis of transformation for others. New life is a life of *upaya* that mediates the kenosis of negation and affirmative compassion of Other-power for the good of all living beings.

This Other-power is in need of what Tanabe calls the "cooperation" of the self for its transformation to bear fruit: "The absolute, which consists solely in absolute mediation, cannot function without their mediative cooperation: it requires the self-negation of their self-power. The former is realized only correlatively with the latter."[26] However, even this cooperation of the self is brought about by the Other-power. In this way a dialectic of mediative cooperation is grounded such that Tanabe can speak of *jiriki-qua-tariki* and *tariki-qua-jiriki*. The self is needed for the realization of mediation, and must exercise its freedom to cooperate with that mediation. And the self needs the Other-power in order to cooperate in the first place and to thereby realize its own transformation in this dialectic. Therefore, the death or kenosis of self is grounded not on self-power as such, but on a negation by Other-power that enables a kenosis that leads to a resurrection of "empty-being" that mediates Absolute Nothingness. Tanabe says:

> The way of *zange* . . . does enable the self to be transformed into a new being within the absolute . . . so that one is allowed to exist by the grace of Other-power and to cooperate as the mediator of the absolute. Metanoesis is action performed by the self, but at the same time it is the practice of abandoning the self. Hence, it originates in the Great Compassion of Other-power. Nevertheless, it is actually the self that submits itself voluntarily to Other-power and performs this action. Paradoxically, metanoesis both is and is not the action of the self.[27]

Here we see that Other-power is a power of compassionate enablement. It is not an autocratic monarch that rules by direct unmediated power. (This unfortunately is how Tanabe sometimes describes the theistic idea of a personal God.) The absolute "is not an ideal or goal that ultimately sublates the relative; it is, rather, a principle that supports us continually wherever we stand and makes it possible for us to engage in authentic action. It is . . . the very force that moves us here and now. Wherever the relative exists, the absolute is there as its correlative."[28] This absolute force that moves as the life-force of relative existence enables us to participate in the dynamic of our own transformation that in turn enables us to be mediators of the absolute for the good of other persons. Our freedom is in need of an enablement that moves one from *metanoesis* to *mediation*. This metanoetic transformation is that "in which the self is enabled to perform the genuine activity of nothingness, even though it is the force of absolute nothingness that does the enabling by turning the self into a mediator of nothingness."[29] So we can now see that the dynamic of death-and-resurrection leads from metanoetics to mediation. Through metanoetics, one's life is transformed so that one can mediate the absolute to others.

This Other-power is also analyzed by Tanabe in what he calls the "trinity of action, faith, and witness (*gyo-shin-sho*)."[30] "Action-faith-witness," an important aspect of the Pure Land tradition, is interpreted in a dialectical fashion by Tanabe. The action that precipitates faith which in turn issues in witness is in fact the action of Other-power. This action is the transformation of the Great Nay-qua-Great Compassion that is realized in the religious consciousness of faith-witness. In one's faithful entrustment to this metanoesis, one is transformed and this transformation *itself* gives witness to the action that brought it about. For example, two modes of this witness to the action of Other-power are joy and gratitude. Joy is not something that comes after the transformation but is part of the process itself. That is, joy is not a feeling that results from a change brought about by the process of metanoesis, but it emerges from the Other-power in the process of transformation. This is because while the negation of the process empties the self, the affirmation of one's empty-being is one of joy. And this joy witnesses to Other-power and in turn leads to gratitude which moves one to cooperate with the Other-power in being an expedient means (*upaya*) in helping others to share in this joy. This becomes the life of compassionate witness that is founded on faith and ultimately on the action of Other-power. The compassion here is a mediation of the Great Compassion. Gratitude for the radiant joy originating in the Great Compassion "issues in an enthusiasm to act on behalf of others (*genso-hoon*)."[31]

There is a spiritual depth to the notion of joy in Tanabe's philosophy because of the negation through which it arises:

> The self-surrender . . . produces the grace of a resurrected self that brings with it the joy of a regenerated life. Needless to say, the suffering of *zange* is accompanied by the bitterness of repentance. . . . This profound pain, however, is at the same time the medium of joy and the source of bliss. Joy abounds in the midst of pain . . . because *zange* turns us toward the bliss of nirvana, however sinful and perverted we may be. The joy and gratitude that stem from our being included in the compassion of the absolute and thus redeemed from our original sin arise neither apart from the pain of *zange* nor after it. The joy and pain of *zange* interpenetrate each other.[32]

So in the midst of the pain suffered through the Great Nay of the kenosis of self, there is joy and gratitude through the affirmation of the Great Love of the Other-power. Death-and-resurrection understood by Tanabe is a total process in each moment of the life of metanoesis. Metanoetics for Tanabe involves the "obedient" submission to the process of transformation that brings the pain of kenosis and at the same time the joy and gratitude of new life.

Another aspect of this way of action-faith-witness is that it is the way of freedom: "Only when the way of action-faith-witness opens up before us does freedom become manifest to us."[33] This "freedom" (*jinen*) is not the unmediated freedom of human will, but the freedom of Absolute Nothingness mediated in the selfless person. Just as the joy and compassion mentioned above are not simply human feelings but rather the concrete expressions of the joy and compassion of the absolute, so too, the freedom of *jinen* is the "naturalness" of the free functioning of Absolute Nothingness. The relative being in its kenosis is enabled to live the freedom of the absolute through the transformation of Other-power. This type of freedom is the free selfless action of new life which in Buddhist terms means "action of no-action" or "action without an acting self."[34] That is, the action of the self is no longer merely the doing of the self, but it is the Great Action mediated by the self. Here again, Buddhists appreciate the statement of Paul that it is no longer he who acts but Christ within him who acts.

So for Tanabe, the affirmation of freedom or naturalness is mediated by the negation of kenosis. Therefore, he says that it demands the "blood and sweat" of kenotic religious discipline. It is not something "beneath ethics," but "beyond ethics" in a Kierkegaardian sense. That is, one must exert oneself to the utmost and then with an awareness of one's powerlessness submit oneself to the grace of the Other-power. In the resulting metanoetic negation, one is enabled by Other-power to live the true freedom of new life for the sake of others: "To submit oneself to the absolute and serve as its mediator means to be free in the true sense of the term."[35] The kenosis of self is completed by grace so that the freedom of new life is made possible. But it is important to note that Tanabe quickly adds that this transformation does not empty out our humanness into angelic perfection: "By following the way of *zange*, we ordinary fools can participate in that freedom just as we are, with all our ordinariness and folly. Once we have set foot on the path of *zange*, access to freedom through the Great Compassion is ours."[36]

One might be inclined at this point to object to this notion of freedom. That is, it seems that one is giving up freedom in submitting one's will to an Other-power. However, Tanabe points out that Other-power in Buddhism is grounded in Absolute Nothingness so that the agent that moves one by Other-power is just the absolute transformation of one's life. There is no "being" as an agent outside the self. Other-power as absolute transformation is a "naturalness" (*jinen-honi*) that is beyond the opposition of self and other. In fact, it is in this regard that Tanabe criticizes Christianity. He feels that in Christianity, God is seen as a personal "other" so that submission to his will makes freedom impossible. The Christian God is outside the transformation process and so cannot be the absolute grounding of the spontaneous freedom of *jinen*. I might add that Tanabe includes Pure Land Buddhism in this critique insofar as it too posits a personal relationship between Amida Buddha and sentient beings.[37]

On the other hand, at one point Tanabe does say that if Christians "identify the will of God with the love of God, and divine grace with the working of divine love, then grace, far from destroying human freedom only draws it out as it fosters and sustains the activity of human will."[38] While this interpretation of the Christian notion of God resembles Absolute Nothingness and absolute mediation, to be the same, the idea of a personal God must be abolished. On the other hand, for Christian spirituality, it is important that the far side of God's reality be maintained as the source of true freedom. For true freedom to be lived by humanity, it must be a living of the resurrection life of the risen one. This involves more than participation only in the process of transformation—it involves participation in the life of the Trinity. The process of the sanctification of humankind is not self-contained, but is the result of the pouring out of that new life from God. This does not deny human freedom but opens it up to its fulfillment in God. The transformation does not lead only to rebirth within its process, but to an eternal life of endless joy, gratitude and freedom within paradise. The negation of kenosis and the affirmation of new life lived by mediating that transformation to others is not, in Christian spirituality, an end in itself. It is a taste of the resurrection life of paradise and thus demands an Other-power with a far side that pours this life forth into human existence and also enables one to participate fully and forever in that far side of paradise in God. But more about this later.

Tanabe refers to true freedom as "ecstatic" in that it involves a kenosis of self, a "breaking through" of the self into a deeper experience of selfhood. This *ekstasis* is the breaking of the limits of self in free action. That is, in true active freedom, the self is ecstatic in that it is no longer merely itself but the realization of Other-power. It no longer acts according to its own plan but acts in a way that manifests a "higher spontaneity."[39] This "action of no-action" is an expression of the Great Action mediating grace for all living beings. And it is certainly this ecstatic condition of freedom that is witnessed to by joy and gratitude. And being restored by metanoesis to "empty-being" (*ku-u*), one is enabled to exist as "being as *upaya*." Tanabe compares this state to the person who works for the "kingdom of God" by submitting to "divine providence."[40] This is similar to Nishida's and Nishitani's notions of being a "servant." For Tanabe, it is the negation of the negation of self by Other-power that affirms the self as mediator of the absolute which is the middle path of "true emptiness, wonderful being."[41] In this way one becomes an axis of transformation for others as "coworkers of God or the Buddha" enabling them to cooperate with God or Buddha even in the midst of pain, suffering and evil as mediators of spiritual peace, joy and gratitude, and the freedom of new life.

Until now, we have been looking at metanoetics as an individual phenomenon, that is, involving personal transformation. But for Tanabe, it has a social dimension as well. For example, another aspect of the new life of action-faith-witness is the unity of love "wrought by the Great Compassion." Within the unity of the Great Compassion, transformation moves the kenotic self to reconciliation with other selves issuing in the realization of "social solidarity."[42] Persons are drawn into this unity by their reciprocal kenotic love, or what Tanabe calls their "reciprocal negation." Here again we see a similarity to Nishida's, Nishitani's and Abe's above-mentioned notions of "merging," "gathering," or "collective sharing." The important thing for Tanabe and the others is that this unity is not contemplated but lived, made real in action. However, unlike with the others, this communal dimension of new life is understood by Tanabe in Pure Land terms. He points out that the salvific work of Amida Buddha is actualized in the context of the community of many divine Buddhas. In fact, he says that Amida Buddha is "nothing other than this 'communion' constituted by the absolute mediation between one Buddha and another."[43] The unity of compassion pervades the relationship between the divine Buddhas. And the communion between relative beings can be the context of a social realization of this unity between the Buddhas.

Therefore, unity in the human community is the realization of this "communion" dimension of Amida Buddha. That is, the reciprocal negation of the members of a community in love and unity precipitates the "reciprocal mediation" of the love and unity that exists in the communion of the divine Buddhas. And the solidarity between the human and divine communities, the "spiritual community of Buddhas and believers," as Tanabe puts it, provides the context for social transformation. Again this is because the human community makes present the transforming presence of Amida Buddha. Amida, as the *tathagata*, "is present in the community of Buddhas engaged in praising one another and reciting the name of Amida Buddha, *and* in the derivative mutuality of sentient beings teaching and guiding one another for the sake of salvation."[44] Thus, Tanabe recognizes the importance of social transformation as well as personal transformation in spirituality. The latter involves the presence of Other-power within one's individual life and the former involves the presence of Other-power in the life of the community. This distinction will be crucial in what I will say about individual spirituality and communal spirituality in the next two chapters.

Tanabe philosophically develops a theory about this communal dimension of metanoetics through his "logic of species" in a manner that clearly shows the influence of Hegel. Each individual does not exist as just a particular form of the universal, for example as a particular form of Absolute Nothingness. Between the genus and the individual is the mediation of the species, namely, in our case, a human community. Contrary to Nishida's "logic of place," Tanabe believes that we do not exist as unmediated forms of and in the "place" (topos) of Absolute Nothingness. Rather, we exist in a community (species) that mediates the universal to us. This makes society, and its ability to mediate the absolute and its unity, of crucial importance to Tanabe. And because of this, he feels that the pressing problem of modernity is the conflict between various societies or communities of humanity. Because of these conflicts, the unity of the absolute is not mediated to humankind by its various societies. In this regard, Tanabe mentions the example of liberal democracy in capitalist countries and real socialism in communist countries. He points out that the ideals of the French Revolution were freedom, equality and fraternity. However, freedom in capitalist countries has led to great inequality, and equality in communism has led to a loss of freedom. Tanabe feels that the unifying factor that can conserve both of these ideals is fraternity. This concrete unity should be the goal of modern society. So the modern philosopher must take up the challenge to establish an ontology of a unified social existence that can aid in the overcoming of the present divisions in our world.

In his philosophy of metanoetics, Tanabe takes up this challenge in the following way. He posits a religious view of society which holds that "only the joy of a trans-individual unity of mutual reconciliation and instruction at work within the human community of individuals mediating individuals" can give meaning to human existence.[45] This is only achieved through love which is the concrete relationship of transforming mediation where kenosis leads to affirmation. And this love can only reach its fulfillment in social existence where it creates unity or "the joy of social harmony." Given this unity, the members of the society will live freely and equally with others for the good of the whole community. That is, people are enabled by the Other-power to live united in freedom and equality. In the ideal sense, this unity that affirms freedom and equality will extend between communities overcoming the divisions of humankind. Again, this is similar to Nishitani's notion of "absolute harmony" except that for Tanabe such harmony or unity is the result of Other-power.

Tanabe points out that for Augustine the meaning of history lies in the establishment of the City of God where love is the pivotal mediator of unity. In this way, God's love is mediated by love of neighbor and God's unity is realized on earth. In Buddhism, Tanabe says, the "mutual correspondence among Buddhas" has a social implication for humanity. It can be lived out in the social solidarity of Dharma fellowship. And if this dimension of religion is not maintained, praxis vanishes into contemplation and religion becomes an opiate of the people: "A religion of the people must offer peace of soul and inspire trust in action."[46] While Tanabe makes it clear that it is only through the action of self-offering for the sake of others that one can be delivered from self-centeredness and return to the absolute, he also notes that growth in this Bodhisattva Way should be in the context of the social interrelatedness of self and other in mutual mediation of Absolute Nothingness. In commenting on "He who finds his life will lose it, and he who loses his life for my sake will find it" (Luke 17.21). Tanabe says:

> Everything in this world exists correlatively to everything else. To seek existence for oneself alone by destroying all others is to forfeit one's own existence as well. Only by giving life to those who exist as others, by seeking coexistence despite the tension of opposition, and by collaborating for the sake of mutual enhancement can the self find life in its fullness.[47]

In this life of metanoesis, one finds oneself "in every other." As an "empty being" in relation to others, one participates in reciprocal mediation in society. Again this is the difference between static and dynamic identity. The transformation of Other-power brings forth this new dynamic identity in unity with others through the mediation of mutual love. This social unity is the realization of the absolute unity of Absolute Nothingness in the life of the community or "species" in a way that can overcome the divisions of our modern world.

Insofar as this unity is realized by a community or state, that species represents, according to Tanabe, a particular determination of the kingdom of God on earth. It mediates the absolute and expresses it in its culture. A transformed culture is a particular social form but also expresses the universal and so can communicate with other cultures the common bond of love and unity that reaches out to all humanity. From all this Tanabe concludes that:

The absoluteness of nothingness that brings us into this society of brotherhood is love; it is Great Compassion. Nothingness is love; and the Great Nay of absolute transformation is the Great Compassion. The action-witness of this fact is itself the building of the Kingdom of God and the fulfillment of faith in rebirth into the Pure Land. It is here that we find the meaning of history: that the Kingdom of God is made actual in the course of history through the action-witness of nothingness.[48]

So it is through the kenosis of the Great Nay that one passes through the enablement of the grace of Other-power into the Great Affirmation of the new life of joy, ecstatic freedom, gratitude, peace, love and unity. This Great Action realizes itself in the faith-witness of new life whereby one mediates Absolute Nothingness to others. But in the context of community, this mediation is also a communitarian life of love and unity that can be realized through the mutual kenosis of its members. This community has present within it the presence of the *tathagata*, the Buddha-reality, as the power of light and truth that illumines and guides its members into a deeper participation in its new life. This community then can become the mediator of this new life to all humanity in a way that overcomes divisions and conflicts in the modern world and builds the kingdom of God on earth.

◆   ◆   ◆

In response to these ideas of Tanabe, I want to begin with the understanding of Other-power in Christian spirituality. Then we can go on to see how this power grounds spiritual transformation both on the individual and the communal level. To examine the Christian notion of Other-power active in spiritual life, especially in kenotic spirituality, one is faced with the relation of the Trinity to the process of kenotic sanctification. In traditional spirituality, it is held that a kenosis within the Trinity is the basis of sanctification. It is with this inner-trinitarian phenomenon that we must begin our discussion of sanctification as a process of Christian spiritual transformation generated by the kenosis of the Other-power of the Holy Spirit.

Within the Trinity, the Son exists through the eternal communication of the divine kenosis by and from the Father. This communication is love. The Son is completely transparent so that this kenotic communication is mutual; he communicates back to the Father the love which he has received. This is a mutual kenosis of love that is the very dynamic life of God. In this way the Father empties his love to generate the Son and in this kenosis he is fully Father. And the Son communicates this love back to the Father clinging to nothing for himself, and in this kenosis he is fully Son. The Son lives so that everything is of and for the Father, that is, his identity is dynamic and not static; he is defined as Son by his relationship of love to the Father.[49] Thus Father and Son exist in a relationship of a selfless mutual indwelling of love. In this circuminsession, the Father and the Son exist outside themselves in an *ekstasis* of mutual indwelling. The "place," so to speak, of this mutuality of love in which they stand united is a single principle of love and unity that generates the Holy Spirit. The Holy Spirit is the very love that unites the Father and the Son, a unity in which, because of their *ekstasis* in it, they are all one. Since the Father and the Son mutually indwell in the Holy Spirit, the Holy Spirit indwells in the Father and the Son. In his kenosis, he keeps nothing for himself but is fully love of Father and Son. This relation determines his dynamic identity as well.

The Holy Spirit, as the self-determination of God's own holy love, of God-Love, is present and active in Jesus Christ since Jesus is the Son of God. The Spirit's indwelling in the Son means that he indwells in Jesus who is the incarnation of the Son. In the kenosis of Jesus on the cross, Jesus empties himself and pours forth that life of the Holy Spirit within him. So Paul finds hope "because the love of God has been poured out in our hearts through the Holy Spirit who has been given to us" (Romans 5.5). This pouring forth of new life, this *paradosis* or transmission of transforming power by the Holy Spirit, is achieved through the *kenosis* of the Holy Spirit. In the kenosis of the Father, there is a pouring forth through the Son of Being that effects beings. But this kenosis of creation was distorted by the negative kenosis of humanity. The kenosis of the Son was a redemptive kenosis that rescues us from this distortion and recovers what was lost. This redemption involves a process of transformation into this new life and this is effected by the kenosis of the Holy Spirit. The Holy Spirit is the Other-power of God that "re-creates" ourselves in the image of God. So Paul prays that: "Out of his infinite glory, may he give you the power through his Spirit for your hidden self to grow strong. . . ." (Ephesians 3.16). Growth of this new self, of the true imaging of God-Love, heals humanity and all creation and restores it to its proper interrelatedness. In this way the Holy Spirit from Christ transforms creation so the Son can return it new and redeemed to the Father.

This notion of Other-power is somewhat different from that found in the philosophy of Tanabe. It is definitely a notion of the absolute that is not "absolutely" identified with the transformative process of existence. However, if one looks at the phenomenon of transformation brought about by Other-power, then we find many similarities. It is from this phenomenological viewpoint of metanoesis that I can affirm many of the insights of Tanabe concerning spiritual transformation. For example, to a Christian, transformation also involves a process of death-and-resurrection. As Tanabe says, it is a process in which the Christian finds union with the death and resurrection of Christ. That is, it is not a change arising from human will, but one that is from the action of God. This action of the Holy Spirit is like the *genso* of Christ, that is, the "returning to the world" of new life through the negation of the cross. This "Other-power" is the force behind Christian transformation or "sanctification." The action of sanctification by the Holy Spirit is a mediation of new life that generates a metanoesis that in turn leads to transforming persons into mediators of God-Love to others in the communal project of building the kingdom of God.

In the rest of this chapter, I want to look at the experience of mediated sanctification in Christian spirituality. And right away it is important to remind ourselves that while there are striking similarities to Tanabe's Buddhist experience, when we go beyond the purely phenomenological description to a theological or philosophical interpretation of the actual experience of transformation, there is at least one important difference. That is, in Christian sanctification, one is opened up to something more than the transformation process itself. One is aware of the mediation of the absolute as being a trinitarian mediation of God-Love that is an activity of the Trinity itself. One recognizes the mediating trinitarian structure to existence, but also sees that this structure reflects something else, something that the Christian calls "Abba, Father." And it is the power of the Holy Spirit that enables one to see this reality as "Abba."[50] Through the kenosis of the Holy Spirit, one possesses the most intimate mystery of divine love and life. Keeping this in mind, I now want to look at the Christian experience of the sanctification of the individual, the community, and the world.

I would agree with Tanabe that the most common mediation of the absolute is through the things, persons and events of daily life. The Holy Spirit touches one's life through the people one meets, the events one experiences and reflects upon, and the movements of nature. And Tanabe is also correct in saying that the secret of spiritual transformation lies in "entrusting" oneself to the Other-power within this process "with total self-abandonment." I am reminded here of the work of Jean-Pierre de Caussade (1675–1751) entitled *Abandonment to Divine Providence*.[51] Caussade taught that the transformative activity of God is found in all things:

It is offered to us all the time and wherever we are. All creatures, friends or foes, pour it out in abundance, and it flows through every fiber of our body and soul until it reaches the very core of our being. . . .God's activity runs through the universe. It wells up and around and penetrates every created being.[52]

Thus, all creatures mediate the absolute to each person through God's providence: "The actions of created beings are veils which hide the profound mysteries of the workings of God."[53] And for this mediation, Caussade says, we should be "grateful to all creatures, cherish them and thank them silently for their good will in helping us, by God's design, toward perfection."[54] For Caussade, each present moment mediates this Great Action, to use Shinran's term, of God's transforming power. Caussade calls this the "sacrament of the present moment." But for it to do its work, one must abandon oneself to its power. It is in need of our "acceptance," "surrender" and "cooperation," in short, our "gentle and wholehearted submission to providence."

Caussade, like Shinran and Tanabe, taught that one's own efforts to generate transformation will fail: "God's action is boundless in its scope and power, but it can only fill our souls if we empty them of all false confidence in our own ability."[55] And also like Shinran and Tanabe, Caussade says that even the ability to practice this kenotic self-abandonment is itself a grace. In this sense, it is what he calls "an art without art." To quote Caussade at some length:

There is a time when God desires to animate the whole of the soul and bring it to perfection secretly and by unknown ways. . . . After several experiences of the folly into which it is led by its efforts to guide itself, the soul recognizes how helpless it is and . . . it abandons itself to God so that it can have only him and receive all things through him. It is then that God becomes the source of its life. . . .[56]

Now it is surely obvious that the only way to receive the impress of this idea is to put oneself quietly in the hands of God, and that none of our own efforts and mental strivings can be of any use at all. This work in our souls cannot be accomplished by cleverness, intelligence, or any subtlety of mind, but only by completely abandoning ourselves to the divine action. . . .[57]

These words certainly echo the teachings of Shinran who also rejected any self-power "calculative thinking" in spirituality. But of course Caussade, like Shinran, also points out that this does not absolve one from following the duties of life and participating in the life of the community. It means only that the True Life is a gift from the Holy Spirit that is to be received through the Great Action of God's divine providence.

The "touch," as John of the Cross calls it, of this action is the Holy Spirit within the heart of the person. It may be mediated by another, but it is, as Tanabe noted, an immanent phenomenon that transforms the person from one's deepest Center and enables the person to be more purely a mediator of God for others. This is what Tanabe calls the movement from *metanoesis* to *mediation*. John of the Cross speaks of this effect of the Holy Spirit in the Center of the person as one that "transforms and clarifies it in its whole being, power and strength and according to its capacity, until it appears to be God."[58] Here John emphasizes the mystical experience of both "transformation" and "manifestation."[59] The Holy Spirit dwells in the Center of one's being: "Do you know that your body is a temple of the Holy Spirit within you?" (1 Corinthians 6.19). And when it transforms a person, that person is clarified so as to reflect or manifest this reality of God to others. One is enabled to image God, to be a purer image of God. John uses the metaphor of a crystal to explain this *transformation* and *manifestation*. He says that when a "pure light" shines on a clean crystal, the light concentrates within it and the crystal becomes brilliant so that it seems to be all light: "And then the crystal is indistinguishable from the light, since it is illuminated according to its full capacity, which is to appear to be light."[60]

Paul points out that "anything exposed to the light will be illuminated and anything illuminated turns into the light. That is why it is said: " Wake up from your sleep, rise from the dead, and Christ will shine on you" (Ephesians 5.13–14). Therefore, Paul concludes that the transformation by the Spirit remakes us in the image of Christ: "All of us . . . are being transformed from glory to glory into his very image by the Lord who is the Spirit" (2 Corinthians 3.18). And this, for Paul, results in a manifestation of God in the transformed person: "For God, who said, 'Let light shine out of darkness,' has shone in our hearts, that we in turn might make known the glory of God shining on the face of Christ" (2 Corinthians 4.6). Both Paul and John of the Cross, like Caussade, also make the point that this is not achieved by us, but by the transforming power of God. It is this "Other-power" that enables us to participate in the new life of the risen one that in turn makes us new persons. Paul calls this "sharing the image of the Son" through which we are rescued from our old ego-self and recover our true or original self as a new self in the image of Christ (Romans 8.29). We are enabled by the transformation of the Holy Spirit to manifest this Christ image in our own unique ways. Again using the metaphor of light as does Tanabe and John of the Cross, Paul says that in this way one "inherits the light" so that the Holy Spirit takes "us out of the power of darkness and creates a place for us in the reign of the Son that he loves" (Colossians 1.13).

This *transformation* leading to *manifestation*, like Tanabe's *metanoesis* leading to *mediation*, is the means by which one discovers the redemptive presence of Christ at the Center of one's being and allows his immanent Spirit of Other-power to manifest itself to the world. To me, this manifestation is the self-determination of the Image itself. Here, I think, is a link between Tanabe and Nishida. The transformation of the person by Other-power leads to the mediation of that Other-power by the person. And in Christian spirituality, this is not a mediation by the self, but is a mediation as manifestation through the "self-determination of the Image itself." This self-determination of God, of the absolute Image, is the source of the mediation as manifestation. The spiritual transformation results from a self-determination of Christ within the person through the mediation of the Holy Spirit. For the Christian, one experiences the Holy Spirit maturing the first fruits of the reign of love, as I prefer to call what Tanabe refers to as the kingdom of God, as it develops the resurrection life within one's heart. Again, this is through the self-determination of its divine nature: "so you might be partakers in the divine nature" (2 Peter 1.4). Through this self-determination, the Holy Spirit generates the Image of God, gives birth to Christ within us as he did in Mary, so that we reflect, or mediate, what we become. Or better, we become what we reflect, namely, sons and daughters of God.

This self-determination of Christ at the Center of our being is the result of the kenosis of the Holy Spirit. What the Holy Spirit is pouring out through this kenosis is the Other-power of divine self-determination. Since this kenosis is experienced as taking place within the self, one could be led to conclude that the transformation process (Tanabe) or self-determination (Nishida) is only immanent to the self and therefore has no transcendent basis beyond the absolute dynamic of the immanent kenosis. But this is not the Christian experience. The immanent dynamic within the Center of one's being opens into the self from the Trinity. The self-determination of the Image of God itself is a self-communication of the trinitarian God-Love through the Holy Spirit. Again, it is "the love of God poured out into our hearts by his Spirit" (Romans 5.5).

When John of the Cross says that we become God by participation in God, he is expressing the Platonic view that, for example, the wise person becomes wise by his or her participation in wisdom. For John of the

Cross, this participation in God takes place at the Center of our being and transforms us as individuals. We are transformed by the inner presence of God until we manifest, or mediate, God. In this individual participation we are individuated as unique images of the Image in which we participate, just as wise persons are unique while all are participating in the same wisdom. And because this new life that is found at the Center of one's being is the divine life of the Trinity, Teresa of Avila calls this Center a "second heaven."

The results of this sanctification by the Holy Spirit are manifold. One certainly recognizes many of these in the description of metanoesis given by Tanabe: the light that illumines our sinfulness and at the same time the grace of God, the sense of enablement and ability to cooperate with the absolute, the joy and gratitude of new life out of negation and conversion, the love and compassion that mediate the Great Compassion, and the ecstatic freedom of spontaneity and naturalness that are marks of true spiritual life. And from a Christian point of view, Tanabe is also correct when he says that the joy, peace, freedom, compassion, etc., are not just psychological effects of transformation, but are the Great Action itself. In Pure Land language, they are the arising of Amida Buddha in the person's faith. They are the joy, compassion, freedom, etc., of the Buddha Mind taking shape in the mind of the person of faith. In Christian language, this is similar to receiving the "mind of Christ" (1 Corinthians 2.16) in the new life of the Holy Spirit so that one can say with Paul: "It is no longer I who live but Christ within me who lives." And only in this way can Tanabe as well as Christian spiritual writers talk about "joy in suffering."[61]

Another result of transformation that is so important to Tanabe, given his logic of species, is "unity." The above mentioned results can be experienced through individual transformation. But real unity requires a communal transformation as well. And in terms of this communal level of transformation, Tanabe is also correct when he points out that the "joy of social harmony" or "unity" is the participation of the members of the community in something that is the result of Other-power. For Shin Buddhists, it is a participation in the communal presence of Amida Buddha. In Christian terms, this is the community living the life of the Trinity which is present among them in Christ. Since the description of unity stemming from kenotic transformation is an important project in this book, I want to spend some time discussing the relation of unity to sanctification.

Masao Abe reminds us that from the Buddhist point of view, all humanity is "a single, living, self-aware entity."[62] And as I said above, for the Christian, all humanity makes up one body created in the image of the Trinity. That is, humankind is created as a whole to image together the love and unity of the Trinity. The negative kenosis of humanity emptied out this imaging into an unlikeness to God. The redemptive kenosis of Christ rescues humanity from this unlikeness and recovers its true imaging of God. So there can be a self-determination of the Image of God not only at the Center of the individual person, but also at the Center of community. And there it can produce a communal imaging of the Trinity. Tanabe says that the unity of the Buddhas can be present in the community of Buddhists. So too, the love and unity of the Trinity can become the life of the community of Christians through a self-determination of the presence of Christ in the midst of the community: "For where two or three are gathered together in my name, there am I in the midst of them" (Matthew 18.20).

Because of this communal presence, Christian spirituality can have a communitarian dimension. That is, while in personal transformation by the Holy Spirit there can be a self-determination of the Image of God within the Center of oneself, in communal transformation by the Holy Spirit there can be a self-determination of the Image of God at the Center of the community. And while individual participation in God at the Center of our being can transform one in personal sanctification, so communal participation in God at the Center of the community can transform both the individual members as well as the community as a whole in communal sanctification. The risen one can be within one pouring forth the new life of the resurrection, *and* he can be among persons pouring forth the new life of unity in the resurrection. In this way, humanity as a whole can recover its dynamic communal identity, its proper interrelatedness that images the interpenetration or mutual indwelling of the persons of the Trinity.

Communal spirituality seeks not only personal sanctification but a communal sanctification that brings not only individual union *with* God but communal unity *in* God. This is the answer to Jesus' last prayer: "That they all may be one, as you Father are in me, and I in you, that they also may be one in us. . . . that they may be one, even as we are one. . . . that the love wherewith you have loved me may be in them, and I in them" (John 17.21, 22, 26). This is also the unity for which Paul was pleading in his letter to the Philippians. Paul saw that this unity depends on the mutual kenosis of the members of the community as they participate in the death and resurrection of Christ: "Continually we carry about in our bodies the dying of Jesus, so that in our bodies the life of Jesus may also be revealed. While we live we are constantly being delivered to death for Jesus' sake, so that the life of Jesus may be revealed in our mortal flesh" (2 Corinthians 4.10–11). Certainly, Tanabe also saw that unity is dependent on death-and-resurrection through mutual or reciprocal negation and the mediation of the Great Compassion. And let me hasten to add that however Buddhists or Christians understand this process of communal transformation toward a unity that reconciles all humanity, both traditions can collaborate together to make it a reality. As Tanabe says, it is not enough to contemplate unity, we must make it a social reality. And in today's pluralistic world, this can only happen through interfaith collaboration.

When we consider all the results of transformation or sanctification from joy to unity, it is clear that from Tanabe's as well as the Christian point of view, one becomes what one receives. And for the Christian, this phenomenon of becoming what one receives is crucial to the mystical life in both individual and communal spirituality. For example, to become joyful, compassionate, peaceful and free by participation at the Center of one's being in the life of God which is marked by these qualities is the fruit of the inner contemplative life. And to share these fruits with others by co-participation together in a communal trinitarian Center makes the members of the community one in love and unity, the unity of God. The former is the self-determination of the Image of God within the person, and the latter is the self-determination of the unity of God among persons. And the way in which one becomes the self-determination of what one receives in these two senses has to do, as Tanabe and other members of the Kyoto School realized, with *ekstasis*.

In trinitarian thinking, the primordial *ekstasis* is found in the heart of the Trinity. As I said above, in the circuminsession of the Trinity, the Father and the Son exist outside themselves in an *ekstasis* of mutual indwelling. This ecstatic unity is love, and that love is the Holy Spirit. In this Spirit of love and unity, God is fully present in its oneness. So wherever there is the Holy Spirit there is the ecstatic oneness of God. This *ekstasis* is the foundation of both the individual and communal *ekstasis* in Christian spiritual life. In Buddhist thinking, *ekstasis* is a "breaking through" of the self beyond the confines of the ego into a deeper spiritual life, the life of Other-power or Absolute Nothingness. For Christians, this breakthrough is into the *ekstasis* of the Trinity. On the individual level, this means a breakthrough, by the grace of Other-power or the Holy Spirit, into the risen life of Christ at the Center of one's being. In this individual *ekstasis*, one participates in the inner presence of the *ekstasis* of God and finds the joy of resurrection life. As Tanabe notes, through this death-and-resurrection one is transformed by the Other-power, or what I am referring here to as the Holy Spirit. We become what we receive, we become images of the Image of God, sons and daughters of God sharing in the joy of the ecstatic resurrection life. And the reception of this new life through grace brings the other fruits of the spiritual life mentioned above as well. Here again I hope it is clear that this spiritual realization is not, as some are claiming, a "natural" potential for all persons, a potential that Jesus Christ realized. Rather, it is a potential for all persons through their participation in what Jesus Christ is, namely in the risen one of God who just is God.

Here we are really talking about the centrality of Christ in Christian mystical life. A Christian mystic is one with Christ in Christ's *ekstasis* in the spirit of love so that he or she can behold and know God the Father in ecstasy. And it is in union with Christ as the Image of God within the Center of the soul, that he or she is in ecstatic union with God. So one actually possesses what one beholds in ecstasy. This is pure joy. It is a participation in the fundamental *ekstasis* of God and thus in the joy of the Trinity. In their trinitarian relationships, each person of the Trinity is in union with the others and yet stands before the others in loving ecstasy. The mystic participates in this condition at the Center of his or her being as a foretaste of paradise where all are one in union with God and yet many in the *ekstasis* of love. Christ is central to all this because it is he within one who pours forth the power of the Holy Spirit whose transforming kenosis in turn pours out this resurrection life here on earth. Through transformation by this Other-power at the Center of one's being, the mystic can have a foretaste of heaven on earth, the ecstasy of God, the joy of the resurrection life to be fully enjoyed in paradise. Here we can see that Christian mysticism is not, as Tanabe thought, a path of *oso*, but is a path of *genso*. Again, one becomes what one receives. What Tanabe saw as the mystic following the ascetic path toward holiness, is simply the cooperation of the mystic with divine grace.

This *ekstasis* of love and unity in the Holy Spirit that transforms human existence on an individual level can also be discovered in communal life. Since Christ can be present in the midst of a community, the mystical experience of the *ekstasis* of God is also possible in a communal context. In the individual *ekstasis*, there is a breaking through of the ego into a deeper life in God. In the communal *ekstasis* there is a breaking through of persons into a deeper life of unity in God. This breakthrough is again the work of grace that opens persons to be united in the *ekstasis* of God. The self-determination of the unity of God in the midst of the community can be an ecstatic reality in which the members of the community can participate and through which they can be transformed outside of their limited selves in unity with one another. This unity is one of ecstatic love, the love and unity of the *ekstasis* of the Trinity lived communally on earth. This is achieved not through human willfulness, but through the kenosis of the Holy Spirit poured out from the presence of

Christ in the midst of the community. This mutual indwelling of persons is a "co-penetration," to use Lubich's term, between persons and is really a participation in the mutual indwelling of the Trinity.[63] This is a mystical communitarian taste of the life of paradise.

So what Teresa of Avila calls a "second heaven" can not only be found within the Center of one's soul, but also at the Center of the community. This "second heaven" is the *ekstasis* of God that is poured through the kenosis of the Holy Spirit into one's heart or into the heart of the community. In either case it enables persons, as Tanabe realized, to be "empty beings" able to live outside themselves for the good of other beings. As Chiara Lubich says, one is enabled to "live one's neighbor."[64] One is enabled to be empty of self in order to take in the joys and sorrows of others. The grace of the Holy Spirit enables one to live the kenosis of self, as Paul was asking for in his letter to the Philippians, in order that unity can become a reality in the community and therefore for humankind.

Since the Holy Spirit is love, through the presence of Christ within each member of the community, the Holy Spirit is the love that becomes mutual in unity. The unity is his not ours. It is the grace of his love, his Great Action that makes us one. Herein lies the source of the ecstatic joy of mutual love in the unity of the community. The Holy Spirit as love disappears in his kenosis in order to put into relief those who are loved. So one sees only the beloved, Christ within oneself, or Christ within one's neighbor to be loved in front of oneself. On the nothingness of the kenosis of the Holy Spirit one sees others to be loved by the light of that nothingness, the illumination of the Holy Spirit as love. For example, Christ is understood as the source of "the light that enlightens all persons" (John 1.9). As Christ, the Image of God, is more and more self-determined in one's life, one finds oneself in a clearing of light that enables one to see oneself, the world and God in a new way. One beholds God in all and through all as a hidden unity that links all things in the providence of his love. One finds that all are brothers and sisters because of the shared original presence of God through the kenosis of the Father. And the unity of this "primary contact" is being realized through a "secondary contact" *and* "tertiary contact I might add. This "third contact," which I add to Takizawa's two other types of contact with God, is the transformative contact with the presence of God resulting from the kenosis of the Holy Spirit. Again, I must add that for me, the secondary and tertiary contacts do not result from the creative kenosis of the Father, which does account for the primary contact, but from the kenosis of the Son and the Holy Spirit, respectively.

Chiara Lubich explains this tertiary transformation with the metaphor of fire.[65] In our individual union with God, a fire *within* us destroys our static identity, our ego, consuming us in a new life of *ekstasis* in God as we participate more and more in it. On the other hand, as we are more deeply united together in a communal participation in God as a fire *among* us, our individualistic selves, like logs on a fire, are consumed until we are made one. In both cases we become what we receive, namely, the fire of God-Love. We can become likenesses of the fire of God-Love within, and likenesses together of the fire of God-Love-and-Unity among us. As individuals and as communities, Christians inflamed by these fires can mediate this transformative reality to others. The kenosis of the Holy Spirit can pour through the person and the community for the ultimate transformation of all humanity and all creation, namely for the building of the reign of love.

Tanabe recognized that unity is not just to be contemplated but "made real in action." For him, the mutual kenosis of the members of the community becomes a context for the mutual mediation of the Great Compassion that reconciles persons into social solidarity. In this way, the community can make unity a social reality that reflects the unity of the Buddhas and mediates their transforming and unifying power to humanity. This mediation of unity can overcome divisions and create a more united world, and ultimately contribute to the reign of love. Like a Buddhist echo of Paul's call for kenosis in his letter to the Philippians, Tanabe says that mutual kenosis mediates compassion that makes unity a lived reality. And in this way, through mutual action-faith-witness of Absolute Nothingness, the reign of God is made a reality on earth. For the rest of this chapter, I want to look at how this social dynamic of sanctification can also be seen in the Christian community, that is, in the church.

When Jesus was baptized by John the Baptist, the Holy Spirit was seen descending upon him "like a dove" (Matthew 3.16). The dove is the symbol of the Holy Spirit, and because of its place in the flood story (Genesis 8.8–12), it also symbolizes the re-creation of a new people of God. So the Holy Spirit is active in Christ *and* in a special way in the new people that participate in Christ's mystical body, namely, the church. The church sees itself as a social form of the sanctifying action of the Holy Spirit in the world. But I must quickly add that this same Holy Spirit is also possessed by and active in all people.[66] Through his sanctification, people of other faiths are guided and impelled toward a new life of holiness. The light of this sanctification enlightens the mind and opens it to the truth while its fire warms the heart and opens it to love. Thus, it guides with the light of truth and impels with the fire of love, the minds and hearts of all people leading them into truth and holiness.

This impelling and guiding is something that is felt at the Center of one's being and is experienced as affecting all one's faculties drawing one into a deeper and more constant metanoesis in the spiritual journey toward the Center of all being. It is something that on the one hand transforms the intellect, will, and feelings, and on the other hand gives certain "gifts" as it draws all people into holiness in the life of God and guides them into the fullness of truth, into "all truth" (John 16.13). The Holy Spirit has given holy gifts to all people as well as to the time-honored religious traditions of all people. These traditions maintain and pass on these gifts to future generations. Today, more than ever before, persons of all faiths are being led by the Holy Spirit to share these gifts in order to inspire one another in our common pilgrimage into the fullness of sanctification and truth. A fundamental gift of the Holy Spirit in Christianity, that is a primary source of aid in sanctification, is the church.

The first occurrence of the Greek word for church, *ekklesia*, is in Paul's first letter "to the church of the Thessalonians" (1 Thessalonians 1.1). The word itself is related to the compound form of the verb meaning "to call out." In classical Greek literature, this word was used for an assembly of citizens officially "called out" together to carry out some responsibility for the larger community. This was a usage with which Paul was certainly familiar. Also the New Testament word for "fellowship" (*koinonia*) is from the verb meaning "to have a share in." So, the church is for Christians a gift of the Holy Spirit *to which* one is "called out" and *in which* one "has a share" for a particular purpose. This is why the New Testament does not present the Christian person as one who lives privately, withdrawn from community. Christians are called out and drawn together by God to carry out some responsibility for the good of the larger community of humankind.[67] And this mission is connected to the fact that Jesus forsaken so emptied himself on the cross that his Holy Spirit poured out into the church. Out of death came new life, a "resurrection life" shared in by the members of the church. The Holy Spirit as love became the new spiritual life of the community drawing it together in unity and impelling and guiding it to finish what Jesus had begun. Christians are like "living stones" in a temple that is an ongoing communal work of sanctification by the Holy Spirit directed toward the end for which Jesus died, the reign of love (1 Peter 2.4). In individual sanctification, one experiences this reign of love within, and in communal sanctification it is found in the midst of the community. But it is yet to be completed for the full harvest of unity, the unity of all persons with one another, God, and the cosmos.

The Holy Spirit has enabled the members of the church to be able to *explicitly* participate in, to "have a share in," the "death-and-resurrection" of Jesus. He enables them to share together as a community, to participate as Christ's very body in his kenosis of love and his new resurrection life of unity. Through this participation in Christ crucified and risen, in oneself and among the community, one experiences the mystery of divine life lived in humanity, the mystery of the incarnate Christ. This mystery of Christ, of divine life lived in *human form*, is given a *social form* through the Holy Spirit as the church which continues this mystery in history. Through the transforming presence of the Holy Spirit, the church is an incarnational social structure of the resurrection life of Christ in humanity. So Christians are "called out" together as the church in the world in order to "have a share in" a mystical and communal lived reality of God communicated through the kenosis of the Holy Spirit. In this way, as the mystical body of Christ, the church can be a particular *communal* leaven of *mediation* and *manifestation*, of sanctification for the reign of love for the good of the larger human community. In understanding this concept of the mission of the church, I believe that the view of the church as "sign," "sacrament" and "servant" given in Vatican II, is invaluable.

First, let us look at the church as "sign." Salvation history has the reign of love as its end. And in Christ there is a revelation of this eschatological fulfillment. The first fruits of this reign of love are discovered in him within us and among us. And the church feels called out together to work for the full harvest of this reign. In so doing, the church is an "inhistorization" of this revelation. To the degree that the church lives the "negation-and-affirmation," the kenosis and resurrection life of Christ, it is more or less a "sign" that manifests the reign of love for which it works. The church functions more or less well in this mediating role insofar as its members participate more or less in the mystery of death-and-resurrection in Christ. This mediation is a functioning for the reign of love, and this is the special gift of the Holy Spirit that the church is for the sanctification of the world. In this way, its mission is to be a leaven of unity. This is the mission of God in the world that defines the mission of the church. One makes that mission one's own by living in unity the resurrection life through kenotic love in unity with others. In this way, the church as a social presence of this life becomes a more tangible communal signification or "sign" of the reign of love.

This description of the church as a sign of the reign of love may be criticized for being too idealistic. And in fact, it is always important for the church to recognize itself as a "church of sinners," to use Karl Rahner's terms. In this recognition, the church also recognizes its obligation to practice metanoesis and constantly re-form itself into a more true sign of the reign of love. The church is always a "sign in progress"; being a sign of the unity of the reign of love is a process for the church. And it must always address both intra-ecclesial as well as extra-ecclesial tendencies and forces that oppose growth toward a fuller, more universal and authentic signification of this reign of love. For example, until today the church has most often been structured by means of the cultural forms of Europe and the West. It has also expressed itself theologically through the philosophical concepts from that same part of the world. For the church to be a fully inculturated *upaya*, or expedient means, for all persons in all parts of the world is something still to be achieved. Therefore, since Vatican II, the church has stressed the importance of this inculturation around the world.

In this regard, Tanabe is correct to point out that the universal is mediated to individuals through the species, through the society and its culture. The mediation, or what I have called signification, of God through the church can be enhanced through interfaith dialogue within the cultures in which the church is located. Toward this end of inculturation, the church is developing a pluriformity of theologies and ecclesial life through local churches in dialogue with their surroundings.[68] In this way, the church will better provide a communal unity of particular communities expressing their common faith, always according to a universal guiding norm, in a plurality of forms appropriate to the different parts of the world. Each will give a particular visible social form or shape to the inner universal dynamic of unity in faith and practice that will best mediate that universal to particular peoples. But each inculturated form must also be a lived guarantee of the unity of the universal church.

This modern development of the inculturation of the church is impelled and guided by the Holy Spirit. But we must remember that living together in love and unity is not simply or purely a result of human willfulness. Rather, it is achieved by sharing in the life of "death-and-resurrection," as Tanabe puts it, leading to a communal participation in the love and unity of the Trinity. It is the self-determination of the unity itself as a communal reality that unites the members of the church and makes them one. And this is achieved through the kenosis of the Holy Spirit. Therefore, we must be careful in the inculturation of the church today because it is the Holy Spirit that gives form to the authentic structures and sacraments of the church. These structures and sacraments mediate or communicate, from the kenosis of the Holy Spirit, a power of transformation within and among persons that bestows and nourishes in a special manner the resurrection life of the risen one for the sanctification of humanity and the cosmos. These special gifts of the Holy Spirit nourish the Christian in the mystical body of Christ. And this body carries a transforming and uniting presence of God. Thus, the church is ultimately a *sacramental* sign, a special sacrament for the unity of the world (*Sacramentum Mundi*).

The church, then, is a people called out by the Holy Spirit to share a True Life together as a sign or *manifestation* of what the world can and hopefully will be, namely, a new and united humanity sharing in a reign of love within a new heaven and a new earth.[69] And with the transforming presence of Christ and the Holy Spirit, the church becomes a sacramental *mediation*, a leaven, for transforming the world toward this ideal. So the church sees itself as a socio-historical sign and sacrament of Christ's presence. It is therefore a sacramental instrument, a sacramental *upaya*, of the creative-redemptive-transformative power of God. It is a presence of what it celebrates, namely, a sacramental presence of "joy and hope" (*gaudium et spes*) for the unity of humankind. Again, this does not mean that the church is the *only* soteriological presence or power of the Holy Spirit in the world. A sacrament is a particular and concrete expression of a broader reality of grace. In other words, it is a particular gift of the Holy Spirit that makes this broader reality tangible in a particular manner and for a particular purpose. For example, in the eucharist, the broader communal presence of Christ in the community is made tangible in the particular bread and wine in order in turn to nourish that broader presence and those people who share in it for the particular purpose of their sanctification. In a similar way, the church is a tangible sacramental sign and presence of an ultimate reality whose broader presence in the world it seeks to express and to nourish.

Such sacramental nourishment, like that of the eucharist, is one of healing, enlightening, enriching and refreshing, as well as encouraging and empowering. And the particular purpose of the activity of the Holy Spirit is to be in this way a leaven for the reign of love. Now I should again add, and I want to underline this, certainly other religions also contain particular expressions of truth and the transformative power of what Christians call the Holy Spirit. And in many cases the depth of this truth is truly profound. So other religions have a positive and unique part to play in the building of the new and more united humanity to which Tanabe, as well as the other members of the Kyoto School, look forward. Therefore, today through interfaith dialogue and collaboration, there can be a mutual enrichment between all religions and cultures leading to their mutual transformation on their common journey toward the ultimate transformation of humanity and the cosmos.[70]

Finally, in all this we can see the image of the church as "servant." Here the image of the kenotic Christ, the "suffering servant," is operative. The kenotic servant is the one who offers himself or herself for the liberation and enablement of others. The church as the suffering servant in this sense is the body of the kenotic Christ offering itself for the good of all persons so they might become full sharers in a more just and united pluralistic world community, the coming of the reign of love. As Tanabe noted, unity is not just to be contemplated but acted. The quest for truth, of being led into a fuller realization of truth, is connected to the quest for justice, freedom, peace and unity. Truth means the disclosure of reality, that is, among other things, the disclosure of a suffering humanity with its limits and its potentials, and also the social-political structures that limit or fulfill human aspirations and ideals. So unity as an ideal calls not just for reflection and meditation, but for existential involvement in an active service to an evolving humanity. It calls for a manifestation and mediation of Other-power that enables humanity to reach the unity of the reign of love. We will look at what this means in concrete terms later when we discuss communal spirituality and its work for building a more united world. But now that we have seen how the kenosis of the Holy Spirit is understood in Christian sanctification, we can turn to how this kenosis is actually lived out on an individual basis in Christian spirituality. Then we can go on to examine how kenosis is lived in communal spirituality not only for the sanctification of the individual but for the divinization of creation.

Chapter Five

Spirituality: The Kenosis of the Individual

At the beginning of the last chapter, I quoted a few lines from the letter that Tanabe wrote to his student Yoshinori Takeuchi (1913–). Takeuchi, who studied under Tanabe as well as Nishitani at Kyoto University, became a Pure Land Buddhist priest of the Takada sect of Shin Buddhism. So on the one hand, through his own training as a Shin priest and the encouragement of Tanabe, Takeuchi studied the religious thought of Shinran with its emphasis on Other-power (*tariki*). On the other hand, he also developed an interest in Christian exegetes and that led him to the conclusion that authentic religious renewal, so needed in modern Buddhism, must look to the origins of its tradition. Therefore, Takeuchi also studied the texts of original Buddhism with their emphasis on self-power (*jiriki*). So, in his book, *The Heart of Buddhism: In Search of the Timeless Spirit of Primitive Buddhism*, Takeuchi attempts to correlate these two seemingly quite opposing orientations in the spirit of Tanabe's exploration of *jiriki-qua-tariki* and *tariki-qua-jiriki*. In fact, it is Takeuchi's view that salvation takes place at the point where a person's "noble quest" for enlightenment understood as *jiriki* meets the "compassionate action" of Amida Buddha understood as *tariki*.[1]

In the first three chapters above, we examined the ideas of Nishida, Nishitani and Abe concerning Emptiness. All of these philosophers were most profoundly influenced by the Zen-*jiriki* tradition. In the fourth chapter, we examined the thought of Tanabe who was influenced more by the Shin-*tariki* tradition. In this chapter we will look at Takeuchi's correlation of these orientations in the context of the actual practice of Buddhist spirituality that seeks personal transformation. Then I will go

109

on to present a parallel approach to spiritual transformation found in traditional Christian spirituality. Indeed, in Christian spirituality, it is also claimed that genuine spiritual experience and growth takes place at the meeting point of the ascetic and the mystical, of the religious quest and the action of grace.

Takeuchi, following his teacher, Tanabe, says that the philosophy of Buddhism "is a metanoetics."[2] For him, Buddhist enlightenment entails a "metanoia of thinking," a fundamental transformation in the way we think *about* the world based on a spiritual change in our experience *of* the world. In the end, Buddhism seeks a new way of being in the world that expresses this metanoia. So then, Buddhism from the very beginning involves a "noble quest" not for answers to metaphysical questions but for a conversion of thinking, an awakening to a new form of awareness and being from which a true Buddhist philosophy of religion can be written. For the Buddha himself, our ordinary mode of thought is grounded on what Abe calls "blind will," an ignorant attachment to self. The noble quest must then involve practical methods of spiritual life by which this ground of dissatisfactory living (*dukkha*) can be emptied so that a deeper and more original ground of selflessness can be discovered. This means that the spiritual quest demands a radical kenosis. Then, on this original ground, a true metanoia of thinking can be found that will provide a basis for Buddhist philosophy. It was for this end, according to Takeuchi, that the Buddha proposed a spiritual path of contemplation that involves a constant and true "detachment" (*upekkha*).[3]

In his exploration of Buddhist spirituality, Takeuchi begins with an explication of Buddhist practice in terms of the three aspects of the Path that became so important in Theravada Buddhism: (1) "morality" (*sila*), (2) "meditation" (*samadhi*) and (3) "wisdom" (*prajna*). As for "morality," he is careful to distinguish it from pure ethical practice. That is, in ethical practice one follows a moral imperative that defines how one ought to behave. In this moral activity, one may in certain situations negate oneself, or what one desires to do, in order to perform a particular moral action. However, Takeuchi believes that the spirit of Buddhist morality can not be fully defined by such ethical actions. Rather, Buddhist morality (*sila*) expresses a type of religious conversion. In this conversion, moral self-negation is a kind of kenosis, self-emptying, that is inspired by a certain spiritual sensibility, namely, a spiritual sense of the impermanence (*anicca*) of all things.

This "first conversion" turns one to a spiritual sense or awareness of one's own finitude and the transitoriness of life. The transitory nature of things and one's own self is not experienced as something positive. Rather it is experienced as "dissatisfactory" (*dukkha*) and "impure" (*adiniva*). Therefore, this sense of impermanence is like a "power of negation," as Takeuchi puts it, that reaches down to the core of one's being and turns one's life upside down.[4] It "nullifies" everything and at the same time interiorizes impermanence. This sorrowful sense of universal impermanence interiorized in the heart of the Buddhist becomes the basis for morality in his or her spirituality. It leads the person to seek purification in the midst of the impermanence of daily life. This purification process involves Buddhist morality. It is lived concretely in asceticism, poverty and through following the moral precepts of the tradition. In pursuing this life of morality, the Buddhist begins to see something more than the dissatisfactory and impure condition of the impermanent world. He or she begins to perceive a purity and a satisfactory mode of existence achievable through the practice of Buddhist spirituality.

According to Takeuchi, this leads the Buddhist to a "fierce struggle." It is a moral and yet at the same time a spiritual struggle between wanting to pursue the spiritual ideal of purity on the one hand, and being enchanted by the pleasures of the impermanent world on the other hand. This struggle is complicated by the fact that given one's new sensitivity to the sorrowful nature of impermanence, one is both attracted by and disgusted with the world. One's conscience is also sharpened and is much more aware of the moral implications of one's deeds and the deeds of others.[5] So as Takeuchi says, the moral struggle is really a spiritual-ethical "struggle for self-denial and self-overcoming."[6] What is called for is a kenosis of self, a purification of all that keeps one from following the noble quest. Here is the spiritual significance of the asceticism of Buddhist morality. It entails self-negation not for its own sake, but for the sake of being able thereby to find the condition of freedom necessary to discover the spiritual ideal taught by the Buddha. This pure and satisfactory ideal entails a life of compassion, of loving-kindness, of ethical living for the good of others and not for the gratification of one's own selfish desires by the possession of impermanent things.

Through this struggle at the moral dimension (*sila*) of Buddhist spirituality, some progress is achieved. However, the Buddhist does not practice morality by itself. There is also the second dimension, namely, the practice of meditation (*samadhi*). In a dialectical fashion, morality can prepare the Buddhist for meditation but meditation can also support morality by developing clarity of insight, mindfulness and control of the senses. In meditation, one can see more clearly which kinds of actions lead to Nirvana and which kinds of actions bind one more strongly to *samsara*. Meditation helps one to become more mindful of the forces within oneself and in the world around oneself that are either freeing or binding. And it can help one to exercise a certain control over these forces. The three abilities (clarity, mindfulness, and control of senses) enable a person to better discern what is good and to better follow the moral life. So because of the need for inner strength in one's moral struggle, one is led naturally to the practice of the second dimension of the Path, namely, the practice of meditation (*samadhi*), or what Takeuchi calls "contemplation."

Takeuchi discusses this second dimension of the Path, namely meditation or contemplation, in some depth. His analysis is focused on the four basic stages of contemplation as given in the *Samannaphalasutta*.[7] The first stage involves a type of meditation characterized by a *gladness* "that springs up within" and a *joy* that also "arises" in meditative practice. The person is at "ease" and is "filled with a sense of peace, and in that peace his heart is stayed." In this meditation, the person is freed from "evil dispositions" and enjoys "detachment." There is also "reasoning and reflection" going on during this meditation. Now, the image for this first meditation is a bather being scrubbed by a bath attendant. The bather is sprinkled with soap and water "drop by drop" until the whole body is completely washed. The image here depicts the purification of selfish attachments so that one experiences the ease of purity with joy and gladness. This is of great value to the moral life because it makes purity so desirable that one can more easily renounce the attractions of worldly pleasure.

So the purification of attachment through meditation results in a detachment and freedom that puts one at ease. This brings joy as an intense feeling that, as Takeuchi notes, results in a quiet sense of gladness, or happiness in the interiority of the heart.[8] Takeuchi notes that as the Buddhist's mind pursues this interiority, it "is already on the way to centering and is caught up in the process of elevation and integration."[9] So, the mind pursues the things of the outer world less and less, and concentrates on the inner life. One's concern is less with the things of the world and more with the things of the spirit, "with religious and absolute truth." And because of this interest in spiritual things, discursive reason and reflection continue to function.

In the second stage of meditation, this reasoning and reflecting no longer takes place. While the first meditation results in a kenosis or self-negation of selfish desires and moral defilements, the second meditation results in a kenosis of discursive reason and reflection that brings peace to the mind and heart. In the words of the *Samannaphalasutta*, the Buddhist "suppressing all reasoning and reflection enters into and abides in the second meditation, a state of joy and ease, born of the serenity of concentration . . . a state of elevation of mind, a tranquilization of the heart within."[10] The image for this stage is quite interesting:

[It is] as if there were a deep pool, with water welling up into it from a spring beneath, and with no inlet from the east or west, from the north or south, and the god should from time to time send down showers of rain upon it. Still the current of cool waters rising up from that spring would pervade, fill, permeate, and suffuse the pool with cool waters, and there would be no part or portion of the pool unsuffused therewith.[11]

The first stage of the spiritual life has to do with moral purification based on the realization and internalization of impermanence in the first conversion. This first turning of the Buddhist toward the inner life, or what Takeuchi calls "centering," is concerned with the purification of the moral life as a groundwork for deeper contemplation. So at that first stage, one is still focused on the external world and one's active life in that environment. However, in the second stage, that focus shifts more fully to the interior life of contemplation. The conditions of the outer world do not affect the person in this deeper meditation. This is represented by the image of a pool with no rivers flowing into it. In this meditation, the outward-directed mind is stilled and one finds "a more profound peacefulness." We will find that there is a similar image with a similar message in Christian spirituality.

Takeuchi points out that in the first meditation, the person's peacefulness and joy are the results of a purity or a profound freedom from attachments to the things of this world. But in the second meditation, the peacefulness and joy are not determined by our purer relation to things without. Rather, they "well up from out of the interiority of contemplation like cool water gushing from its source underground."[12] This inner peace may from time to time be affected by a special joy like a holy rain, sent by a transcendent god, which further "washes" away one's attachments and defilements. However, what permeates the mind and heart is a joy and happiness that refreshes the whole person from a deep inner Center. In this refreshment of the second stage of centering, the mind of the person is quieted or emptied through an inner spiritual kenosis that presupposes the moral kenosis of the first stage.

This process of negation continues in the third stage of meditation where the emptying becomes even more radical. Here the feeling of joy experienced in the first and second stages is negated. Takeuchi notes that joy is not the goal of the Buddhist spiritual life. It is superseded in the third stage by a condition of "self-possession," "mindfulness" and "equanimity." That is, the person finds an inner strength that comes from the Center discovered more deeply in this third stage of centering. This strength empowers the person to be more self-sufficient, to be "self-possessed." "Mindfulness," as it is used here, implies that the person is more clearly aware of the true meaning and value of all things. And "equanimity" is a stability of mind and heart that remains no matter what happens; it is an inner sense of ease and an acceptance of whatever life brings.

This condition, according to both Buddhist and Christian spirituality, is the basis for many concrete results in daily life. In fact, the image for this third stage of contemplation is various colored lotus flowers that have grown in a pool of water. Each of the lotus flowers is "permeated" by the cool water of the pool. It is said that these flowers are the fruits of the more stable spiritual life of the third stage and are visible to the world. The point seems to be that the result of Buddhist spiritual life is not a feeling of joy entertained within the self. Rather, it is a selfless and stable life permeated by a spiritual nourishment from the Center of one's being. All aspects of one's being and all one's actions flower from this enlightened attainment in a manner that is visible to the world. As Takeuchi puts it, one's inner and outer lives are connected at this stage like the strong stem of a lotus plant connecting the roots at the bottom of the pool with its many flowers on the surface.

Finally, we come to the fourth stage of meditation. Here we find true spiritual freedom which is much more than the moral freedom or purity of the first stage. It is the freedom from self, from ego-centeredness. It is a condition of self-forgetful freedom, of a selfless living of the true Buddhist life. This condition is described as one of greatest "equanimity" where there is "the putting away alike of ease and of pain . . . the passing away alike of elation, any dejection, he had previously felt. . . ."[13] This state seems quite similar to the classical Christian notion of *apatheia* or the Ignatian notion of *indiferencia*. Ignatius of Loyola described this latter condition in the following way:

> Therefore, we must make ourselves indifferent to all created things, as far as we are allowed free choice and are not under any prohibition. Consequently, as far as we are concerned, we should not prefer health to sickness, riches to poverty, honor to dishonor, a long life to a short life. The same holds for all other things. Our one desire and choice should be what is more conducive to the end for which we are created.[14]

In fact, Takeuchi compares this fourth stage to what Eckhart calls *Abgeschiedenheit*. This "poverty of spirit," which is a condition of spiritual freedom, is a result of the kenosis of the ego-self in Eckhart's mysticism. However, this is not the final goal of Christian spirituality. Eckhart underlines the fact that this poverty enables the person to live a more perfect life of charity. According to Ignatius, to serve God in a life of charity is the "end for which we are created" and to which he is referring in the above quotation. Or as Eckhart often points out, it is better to leave God for God's sake, that is, to leave God in contemplation to serve him in a person who is in need. The freedom of this poverty of spirit enables one to forget oneself, even one's own spiritual state or graces received, to live more fully the Christian life of charity. Takeuchi understands this fact and compares it to original Buddhism: "The purified spirit of a monk is revealed in compassion. Compassion is seen as the consummation of contemplation and contemplation as the realization of compassion."[15]

The image for this fourth stage of meditation is a person sitting and wrapped from head to foot in a clean white robe. This person in white, according to Takeuchi, is a new person cleansed in the pool of contemplation "resurrected to a new religious life" with a "truly free mind and pure heart." Like the Christian "poverty of spirit" and "purity of heart," this Buddhist state is one of freedom where one no longer clings even to the holy joy and happiness of spiritual life. Rather, one is elevated beyond the opposition of happiness and sorrow so that one can live more fully a life of compassion for the good of others. Therefore, kenosis, self-renunciation, and negation are part of living out the first conversion, that is, the turning from the world to the interior life. However, when this "centering" process reaches its summit, one is turned back to the world transformed and enabled by one's religious life to live compassionately for the good of others. In the end, one is free from self-concern, from the desire for joy (even spiritual joy), and from fear of sorrow so that one can use one's "lotus flowers" for the good of others without a binding concern for self.

This is Takeuchi's description of the "noble quest" in the spirituality of original Buddhism. Since he is directing his attention to the stages of Buddhist contemplation, he does not present a sustained analysis of the third dimension of the Path, namely, "wisdom" (*prajna*). I would just add that in the process of kenotic purification and contemplation, one is transformed such that a new way of seeing emerges. One sees oneself and the world in a different way. The power of the "blind will" that pollutes the waters of the interior life is overcome. The ignorance that binds one in a dissatisfactory life is reduced. One is able to see more clearly the truth about our dissatisfactory human condition and the factors that contribute to that condition. One sees the truth about the factors of hate, greed and confusion that are the root causes of our negative condition stemming from the ignorant desires of our blind will.

This insight helps one to become free from these negative factors of human existence and to live a new life wherein the Buddhist virtues of loving-kindness, compassion and joy for others are not compromised by self-concern.

This state in which there is a cessation of these negative factors of existence that condition ordinary human life is called Nirvana in original Buddhism. It is best characterized by the description of equanimity given by Takeuchi. That is, it is a condition of detachment, of freedom and stability of mind that is not shaken by gain or loss, respect or disrespect, praise or blame, happiness or suffering. The person certainly continues to experience positive and negative feelings and sensations, but is unmoved by them.[16] Therefore, he or she does not generate the defiling states of consciousness such as hate, greed, confusion, attachment or clinging, that can pollute the clear water of interiority and compromise the lotus flowers of this pool of contemplation, namely, the compassion, loving-kindness and other virtues of the enlightened life. The Buddhist is able to maintain this state through a life of morality and meditation supported by a wisdom that properly understands all the factors of experience and thereby realizes which are and which are not conducive to Nirvana.

Now the question arises as to how this ascetic path is related to the path of grace found in Takeuchi's Pure Land tradition. Where does the ascetic noble quest for enlightenment by self-power (jiriki) meet the grace of the compassionate action of Other-power (tariki)? Takeuchi's answer to this question presents us with a fascinating phenomenology of Pure Land Buddhist experience. What Takeuchi does is to show how in Shinran's Kyogyoshinsho, one can find three stages of religious consciousness. These three stages take place as one attempts to follow the noble quest and finds, along the way, the grace of Other-power.

The first stage is what Takeuchi, certainly influenced by Kierkegaard, calls the "aesthetic and ethical stage." Here, the Buddhist tries, on the basis of his or her own willpower, to pursue the noble quest toward enlightenment. But Shinran believed, based on his historical and eschatological consciousness, that we are living in "degenerate times." We are so affected by this historical condition that there is no hope of achieving enlightenment through our own efforts. So Takeuchi says that: "Only the grace of Amida Buddha can bring redemption in this time."[17] Today, persons on the noble quest are not able to center their minds as the sages of old were able to do. One only encounters within oneself a dispersion of mind and heart because of the radical evil in and around us that pollutes any religious practice. So we are all "unenlightenable" beings; or as Shinran taught, we are all "foolish beings" (bombu). It is when one comes to this self-knowledge that one is led to a condition of spiritual and moral despair. However, this situation has a positive side, for it can be the opportunity for the encounter with the name of Amida Buddha who comes to one from the far side out of compassion for humanity.

This encounter, according to Takeuchi's reading of Shinran, leads to the second stage in religious consciousness. As one follows the noble quest, the sense of finitude intensifies into a feeling of despair over not being able to achieve the goal of the quest. One can never be free from the radical evil at the core of the human condition that always compromises the noble quest with a pollution of egoism. But it is precisely in the face of this finitude and sinfulness of the human condition, that the Buddhist turns to the powerful grace from the far side. This turning is itself the result of grace, of the reaching out of Amida Buddha from the far side drawing the Buddhist into his mercy. It is exactly at this point that there is the contact between Other-power and the Buddhist on the noble quest. And this is the point at which there is the most radical turning in religious consciousness. It is a metanoia that defines the authentic religious life of the disciple of the Pure Land tradition.

However, according to Takeuchi, it is in this second stage of religious consciousness, that one finds a new and more subtle contradiction. On the one hand, one has a genuine will to surrender totally to a dependence on Amida Buddha's grace. On the other hand, this action of surrender becomes itself a source of pride and Amida's grace becomes an object of self-centered manipulation or what Shinran calls "calculation" (hakarai). The problem here derives from what Shinran calls the "misappropriation of the name," that is, one's surrender to the name of the Buddha is compromised by the same radical evil that compromised the previous noble quest. Again we encounter the power of the ego, the blind will at the core of our being. Takeuchi says that in this way we are led to the realization of just how deep "the abyss of nihility of ego" really is.[18] The goal of spiritual freedom of the Pure Land seems to be at an infinite and insurmountable distance.

It is precisely in wandering in this desert of true self-knowledge, that one is able to meet the true grace of Amida Buddha and find the third stage of religious consciousness: "One must wander perseveringly through the many torments of the heart so that the genuine achievement of an encounter with the name of Buddha (the steadfast utterance of the name) can take place in one's innermost being."[19] To describe this situation, Takeuchi uses the image of a person excavating a well who must bore through many layers until reaching "the real, richest underground watercourse." This grace of Other-power generates a "trans-ascendence" to a new life of freedom (jinen). But for this to take place, a Pure

Land Buddhist must first "trans-descend" through ever deeper experiences of painful self-knowledge until being lifted up by the grace of Amida Buddha.

I must conclude from Takeuchi's analysis of this third stage of religious consciousness that this underground watercourse is the true source of the deep pool of clear water referred to in the Theravada image mentioned above. That is, the grace of Amida is the Other-power needed for the kenotic purification of ego so necessary for the practice of a Buddhist way of life. It is not that one can come to know who one is by oneself, by self-power. Rather, one is made to know who one is. What Shinran calls the "deep mind" involves the insight into our miserable condition, our being lost in the world as "unenlightenable ones." But to see this is itself a grace. The deep mind is not just one's own insight, but it is really the "Buddha mind" making one aware of this condition. So the deep mind is the "mind of faith" which is in turn an arising of the Buddha mind at the root of a person's consciousness. The self-knowledge one finds in the deep mind is a result of Other-power at work in the depths of one's being. This Other-power is like a fire that first illumines our miserable condition only to then burn away what needs to be negated for our salvation. The purification will result in true faith and the enablement to follow the Buddha Path unhindered by the many faults and weaknesses of our humanity that, given our finitude, will remain with us until death. Finally, it is this dialectic of the religious life in Pure Land spirituality that Takeuchi sees as the dynamic of transformation found at that point where the noble quest for enlightenment meets the Other-power of the Vow of Amida Buddha. In this dialectical encounter of the far and near sides of spiritual transcendence, Takeuchi locates salvation.

In the first chapter above, I argued for maintaining the distinction between the near-side and far-side dimensions of God. So, too, Takeuchi wishes to maintain the dialectic between the "yonder shore" and the "hither shore." For him, the far-side reality is "the Pure Land Paradise in the West." This reality transcends this world and also entails a dimension that is experienced as "thou." It is in the dialectic of an I-thou relationship between oneself and this reality that religious transcendence and transformation take place. From the human side, there is a transcendence from hither to yonder shore. But this movement is made possible, Takeuchi believes, by the corresponding "ad-vent" (*Zu-kunft*) from the yonder shore to the hither shore: "Transcendence thus requires the encounter of these two processes."[20] And for Takeuchi, as a Shin Buddhist, the "bridge" that connects these sides or shores is the ad-venting of the sacred name of Amida.

In the face of the modern spiritual crisis caused by secularization, Takeuchi suggests that the notion of the beyond must be made relevant to daily life. That is, we must find a means of transcendence to a fuller spiritual life in the common actions of daily life. This means, given Takeuchi's understanding of transcendence, that the transcendent cannot be understood as something apart from our world but as something that ad-vents into daily life: "True transcendence is something that emerges into the present ad-venting in real transcendence *toward us.*"[21] This Other-power is relevant insofar as it transforms one in contemplation *and* in daily life. God or Buddha must ad-vent into secular life bringing the possibility of transcendence to ordinary people in everyday situations. Again, for a Pure Land Buddhist, this provides the spiritual reason for *nembutsu* practice, that is, the recitation of the name of Amida Buddha. For the name of Amida is the presence of Amida. The reciting of "Namu Amida Butsu" in a coffee shop, Takeuchi notes, can make that place a locus of the ad-venting of the transcendent into the midst of the secular world.

This ad-venting in religious practice is a means for both personal transformation and social transformation as well. In this way, grace not only meets the noble quest of the individual Buddhist but meets the noble quest of society as well. To provide for an ad-venting of the transcendent far side into the near side of our social life can become the basis for social transformation. In Tanabe's terms, this can become the ad-venting of the kingdom of God in our world. In addressing this issue, Takeuchi, like Tanabe, emphasizes the image presented by Shinran in discussing the seventeenth vow in the *Kyogyoshinsho*. This is the image of all the divine Buddhas praising each other and exalting Amida Buddha. In that Buddha world, everything mirrors everything else united together in the Great Compassion.

This reality can be lived in this world as well. It can be "mirrored" in the human practice of *nembutsu* so that "the Pure Land and this world, all Buddhas and all living beings, the cosmic chorus sounding the name throughout 'the ten quarters' and the career of the historical *nembutsu* on earth combine in this symbolic action to form a locus of *Geviert.*"[22] Takeuchi uses here a term from Martin Heidegger's philosophy. *Geviert,* or "quadrate," symbolizes a possible unity binding the gods, sky and earth, and humanity. For Takeuchi, this image represents the possibility for an ad-venting of a unity between those in the Pure Land, humanity on earth, and nature. This ad-venting is the locus for the I-Thou encounter of a person with Amida Buddha. As these two meet on the bridge of the sacred name of the Buddha, subject and object penetrate each other such that the Pure Land ad-vents into our world and transforms it by its wondrous power and creates I-thou relationships of unity between persons and nature on earth that mirror the unity of the divine Buddhas. And here is a Shin Buddhist ideal of social transformation and harmony.

The I-Thou encounter with the Buddha, as a basis for I-thou relationships between persons and even with nature is, according to Takeuchi, arrived at "ek-statically."[23] That is, the person reaches his or her ground and in a transcendence beyond the ego is emptied of self and enters a condition of "true living." This true living is the living of Amida Buddha in and through the person. That is, for the Shin Buddhist, being ek-statically in one's home-ground is not just being in the place of Absolute Nothingness. It is not simply being fully a self-determination of Absolute Nothingness. Rather, it is also being lived, in a graced kenosis of self, by Other-power. In that true life of self-forgetfulness is a freedom (*jinen*) where one is conscious of Amida Buddha working as Other-power within oneself. This Other-power functions in a way that "makes one so of itself" (*jinen-honi*) and is the basis of "true living" such that one can act spontaneously with the clear mind and compassionate heart of Amida Buddha.

So in the end, we see that for Takeuchi and Shin Buddhism, the noble quest of self-negation, with its kenosis of impurity, reason and reflection, joyful feelings and any attachment to the things of the world, is a path that will eventually lead to "shipwreck" because of the radical evil of our human condition. Takeuchi sees this shipwreck as the occasion for the encounter with the name of the Buddha which comes to one "like a great ship from the yonder shore over the sea of life and struggle to help humanity."[24] Here the noble quest for enlightenment meets the compassionate action of Amida Buddha. Yet the new life of grace can be compromised by a misappropriation of the name by ego-centered self-seeking and pride. However, with perseverance one is purified by the realization of this condition through self-knowledge and the further grace of Amida Buddha. This results in a more radical kenosis of the self that brings a new freedom and true living of the Buddhist ideal of compassion and unity. And living this way of life with others can be the occasion for the ad-venting of the purifying grace of Other-power for the transformation of society in a manner that brings forth a mirroring of the Pure Land here on earth.

Before going on to the Christian approach to individual spirituality, I want to say a few words about the Zen tradition. We have already looked at the process of Zen transformation when we discussed the philosophies of Nishida, Nishitani and Abe. Also, analyses of this process in Zen spirituality as it compares to Christian spirituality have already been made by various scholars.[25] However, since Takeuchi emphasizes the

Shin tradition, and because of the obvious kenotic nature of Zen practice, let me just mention a few points about Zen that relate to what we
have been discussing.

The practice of Zen is a "trans-descending" by the emptying of the
mind and heart: "All thoughts, images, fears, feelings, anxieties, plans,
ambitions, envies, whatever it may be—all are emptied out of the
mind."[26] The mind then becomes concentrated in that emptiness until
it reaches deepest meditation (samadhi). This "non-ego" (muga) Center
is the field of Emptiness. And the realization of this non-self, this True
Self, is an "insight into one's essence" (kensho) that is ultimately transformative. It brings a freedom from self and every worldly condition.
Therefore, H. M. E. Lassalle refers to Zen meditation (zazen) as "a way
of purification, indeed, it is the most radical form of spiritual
purification."[27]

Living in and from this deeper Center of non-self, discovered
through zazen practice, results in a life characterized by virtue, freedom
and compassion. This new quality of life is advanced by a renewal of
kensho over and over by the further practice of zazen. Now, it is important
to note that this lived Emptiness empties itself out as compassion. It is not
the case that one lives Emptiness compassionately through an effort of
one's own will since that very willful effort must itself be emptied out.
Rather, one is lived by Emptiness. This is the Zen experience of jinen. It is
a freedom from the ego-self that is accomplished by the kenosis of Emptiness itself: "The self or ego must therefore completely disappear . . .
and this is precisely the center of focus of Zen. A person must literally no
longer be conscious of his self, he must be selfless."[28] One cannot make
oneself this way; one must be made this way by the free functioning of
Emptiness itself.

So, if a person tries to experience and live Emptiness by a kenotic
practice driven by the will, that effort is doomed to failure. It leads to a
kind of shipwreck that is similar to what happens in Shin practice. One
sees that the goal is impossible to attain by one's own effort. However,
while in Shin this realization leads to abandonment in tears to the grace
of Other-power, in Zen it leads to a deep metanoesis, weeping and ultimately to a more humble perseverance in Zen practice. Therefore, the
final kenosis in Zen is not something produced by the person but by the
ground of the person, by the dynamic power of Emptiness itself. This
True Self overcomes the ego and empties it in deepest samadhi. Here,
there is an emptying of all duality between subject and object, and one
realizes that one is, along with all other things, a self-determination of
Absolute Nothingness. In this ultimate emptying, as William Johnston
puts it, "It is not that something different is seen, but that one sees

differently."[29] By experiencing life from a new Center, from one's home-ground, one discovers one's True Self as an original mode of being that is free, selfless and compassionate.

Shinzuteru Ueda has explained this process of kenosis of the self in his study of the Ten Oxherding Pictures.[30] He points out that the first six pictures portray, step-by-step, the practice of the Zen path of meditation (*zazen*) leading to deep "self-integration." This practice is certainly kenotic in nature, as I have described above, and its negation leads to the seventh stage where there is a unification of the person, represented by the herder, and his or her True Self, represented by the ox. However, this is not the end of the journey. Just as a person's surrender to the grace of Amida Buddha in Shin Buddhism can be compromised by the ego, here too the person can feel self-sufficient and self-confident. The person may have emptied himself or herself by Zen practice, but the ego remains to be fully emptied by its ground and can compromise Zen practice by pride in its achievement. So in both Shin and Zen, self-centered pride distorts the religious life into expressions of religious egoism or elitism.

It is because of this that Shin Buddhism teaches the need to pass through a final negation or kenosis by the power of Amida Buddha's grace. In Zen, Ueda says, one must leap into pure nothingness and die the Great Death.[31] This is the eighth stage symbolized by the empty circle. It is an absolute negation by Emptiness itself. It is a final kenosis, that opens from and into Absolute Nothingness. Paradoxically though, this negation empties itself out as an affirmation. Out of death comes resurrection and new life. The ninth picture depicts the fullness of nature. It represents wondrous being as a fullness which just is the functioning of Emptiness. In this identity of Emptiness and the fullness of wondrous being, one discovers "the play of the selfless freedom of the self."[32] Again, this is the Zen experience of *jinen*. For the Zen tradition, this *jinen* is not the free activity of compassionate Other-power as understood in Shin Buddhism, but it is the compassionate activity of Emptiness itself. It is Emptiness in its compassionate dynamic as fullness.

Ueda says that the tenth and final stage is where "the true self resurrected from nothingness is at work between individuals, or comes into play there, as a selfless dynamic of the 'between.' "[33] The tenth oxherding picture shows an old person meeting a young person. In this I-thou relation, the concerns of the young person are the concerns of the old person. This is because each person "split open by absolute nothingness . . . spreads out and unfolds itself selflessly into the *between* where the other in its otherness belongs to the selflessness of the self."[34] Ueda says that this is "a matter of making oneself a nothingness before the other. . . ."[35] In the "place" of Absolute Nothingness where this is possible, both persons in mutual self-negation or kenosis can discover a true I-thou relationship. And it is in such a relationship that one can "step outside of oneself" in what Ueda calls *ex-sistence*. This, like Takeuchi's use of the term *ek-stasis*, implies that the freedom of persons in an I-thou relationship resides in a deeper reality transcendent of the ego. For Zen, it is in Absolute Nothingness as the near-side locus of True Life. For Shin, this is the ad-venting of the Other-power from the far side found at the depth of Emptiness. For both Zen and Shin, this ground, however conceived, is the basis of both personal and interpersonal transformation.

To conclude, Zen may give more credence to the "noble quest" than Shin Buddhism, but both agree that the ego can cause shipwreck in reaching one's goal. For Zen, one can become religiously egotistic at the seventh stage and must go through the purification of the absolute kenosis of the Great Death. For Shin, one can misappropriate the name of the Buddha and practice *nembutsu* in a self-centered and prideful way. So, he or she must undergo a further kenotic purification by Amida's grace. The result in both cases is *jinen*, understood in Zen as the spontaneity of Absolute Nothingness, or understood in Shin as the dynamic of Other-power. In this new life, the Buddhist establishes authentic I-thou relationships, understood in Zen as mirroring the compassionate unifying dynamic of Absolute Nothingness, or understood in Shin as mirroring the compassion and unity of the divine Buddhas. For Zen, this unity is a self-determination of the unification of Absolute Nothingness in which humanity and nature merge in compassion and peace. For Shin, this unity is an ad-venting by Other-power from the Pure Land that unifies humanity, nature and the Buddhas in compassion and peace. In either case, we are presented with highly relevant ideals for our modern world.

◆   ◆   ◆

Christian spirituality, in the most general sense of that term, is a mode of spiritual living that enhances one's transformation in God.[36] This spiritual growth is understood in Christianity to involve the sanctifying activity of the Holy Spirit. One can discern two aspects of Christian spirituality. First is the way in which the person actively prepares for, responds to, and cooperates with this action of grace. And second is the manner in which God works in the sanctification of the person. The former has to do with the ascetic life and the latter has to do with the mystical life. Actually, both are two parts of one growth process, the growth of a relationship between God and a person. This life is one of participation in God by which God transforms the person so that the person manifests God-Love more and more in his or her living of the Christian gospel of love.

In the history of Christianity, many particular spiritualities have developed over the centuries.[37] These spiritualities were especially suited to the needs of the people who were living at the times of their foundation, and they continue to lead their followers into a fuller transformative participation in God. They carry a charism that aids those persons, who are called by God to follow them, to grow in sanctity, in the sanctification of the Holy Spirit. And while each one is in many ways quite unique, each also has the two aspects of the Christian spiritual life, the ascetic and the mystical. Because of these two dimensions, Christian spirituality is in some ways similar to Zen and in other ways similar to Shin Buddhism. Therefore, I find Tanabe's notion of *jiriki-qua-tariki/ tariki-qua-jiriki*, and Takeuchi's exploration of the "meeting" of the "noble quest" and the "compassionate action of Amida Buddha," both to be very suggestive for Buddhism's dialogue with Christian spirituality.

Christian experience demonstrates that these two sides of the spiritual life are two sides of the same coin. On the human side, it is the case that a person can actively prepare himself or herself for, and reduce the barriers to, the action of God's loving grace. One can make ethical choices and remove moral impediments to God's saving work. One can also allow that Other-power to work, respond to its promptings, and cooperate with its action. And yet this can only be successful through a prior and enabling grace of God. Therefore, because of the divine side, there is a sense in Christian experience that one is being empowered by an "Other-power" to live the Christian life from the very beginning. Whatever progress the person makes, it is through the sanctifying activity of God transforming the person so that he or she can find a more intimate knowledge and love of God. And it is this life of grace that makes the person a fuller self-determination of that Love for the good of others. It is initiated *by* God, developed *through* God and completed *in* God.

As I have said, there are many Christian spiritualities by which this ascetic-mystical life takes concrete shape. It is impossible to compare all of these spiritualities to the various forms of spiritual life we have mentioned in the first part of this chapter. So what I want to do here is simply to present one particular Christian spiritual tradition, the Carmelite spirituality of Teresa of Avila and John of the Cross, in comparison to Takeuchi's analysis of Buddhist spirituality outlined above. In this presentation, I will emphasize the role of kenosis in spiritual life. We must remember that Paul in his letter to the Philippians stressed that the

Christian's "own attitude must be the same as that of Christ" (Philippians 2.5). That is, Christ "emptied" himself in a kenosis of love and humility, and this emptying in both its ascetic and mystical dimensions is an important part of Christian spirituality.

Takeuchi begins his exploration of early Buddhist spirituality with a discussion of Buddhist morality (*sila*). We saw how true Buddhist moral life in the Theravada tradition is tied to a spiritual realization of the impermanence, finitude and impurity of one's life. This leads to a moral discipline that purifies that life through asceticism and poverty. Teresa of Avila's spiritual classic, the *Interior Castle*, presents a castle as an image of the human person.[38] In this image, the self is like an interior castle that has seven concentric sets of mansions leading to the innermost chamber where Christ is at the Center. The Spanish word for mansion is *Morada*, from the verb *morar* meaning "to dwell." So, the seven concentric sets of mansions are really seven ways or levels of dwelling or participating in God. Teresa believes that many people live outside the castle paying no attention to the inner life. Outside the castle, these people live with "snakes and vipers and poisonous creatures" that represent the impure and vain things of the world. These negative things of the world so attract, tempt and disturb the persons that they give in to an immoral life, and in so doing "they have become almost like them [the creatures]."[39] When these persons try to enter the castle, the creatures pursue them and turn them back to their old way of life. It is a realization of this condition that ties morality to Christian spirituality. To begin the spiritual life means, in part, to be sensitive to and attend to the effects of these creatures on one's life.

As in Buddhism, there is in Christian spirituality a realization that the impure conditions of life (the poisonous creatures) are within oneself. That is, these creatures also represent our own disordered affections and attachments. Teresa refers to this discovery as entering the "rooms of self-knowledge."[40] These are the most important rooms in the first sets of mansions because they teach one humility. One is able to discern just how much one is attached to worldly affairs, pleasures, honors and ambitions. These attachments, Teresa says, keep one from freely living the more spiritual life. What should one do? On the one hand, Teresa suggests the development of a moral life based on charity and compassion, the love of God and love of neighbor. One is reminded here that the first aspect of the Buddhist Path is morality. On the other hand, Teresa also suggests vocal prayer which can help the person to turn his or her attention to God. This attention to God is quite important and serves as an antidote to one's inordinate attention to worldly things. In fact, Teresa says that without this attention in prayer, "I do not consider that he is praying at all even though he be constantly moving his lips."[41] Here we might note that in Shin Buddhism, too, the "mere recitation itself is insufficient unless it is inspired by a deep trust in Amida Buddha's Vow."[42] For the Christian, this attention directed toward God is the beginning of meditation. So, in Christian spirituality, as in Buddhism, morality is also related to and enhances meditation.

Teresa presents a water image to clarify the difference between being rooted in a life of attachments and being rooted in the inner spiritual life. One can note a similarity to the images Takeuchi quotes from the Theravada tradition. Teresa says that:

> just as all the streamlets that flow from a clear spring are as clear as the spring itself, so the works of a soul in grace are pleasing in the eyes both of God and of men, since they proceed from this spring of life, in which the soul is as a tree planted. It would give no shade and yield no fruit if it proceeded not thence, for the spring sustains it and prevents it from drying up and causes it to produce good fruit. When the soul, on the other hand, through its own fault, leaves this spring and becomes rooted in a pool of pitch-black, evil-smelling water, it produces nothing but misery and filth.[43]

Now it sounds like the person is going from one spring to another pool. However, Teresa notes that the spring is at the Center of the soul and is always within oneself. Leaving the spring for a pool is rather a way of saying, as Nishitani himself says, that one abides in the world unaware of, and lost from, his or her spiritual home-ground. The spring, or home-ground, is still there but has little effect upon the person's life because one is not attentive to it. Teresa says that one's senses are instead "distracted" and one's mind is "blind . . . and ill controlled." That is, one is not free to live from one's true spiritual Source, but is distracted and controlled by one's attachments, by the "snakes and vipers and poisonous creatures."

As one becomes attentive to this inner spring of True Life, Teresa says that one realizes that the good one is able to do comes ultimately from this Source. This shows the person that real purity comes from this inner spring of life, and the person is thereby more attracted to this pure reality. This meditative attention to the things of the spirit leads to a metanoesis, a purifying repentance and turning to God. And the person also realizes that this very turning is already a sign of grace. It is a good action and so it must come from the inner spring of God. One's desire for God is itself God's desire for oneself. As Shinran said, "Amida

Buddha also gave the mind which precedes and moves the individual to take up the discipline."[44]

This "first conversion," as Takeuchi calls it, this turning to the spiritual quest, the inner journey to the Center, is in part an act of the person and also a result of the inner spring of God's grace. And as Takeuchi also says, it is at this point that true transformation takes place. For Teresa, this means a movement deeper into the interior castle that reaches the second mansions. In these second mansions, we have something similar to what Takeuchi calls the "fierce struggle." It results from the desire to pursue the spiritual ideal of purity and being pursued by the creatures of the impermanent world. Shan-tao (613–681), a Chinese Pure Land Buddhist sage, said that this situation is like a person traveling west to the Pure Land on a narrow path between two rivers pursued by "evil beasts" and "poisonous insects."[45] Shan-tao's advice is similar to Teresa's, that is, to practice detachment, single-hearted perseverance, and entrust oneself to God's grace.

Besides this advice, Teresa also emphasizes the necessity to persevere in the moral life by bringing one's will into accordance with the will of God. This certainly requires the kenotic type of "self-denial and self-overcoming" to which Takeuchi also refers. Teresa's friend, John of the Cross, strongly emphasizes the need to conform one's will to the will of God at this particular stage. To enter what he calls the "active night of the senses," or an active and ascetic purification of the self, he suggests two things:

> First, have a habitual desire to imitate Christ in all your deeds by bringing your life into conformity with His. You must then study His life in order to know how to imitate Him and behave in all events as He would. Second, in order to be successful in this imitation, renounce and remain empty of any sensory satisfaction that is not purely for the honor and glory of God. . . . By this method you should endeavor, then, to leave the senses as though in darkness, mortified, and empty of pleasure. With such vigilance you will gain a great deal in a short time.[46]

This ascetic kenosis, with the help of the grace of God, aids the person in departing from what John of the Cross calls the "house of the self-will" through a mortification of the senses. This mortification seems similar to what Takeuchi calls the "control of the senses" and "self-possession." For John of the Cross, this asceticism "empties" self-centeredness and makes God's will the motivation for living. For both John of the Cross and Teresa, this kenosis of the "self-will" by conforming to the will of God provides the "firm foundation" of morality that is needed for the practice of meditation and contemplation as one continues the spiritual journey to the Center.[47]

However, this ascetic kenosis is not an easy practice. The emptying of self-will is, in fact, impossible to complete when it is attempted only by the will itself. Ascetic emptying of the self is more like the choice of a direction in the spiritual life of centering. One needs something else to reach the goal because, as Abe points out, the self cannot empty itself of attachments that stem from a deeper "blind will." So as in Zen and Shin, one is led to a "deep sorrow" over this situation, and even to "shipwreck." Teresa says that at this second level of spiritual dwelling, God calls the person "unceasingly" and that "this voice of His is so sweet that the poor soul is consumed with grief at being unable to do His bidding . . . it suffers more than if it could not hear him."[48]

To draw on the spring image, the person feels the purity of the water from the inner spring of life and realizes the impurity of his or her own life. This poor person sees more clearly and is more mindful of the difference between good and evil and between what one seeks and what one is. In this spiritual situation, the person experiences more painfully the attacks of the reptiles that have followed him or her into the castle. He or she may want to leave the castle and yet feels impelled to stay. Or the person may even wish that he or she had never entered the castle in the first place, and yet feel that one should be in the castle. This is a time for deeper and more painful "self-knowledge" in light of the ideal of the spiritual life. I am reminded of Shinran's sensitive statement: "I do not rejoice that I have entered the company of the truly assured; I do not enjoy the fact that I am approaching the realization of true attainment. O how shameful, how pitiful!"[49]

For the Christian, it is by the combination of practice and grace that one makes progress in the spiritual life. So in order to move beyond this struggle with oneself in the ascetic kenosis of the second mansions, Teresa says that one must practice with perseverance and depend on the grace of God: "To those who by the mercy of God have overcome in these combats, and by dint of perseverance have entered the third mansions, what shall we say but 'Blessed is the man that feareth the Lord?' "[50] (Psalm lll.l). In the more peaceful third mansions, one finds a new and deeper experience of prayer. It is an experience not unlike the first stage of Buddhist meditation, discussed by Takeuchi. There, the Buddhist (1) utilizes reason and reflection, (2) finds peace, gladness, and joy, (3) is freed from attachments, and (4) becomes more focused on religious truth. We can find these same qualities in the third stage of Teresa's spirituality. For example, Teresa says that in the third mansions the

Christian (1) experiences "discursive meditation," a prayer state in which one is illumined by God through reasoning and reflecting on scripture and theology. This in turn brings (2) peace and happiness to the soul. There is also "affective meditation" in which God stirs feelings of love, reverence, gratitude and joy. All of these experiences sharpen one's attention and attraction to the pure spiritual life and this (3) enables the person to better leave behind the life of attachment and selfish desire. In this way the person (4) acquires a taste for, and is nourished by, the knowledge of spiritual truths.

It is interesting that Teresa, like the *Samannaphalasutta*, uses a water image to describe this stage of meditation. In her *Interior Castle*, she refers to water basins on two fountains which can be filled with water. She says that "the water in the one comes from a long distance, by means of numerous conduits and through human skill. . . ."[51] Elsewhere, she uses the image of drawing water from a well which she says "involves a lot of work. . . ."[52] The point is that in discursive and affective meditation, one expends a great deal of effort. The focus in such meditation is on the ascetic dimension of purification rather than the mystical. One could compare this to the image in the Buddhist story of the bather being scrubbed by a bath attendant who sprinkles water "drop by drop." This also carries the connotation of purification through great effort.

The virtues that are needed to deepen this purification, according to Teresa, are humility and strength, perseverance and detachment, abandonment of everything and resignation to God's will in all things. This takes, of course, a certain kenotic self-forgetfulness and spiritual poverty. However, because of the spiritual fruits in this third set of mansions, the person often focuses on his or her own efforts and achievements. With this new spiritual self-centeredness, the ego compromises religious practice in a manner similar to "the misappropriation of the name" in Shin practice. Teresa says the "good" religious person at this stage becomes "careful," "upright," and "orderly."[53] The underlying blind will "prevents us from making progress" because one is always concerned about how to improve or maintain one's spiritual status.[54] Teresa says that this is like a person who always checks his or her spiritual temperature to see how holy he or she is and then tries to increase that holiness for his or her own sake. This not only prevents progress, but can lead, as in Shin Buddhism, to a second shipwreck.

What is needed for the passage to the fourth mansions is a purification that comes from the inner spring that is deeper than the blind will that so compromises religious life by its selfish desires. This is not an active or ascetic kenosis, but a passive and mystical kenosis of grace where God is active and the person is passive. Hence, John of the Cross calls this "the passive night of the senses." John also analyzes the defects of the heart that compromise the spiritual life in terms of the seven deadly sins.[55] For example, the sin of pride refers to one's attachment to spiritual attainment. Because of this attachment, one cannot stand to see any imperfections in one's self or in others. One is therefore constantly obsessed with one's own spiritual condition and the condition of others. Another example is the sin of avarice which is a possessiveness or attachment to spiritual things such as holy knowledge, religious objects, spiritual experiences, spiritual teachers, and so on.

Underlying these defects and the defilements they cause to self and others is a "blind will," to use Abe's term.[56] And this phenomenon cannot be rooted out by moral or religious actions on a purely volitional level. The spiritual humility, poverty and self-forgetfulness needed can only arise from a deeper source of freedom and non-attachment. What arises from the inner spring of True Life is a passive purification of the self that empties any sensory satisfaction or sensual gratification in all things, including religious practice. This graced kenosis of the spirit enables one to develop a level of detachment not achievable by purely ascetic effort. And out of this cross or death comes a resurrection of new spiritual life. This is the life of contemplation that characterizes the fourth mansions.

The purifying waters of the night of the senses are the same waters from the inner spring that flow forth from the Center of one's being in contemplation. For Christians, contemplation is different from meditation. The latter involves reflective and affective states found in the discursive and affective meditations mentioned above. The contemplative experience is deeper and one is very much aware that it is "infused" into one's consciousness from a deeper source than one's own mind or affections. Here we move from the more ascetic to the more mystical dimension of spirituality. Again, the image that Teresa presents for this new dimension is strikingly similar to the Buddhist image for the second meditation discussed by Takeuchi. The Buddhist image is of a deep pool fed by the water from a spring beneath with no inlet from any outside source. The spring permeates the whole pool with its cool waters. The Buddhist becomes "centered" by this inner source, his or her reasoning and reflection are stilled, and his or her heart is filled with peace and joy from this spring of contemplative waters.

Teresa also uses a water image for the fourth mansions that differs from the image used for the third mansions. The earlier image was of a basin filled by numerous conduits. The new image is of the basin of a fountain that is constructed over the water source. Teresa says:

To the other fountain the water comes direct from its source, which is God, and, when it is His Majesty's will and He is pleased to grant us some supernatural favour, its coming is accompanied by the greatest peace and quietness and sweetness within ourselves. . . . later the basin becomes completely filled, and then this water begins to overflow all the mansions and faculties, until it reaches the body. . . . I do not think that this happiness has its source in the heart at all. It arises in a much more interior part, like something of which the springs are very deep; I think this must be the centre of the soul.[57]

Teresa says that at this fourth stage of spiritual growth, there are two types of contemplation. First is the "prayer of recollection." Here, one feels oneself being emptied, stilled and integrated by God. One's mind and senses are involuntarily quieted and one is drawn within oneself like "a tortoise withdrawing into itself."[58] The effect of this purifying water is an "enlargement of heart." Teresa says that this is like the enlargement of the basin of the fountain. This enlargement enables the person to love God and others more deeply, that is, from a deeper Center. Teresa says that with the stilling of reason and reflection, one is better able to realize that progress in the spiritual life of contemplation comes not from think-ing but from loving: "The important thing is not to think much, but to love much. . . ."[59] Not only is the heart affected, but the body as well. Again, this is like the Buddhist image where the entire person is "suf-fused" by the waters from the inner spring of contemplation.

A second type of contemplation that one encounters in these fourth mansions is the "prayer of quiet." It lasts for only a minute or so, and is characterized by a deep sense of peace and quiet welling up from within, which not only affects the mind but even stills the body. Both of these types of prayer bring "ineffable blessings" which include more firm vir-tues, freedom from self-concern, a more total detachment, and true humility. Detachment and freedom advance one's "poverty of spirit." And strength in virtue and self-forgetfulness advance one's "purity of heart."[60] However, one of the most important effects is a more radical kenosis of purification. In the previous mansions, especially in the dark night, the will became more conformed to the will of God. But in that conforming process, the mind was affected in such a way that it became overly active, even restless and distressed. So the mind must be emptied and purified through this kenosis that stills its functioning in prayer in such a way that one is more mentally peaceful even in daily life. And since the mind and body are so connected, the body is also affected.

It should now be clear that in the prayers of recollection and quiet, there is less ascetic and active self-emptying, and more of a passive and mystical experience of "being emptied," or recollected and quieted by God. This passive experience of "being prayed," as it were, that characterizes Christian contemplation may in its dynamic be similar to the Zen experience of "being meditated," that is, experiencing one's meditation as stemming from a home-ground beyond one's willpower. In any case, the Christian experience of recollection and quiet empties the mind and leads to an inner stillness in prayer. And John of the Cross teaches that this kenosis plays an important role in preparing a person for union with God. He says that the ordinary way one discriminates with one's mind creates a disordered mode of being in the world. In this way, one creates a false self alienated from one's real self, one's dynamic imaging of God, and therefore from God himself. So to find union with God, to discover one's true identity and image God-Love in one's own life, one must undergo a mystical kenosis. In order to receive, we must be empty: "It is impossible for the highest wisdom . . . which is contemplation, to be received by anything less than a spirit that is silent and detached from discursive knowledge and gratification."[61]

This mystical kenosis prepares the body, mind and will for the next set of mansions, the fifth mansions in which one begins to experience union with God. Teresa gives a phenomenological description of the first type of union with God, sometimes called "simple union," found in the fifth mansions. Her description of the prayer state of simple union sounds similar to the Zen description of deepest meditation or *samadhi*. Teresa says that a person in this prayer "neither seems asleep nor feels awake."[62] There is no power nor desire to think, and the person barely breathes and does so without realizing it. The body does not seem to be able to move and one feels that one has come into "close contact and union with the essence of the soul. . . ."[63] The experience seems to penetrate "to the marrow of the bones. . . ."[64] And finally, after the experience there is an absolute "certainty" about the validity of one's experience that always remains. This certainty is so strong that no one can make the person believe otherwise.

On the other hand, while this state may have some similarities with Zen *samadhi*, it is important to add that it is also seen by Teresa to be a result of the "ad-venting," to use Takeuchi's term, of God at the core of one's being. So in this sense, the experience is also like that of Pure Land Buddhism. The person is passive and God is actively bringing about this profound transformation of the person's life. It is part of the process of death-and-resurrection. Beyond a kenosis of self-will, self-love and attachments, this mystical emptying in and through union with God brings a death-and-resurrection that Teresa compares with the metamorphosis of a silkworm into a butterfly. Our ascetic kenosis is like spinning a cocoon. However, the actual metamorphosis is effected by the mystical kenosis of God, the pouring forth of new life from the Holy Spirit at the Center of our being. This transforms one in such a radical way that one becomes a new creature. In this mystical union, the life of God becomes more and more the life of the person. This life is not created by self-power, but by the action of Other-power. Therefore, one learns in this prayer of union to "allow his Majesty to work."[65] This allowing is itself achieved by the "water of grace" from the Center of one's being that "softens" the person to be more gentle and receptive to God's inner transformative action.

This transformation makes the person more free, like the freedom of a butterfly over the bondage of a silkworm in a cocoon. And, of course, there is a sense of peace and contentment. However, the end of this contemplation is not the peaceful state itself, but being moved back to the world to live for others. Teresa says that the person at this stage will seek a greater active life of charity. She warns that people should not:

> think the whole thing [union] consists in this [being wrapt in prayer]. But no, sisters, no; what the Lord desires is works. If you see a sick woman to whom you can give some help, never be affected by the fear that your devotion will suffer, but take pity on her: if she is in pain, you should feel pain too; if necessary, fast so that she may have your food. . . . That is true union with His will.[66]

In a way that is perhaps similar to what Takeuchi says about Shin practice, one is here led to I-thou relationships with others based on the I-Thou relation with God in the prayer of union. One's actions are a reflection of one's new being. One manifests God who is Love in one's actions which are charity. This charity does not derive from a forced willfulness but from an empathetic "merging" with the other, to use Nishida's term, so that one feels the pain and joy of the other.

So as this union deepens, Teresa says that the person does not attach himself or herself to the consolations and joys of prayer. Rather, the person, like a butterfly, does not rest in anything but goes about doing good for everyone. Like the third meditation of the Theravada tradition discussed by Takeuchi, one becomes unattached to the joys of one's own spiritual life and then from this self-forgetfulness many beautiful lotus flowers blossom. These fruits of a more stable and selfless spiritual life are "permeated" by the waters of the inner spring. One's actions flower from this depth, this Center. Yet, while Teresa says all these beautiful things about action stemming from contemplation, she quickly adds that the person is not perfect for there are "many faults that we always commit, even in doing our good works."[67] Even at this advanced state, Shinran is correct when he says that we remain "foolish beings" in need of the compassionate action of Other-power.[68]

It should be remembered that in the third stage of meditation in the Theravada Buddhist tradition, the joy that is characteristic of the two earlier stages is emptied out. However, it is also the case that in the Theravada tradition, the enlightened person has the nirvanic virtue of *mudita* or "selfless joy in others." And in the Zen tradition, the experience of *kensho* is characterized by "ekstatic" joy since it transcends the ego into our true home-ground. And in Shin experience, the action of Other-power often takes one beyond oneself and even brings one to "ekstatic" joyful glimpses of the Pure Land. As one moves into the sixth mansions, Teresa says that the Christian mystic happens upon a number of " ekstatic," joyful experiences. Now in Zen, many of these may be dismissed as *makyo*, or illusion, since they often involve a "revelation" of a far-side reality. However, in Christian spirituality, these mystical experiences have a certain truth value concerning this far-side dimension of existence. They are seen as part of the mystical life, generated by the action of Other-power, that may happen when one follows the spiritual quest. So let me say a few words about them.

Teresa discusses certain examples of such mystical phenomena as ecstasy, raptures, locutions and visions. Again, people often and incorrectly think that these phenomena are the goal of the ascetic/mystical life. However, they only make up a small part of the life of grace and are in the sixth mansions, not the seventh. In fact, some mystics do not experience these phenomena at all. And both Teresa and John of the Cross caution their readers not to seek for, be attached to, or be concerned about these phenomena. Be that as it may, the first type of mystical experience that sometimes happens as one's union with God deepens is ecstasy. This is not an extraordinary state of prayer. Rather, it is an ordinary part of spiritual growth where the faculties are stilled in a "sweet and gentle reflection on God." A person can be so caught up in this state that he or she may seem to be in a trance. On the other hand, a rapture is extraordinary. Unlike ecstasy that grows gently out of prayer, rapture happens suddenly and even explosively. In explaining this phenomenon, Teresa again uses the water image. She says that while the water basin was before filled gently and quietly, "now this great God . . . has loosed the sources whence water has been coming into this basin; and with tremendous force there rises up so powerful a wave that this little ship—our soul—is lifted up on high."[69]

In this enrapturing, God may show the person "some little part of the kingdom which she has gained. . . ."[70] This may involve a locution, that is, hearing something supernatural; or a vision. Such a vision may be of the near side or the far side. An example of the former would be what Teresa calls a vision "in which is revealed to the soul how all things are seen in God, and how within Himself He contains them all."[71] John of the Cross also speaks of seeing God as phenomena because they are nothing in themselves; they receive all they are from God at the Center and show this fact to the mystic's eye.[72] An example of the latter would be a glimpse of paradise. As with the glimpse of the Pure Land in Shin Buddhism, this vision, to be valid, requires the existence of a far-side dimension to reality. So from the Christian point of view, these experiences need not be dismissed as *makyo*, but may be authentic experiences. Of course, Teresa is careful to point out that any such experience must be carefully discerned since it can come from another source such as one's own overactive imagination. In fact, a great deal of the material in her description of the sixth mansions has to do with rules of discernment.

Teresa discerns three types of visions: external, imaginary, and intellectual. The first happens when one sees something external to himself or herself. The second takes place when the object seen is experienced as an image only within one's mind. The third type of vision is an imageless or intellectual vision where one does not actually see something but realizes a deep spiritual truth within the Center of his or her being. For Teresa, this type of imageless vision is the most important type. The other two can more easily be the product of self-deception. The signs of authenticity include the following: the person is left with a great sense of peace and tranquillity, a deeper knowledge of God's greatness, more clear self-knowledge and humility, detachment from things, and a more profound love for God and neighbor. All of these effects reflect the kenosis of self-interest and self-centeredness that is taking place throughout this mystical period of death-and-resurrection.[73]

One thing that Teresa stresses at this point is the importance of meditating on the humanity of Jesus. She says that one could come to believe that at this point one has gone beyond the need for such meditation and should rather focus on the Godhead. This, for Teresa, is a spiritual deception because for the Christian, Jesus always remains the guide that leads to the Center.[74] In fact, the underlying kenosis of grace behind this centering is a participation of the person in the death-and-resurrection of Christ. Even at this stage, there are many painful trials to be endured which are the way one passes through the wounds of Christ, or the cross, into a fuller participation in the resurrection life. In this passage, meditation on the Way of passage, namely Jesus Christ, is essential. Teresa confesses that one of the mistakes she herself made at one time was to not meditate on the humanity of Jesus and instead "go about in that state of absorption, expecting to receive spiritual consolation."[75] Finally, one should always remember that it is this spiritual passage of death-and-resurrection into a new life of freedom that is important and many people complete this passage without experiencing any of these mystical phenomena. They are not a necessary part of spiritual growth and can even get in the way of that growth if one becomes attached to them and gives them undue importance. On the other hand, if one should receive such experiences as part of God's action, then they must be discerned and accepted for what they are.

At the end of her discussion of the sixth mansions, Teresa mentions a type of purification in the process of mystical death-and-resurrection that leads one into the seventh and last mansions. She refers to this purification as something like a "death" that afflicts the person from time to time for a period of a few hours.[76] This is an aspect of the dark night of the spirit that John of the Cross describes and explains so well.[77] While the dark night of the senses mentioned above purifies one from an ego-centeredness that affects one's motivation in living the religious life, this second and last dark night purifies the very foundation of that religious life. That is, the deepest parts of oneself are united by grace to the kenosis of Jesus crucified and forsaken on the cross, and through that union one eventually finds the fullest expression of new life that is possible to attain in this world. This is the final phase in the process of death-and-resurrection, kenosis and new life, negation and affirmation that have characterized the whole process of spiritual growth from the beginning. Out of this absolute fundamental negation of the whole person comes the Grand Affirmation in the home-ground of our being and all creation.

John of the Cross describes the kenosis of the faculties of the spirit: the intellect, will and memory. In the intellect, there is a kenotic darkening of the understanding that results in an emptying of, or loss of, faith. This kenotic darkness is really the result of being blinded by a great infusion of the light of God from the Center of one's being. And the effect of this kenosis of the intellect is a painful experience of deepest self-knowledge. In light of the purity of God, one feels impure, in light of the strength of God, one feels weak, in light of the unity of God, one feels disintegrated, in light of the fullness of God, one feels empty. The will is left in affliction because of the immense love of God that, like too much light causing blindness, makes one feel only an absence of love with great sorrow and pain. The memory, which for John of the Cross is the source of hope, is so affected by the great presence of God that one feels emptied of that presence in a hopelessness that seems endless. In this emptiness, one is united with Jesus crucified and forsaken and is overwhelmed by the negation of the cross. So one does not understand anything, one does not love anything and one does not hope in anything. This mystical kenosis of the whole person leads one to be detached from everything. One finds no support in anything, lets go and simply lives the cross to the end. And in the end, the affirmation of death-and-resurrection, which is the overflowing of new life from the side of Christ (John 19.34), makes one a child of the light.

All the suffering one experiences in this state is not inflicted on the person by God, rather it is a result of the nature of the person. That is, it is the result of the negative kenosis of our humanity. This negative kenosis must be emptied out by the transforming action of the Holy Spirit so that one can image his or her "likeness" of God. God in the dark night of the spirit empties out this negative condition to fill it with himself. Then the light by which one understands will be the light of God, the love by which one loves will be the love of God, and the presence of that for which one hopes will be given in the joy and delight of God. One understands like God, one loves like God, and one delights in the constant presence of God, all by participating in God at one's home-ground wherein one regains one's likeness to God.

These effects of the dark night of the spirit are discussed by Teresa in her treatment of the seventh mansions. As one enters these mansions, one loses any fear for what may happen to oneself, "is very much more detached," and wants only to continue to participate in God.[78] This participation in God in the seventh mansions is called "transforming union." It begins, according to Teresa, with an intellectual vision of the Trinity and a constant awareness of this triune presence within oneself and within all things. One always abides in this trinitarian home-ground no matter how active one may be. And as in the final stage of Zen practice, one finds oneself, at the very same time that one is always in that home-ground, "entering the marketplace" continually living for the good of others. In point of fact, the last ten years of Teresa's life were her most active. Teresa presents a number of images to picture this state:

> But here it is like rain falling from the heavens into a river or a spring; there is nothing but water there and it is impossible to divide or separate the water belonging to the river from that

which fell from the heavens. Or it is as if a tiny streamlet enters the sea, from which it will find no way of separating itself, or as if in a room there were two large windows through which the light streamed in: it enters in different places but it all becomes one . . . for it is here that the little butterfly to which we have referred dies, and with the greatest joy, because Christ is now its life.[79]

In this union, Teresa says that the "spirit is verily made one with the celestial water of which we have been speaking. . . ."[80] So one may experience the ups and downs of life, but, as with the "stability" or "equanimity" of the fourth stage of Theravada meditation, "they are not of such a kind as to rob the soul of its peace and stability. . . ."[81] Of course, for Teresa, the source of the water from the Center comes from the Trinity of which she is constantly aware. This living water is Christ. So when in the prayer of union, one cannot separate this water from oneself, one can say with Paul, "It is no longer I who live, but Christ within me who lives" (Galatians 2.20). This is the new life, the resurrection life, that comes from the kenosis of the butterfly. For the Christian, this is the purified person wrapped in a clean white robe from head to foot, to borrow the Theravadin image for the fourth meditation.

What is a person like in this state? Teresa says that the unusual mystical phenomena, such as raptures, rarely happen or simply do not happen at all. The person's life is almost always tranquil and stable. And one is frightened of nothing. There is a condition of "self-forgetfulness" and "humility" that is associated with a deep appreciation for even the simplest things in life. And one acts with great love and compassion in serving God in all things. One is able to embrace the sufferings of life and transform them, united with Jesus crucified and forsaken, into a compassionate love for others. All of these actions are not forced by the will, but seem to come about in a natural, simple and spontaneous fashion that reminds one of the freedom of *jinen*. John of the Cross says that the emergence of a person from the dark night into transforming union with God is an experience of new freedom. One freely lives by the grace of God what before one could only hope to live.

After exploring the spiritual journey of Christian contemplation, one must agree with Takeuchi that spiritual transformation happens at the meeting place of the ascetic noble quest of the person and the mystical compassionate action of God. This meeting place is, for the Christian contemplative, found in the interior castle, at the Center of our being, at our home-ground. The meeting that takes place results in a metanoetic process of death-and-resurrection, of ascetic/mystical kenotic purification and conversion into new life. On the one hand, there is the ascetic kenosis that involves a moral struggle of self-overcoming and self-negation of the ego not for its own sake but to attain a selflessness or self-forgetfulness in God. This condition is one of freedom *from* attachments and freedom *to* love God and others. On the other hand, there is a mystical kenosis, a being emptied by the ad-venting of God, especially at times of spiritual shipwreck, from an inner spring of spiritual grace. This mystical kenosis illumines, purifies and overwhelms the person with painful self-knowledge and even spiritual death. But at the same time it pours forth and fills the emptiness and humility with an overflowing from the inner spring of the new life of freedom for which one seeks.

Joseph Ratzinger, in his letter on the relation of Christian meditation to other forms of meditation, says that ascetic spiritual "emptying . . . creates an empty space which can then be filled by the richness of God."[82] He says that this emptiness involves an emptying of selfish attachments so one cannot remain "in oneself" but must pass beyond the self into the mystery of God. Ratzinger concludes that one cannot achieve this passage by one's own efforts, but needs a graced kenosis: "God is free to 'empty' us of all that holds us back in the world, to draw us completely into the Trinitarian life of his eternal love."[83] One could further conclude that through these two forms of kenosis, ascetic and mystical, there is a purification and transformation of the person in the cross and resurrection of Christ. This process brings about a poverty of spirit that is free *from* self-concern and is free *to* live the compassion that comes from the inner spring for the good of others and the service of God.

It is important to remember that this new condition is actually the full actualization of the fundamental condition of our original union or participation in God that was emptied out in the negative kenosis of humanity. Therefore, this fundamental condition is now something to be discovered and actualized.[84] It is for this actualization that the contemplative enters the interior castle so that the Holy Spirit can transform the person into this condition through a deeper participation in God at the Center of one's being. The entrance and further movement into the castle is made possible through the kenosis of the Holy Spirit. This process of sanctification is not forced upon the person but requires an assent, an ascetic and kenotic cooperation, a correspondence to the grace one receives. By this grace, one is sanctified and can begin to manifest a dynamic imaging of God-Love. In this way, the person can be a presence of God-Love for others, that is, be an image of the Image for it is no longer he who lives but the Image of God itself who lives. As Thomas Merton puts it, we seek a transforming union with God which is "the perfect coalescence of the uncreated Image of God with our created image not only in a perfect identification of minds and wills in knowledge and love, but also above all knowledge and love in perfect communion."[85] So by the force of this Other-power, one becomes a unique self-determination of the Image itself, that is, discovers, recovers and lives one's true identity as a child of God.

So Christian spirituality is not a self-calculating asceticism of the ego directed at the possession of some God-object it presently lacks. Rather, it is a kenosis of the ego that opens one to being more fully possessed by a God whom one has never lacked. The negative kenosis of humanity was the emptying out of our dynamic true-identity into a static ego-identity in alienation from God, other persons and all creation. The positive kenosis of spirituality, both ascetic and mystical, is the emptying out of this false self into our original dynamic interrelatedness with God and creation. This negation of the first negation is ultimately beyond one's control. It is not something that one can make happen, but is something that happens to one from the depths of one's being. As Lassalle notes in his own study of Christian mysticism and Zen, "In spite of all his efforts and abandoning everything with a sincere will . . . his own ego bars the way."[86]

In Christian spirituality, as well as in Shin and Zen Buddhism, the realization of this situation leads to a spiritual "sorrow" that may last for many years. But with perseverance and patience, one can move through death-and-resurrection into a new life. For the Christian, one can do things that cooperate with this process, but in the end it breaks into oneself from an Other-power that leads to this affirmation of new life. One can discover in this true living one's lost likeness to God. One can image more clearly the likeness of God who is Love in daily life, in one's personal relationships with others. Through this sanctification of the Holy Spirit, one possesses by the grace of this Other-power of the Holy Spirit what Christ possesses by nature. One is divinized through the mystical kenosis of the Holy Spirit so that one can, as John of the Cross puts it, "appear to be God."[87] In this way, in the way of the cross, in the kenosis of Christ, one can be transformed by God-Love to such a degree that he or she can manifest the truth of his or her original participation in God-Love in a true living that reflects the compassionate and humble self-giving and self-emptying love of Christ's own kenosis in the manner for which Paul is asking in his letter to the Philippians.

This true living in one's home-ground is an *ekstasis* in God. From the Christian point of view, as Abe correctly understands it, this *ekstasis* is a free and dynamic living (*jinen*) of the self-emptying love of God that can establish one beyond oneself in a relation of trinitarian unity with others.

So, the depth of contemplative prayer can lead to a self-trans-descendence that can be the basis of true self-transcending I-thou relations. Living such I-thou relationships with others can be the mutual imaging of the Trinity on the near side of human interaction. But, what does this living of the Trinity in community really entail? Teresa and John of the Cross concentrate in their writings on the inner life of prayer and therefore on "the personal divinization of the mystic."[88] So we need to look elsewhere for an in-depth answer to this important question.

We have seen that Tanabe and Takeuchi both recognize the social implications of Dharmakara's seventeenth vow, that is, that the compassion and unity of the divine Buddhas can be lived by the human community of Buddhists. We have also seen that the Zen-influenced members of the Kyoto School, such as Nishida, Nishitani, and Abe, all emphasize the need for a more united humanity today. For them, the dynamic force of Emptiness gathers persons in their home-ground where they can "merge," "gather" or "make themselves one" in order that there can be a self-determination of the original unification of Absolute Nothingness for the unity of humankind. As Ueda points out in discussing the final stage of Zen practice, Emptiness must be expressed as the selfless dynamic of the "between" in I-thou relationships. How are we to understand this kind of communal spiritual phenomenon from the Christian perspective? What type of spirituality can engender a mutual kenosis of persons, on both the ascetic and mystical levels, such that through the action of Other-power, of the Holy Spirit, a self-determination of the unity of the Trinity can be lived by a Christian community? It is to this type of communal spirituality and the kenosis it entails that we must now turn.

Chapter Six

Spirituality: The Kenosis of Humankind

In the previous chapter on spirituality, we examined the dynamics of individual spiritual growth in Buddhism and Christianity. The focus of that chapter was on this dynamic in the life of the religious individual. But at the end of both the Buddhist and Christian sections of that chapter, we saw that spirituality can have a communal dimension with a social impact, that is, it can contribute not only to personal transformation but also to the social transformation of humankind. It is my view that in the future, spirituality East and West will emphasize more and more this communal dimension for the benefit of social as well as individual transformation. So in this chapter, I want to explore this potential in both Christian and Buddhist spirituality. In doing so, I will examine the role of Emptiness in a Buddhist spirituality dedicated to this goal, and the role of kenosis in a Christian spirituality also dedicated to social as well as personal transformation. Specifically, I will present the lives and spiritualities of two contemporary individuals who have made significant contributions to the history of spirituality. As we shall see, both have visions of a new and more united humanity in the future, and have also established organizations devoted to the realization of those visions through the practice of new forms of spirituality. The Buddhist member of the Kyoto School whose spirituality I want to consider is Shin'ichi Hisamatsu, founder of the F.A.S. Society. The Christian whose spirituality I want to explore is Chiara Lubich, founder of the Focolare Movement.

Hisamatsu's philosophy and spirituality can be better understood by looking first at his life. Hisamatsu was born in 1889 to orthodox Shin Buddhist parents. While at times he was interested in particular political issues, such as the Russo-Japanese War, his primary interest was religion. He even planned to enter what is now Ryukoku University, a Shin Buddhist institution in Kyoto. However, as he acquired more and more scientific knowledge before going to the university, "his indestructible iron faith, of which he had been so proud, eventually crumbled."[1] Hisamatsu refers to this change as a conversion from what he saw as a "medieval form of religious life" to a "modern critical rationalism." He gave up a "medieval faith" in the Buddha and the Pure Land for a "modern faith" in the self-conscious individual person as a rational and moral agent in this world.

Given this new "modern standpoint," Hisamatsu went to Kyoto University to study philosophy. He had heard of a new professor at Kyoto University whom the head of his middle school thought would become a great philosopher. This new professor was Kitaro Nishida. And, as it turned out, Nishida became Hisamatsu's mentor. After eight years of studying philosophy, Hisamatsu was about to graduate but found himself confronted with a variety of problems. As he dealt with each particular problem, he felt that he had uncovered a more fundamental existential problem which he could not solve by the rational-critical method of philosophy. This was the fundamental problem of sin and death. He realized that his own moral life was constantly being compromised, or "poisoned" to use his term, by an evil at the depth of his being.[2] He felt that his True Self was poisoned so that he could not do what he wanted to do, and ended up doing what he did not want to do. It was as though his True Self was "shackled," "impotent" and "choked by the clinging web of the spider of sin" to the point that it was as if he were "paralyzed" and in a "prison."[3] In this spiritual condition, and wanting a "new freedom," Hisamatsu wrote the following to Nishida:

> I want to rid myself of my present dilemma, and turn my daily life into an outflow from the pure, clear spring of the true self. I want to find new significance in all of my actions—from such daily acts as getting dressed or wearing a hat to putting morality into practice, doing social work, and serving humanity—and to be able to live in the realm of sacred light. Until I realize such freedom, all of my acts will be sinful.[4]

For Hisamatsu, this spiritual crisis seemed to be penetrated with death. In this sinful condition, he felt that he was facing death itself. And he realized that purely rational philosophy could not help him with this existential condition, nor did he feel that returning to his earlier Shin faith would help. In despair over the powerlessness of philosophy to solve this fundamental problem, and seeing no turning back to a simple life of faith, Hisamatsu spent days in his room lost in silent thought.

Finally, he resolved to break through this situation by means of Zen. And although he had not defended his graduation thesis, he decided to leave the university. In the middle of the night, he slipped out of his rooming house, and on the way, he went to tell Nishida of his decision. Nishida convinced him to finish his graduation and then go to a Zen temple. Despondent, Hisamatsu returned to his rooming house and later graduated. After a few months, Nishida arranged for Hisamatsu to enter Myoshin-ji Monastery to attend a *sesshin*, or Zen retreat, under the guidance of Shozan Roshi.

In December of 1915, Hisamatsu participated in his first *sesshin*. In fact, it was the first time he had ever practiced Zen meditation (*zazen*). However, during the third day of the *sesshin*, in the midst of great physical pain from the sitting and great spiritual struggle, Hisamatsu's whole being became a "dark mass of doubt." It was not as though he had reached an impasse in solving his problem, but rather that he had become a "single Great Doubting Mass." Fully entering the Great Doubt, Hisamatsu found that it all "melted away like ice from within." And Shozan Roshi also melted away without a trace, "leaving not even a hair's space between the student and the Roshi."[5] Here, in this unity, Hisamatsu awakened to his Formless Self seen in the True Face of Shozan Roshi for the first time. And in that Awakening, he solved all his problems at their root, at their source, in Absolute Nothingness prior to life and death, and good and evil. Speaking about himself in the third person, Hisamatsu says that:

> From then on, he devoted himself to two inseparable matters. First, living this True Self . . . he initiated the "religion of Awakening." Second, by the True Self being conscious of itself objectively . . . and thereby attaining objective knowledge of the self, he established a "Philosophy of Awakening." The completion of this Religion of Awakening and Philosophy of Awakening was his primary concern and his eternal task.[6]

Reflecting on this event in Hisamatsu's life, Masao Abe reminds us that Zen Awakening is both universal *and* particular.[7] The particular dimension of Hisamatsu's Awakening illumined the crisis that he took into that Great Doubt Mass, namely, the crisis that he experienced because neither "medieval faith" nor "modern reason" could overcome the existential problem of sin and death. In a sense, this was his third conversion, a conversion beyond the medieval and the modern to what he would later call the "post-modern." That is, his Zen experience gave him a means of overcoming the limits of modern autonomous reason without returning to medieval faith. And this Awakening became a new standpoint from which he philosophically criticized the standpoint of the modern world and went on to propose the religious creation of a "post-modern" world. We will look at the content of this philosophy and new spirituality later. But for now I want to turn to the next chapter in the story of his life.

During the Second World War, in 1942–43, the Young Men's Buddhist Association of Kyoto University was holding lectures only a few times a year. These events constituted the entire program of the organization, and some students were dissatisfied with the lack of spirituality. A professor who was president of the association called in two students, Shiro Nakamae and Masao Abe, to discuss reforming the organization.[8] The two students agreed to explore how this reform could be done. In their meetings with other students, the suggestion was made that the standpoint of the reform should be "Common Buddhism," or what all Buddhism has in common, in order to avoid Buddhist sectarianism. However, there was a concern that this approach would ignore Buddhist practice. Another suggestion was to make "Original Buddhism," or the original teachings of the historical Buddha, the standpoint of the reform. However, this approach would ignore the development of later Mahayana Buddhism.

Having reached this impasse, the students thought of visiting Hisamatsu at Myoshin-ji. At that time, he was an associate professor of Buddhist Studies at Kyoto University. The students met for the first time with Hisamatsu in December of 1943. Hisamatsu suggested a third alternative, namely, taking "Fundamental Buddhism" as the standpoint of the organization. This meant to expand the focus of the group to an examination of the fundamental Awakening of the Buddha. And for Hisamatsu, this Awakening is the fundamental realization of reality attainable by all humankind. Therefore, although the Buddha was the first to realize it, it actually goes beyond the limits of Buddhism. So, Hisamatsu also suggested that the group take a new name that did not include the word "Buddhism." The group was greatly impressed by Hisamatsu and decided to take his advice.

For the first three months of 1944, the students gathered weekly with Hisamatsu to discuss what the new name for their organization should be. Abe's description of those months makes them sound truly extraordinary.[9] At that time, the temporary draft exemption had been abolished and many students were forced to go to the war. One by one, members of the organization received their induction notices. So, as the students gathered together, they carried into their meetings the personal crisis of facing their own deaths. Their existential problem of the meaning of life and death provided a spiritual depth to the meetings. They would often stay up talking until two or three in the morning. Also, Hisamatsu himself was quite serious during those meetings. He carefully listened to the students, taking their problems as his own. He made himself "one" with them in a deep kind of unity that expressed his great compassion for their situation. Abe says that "the teacher and the students became one. . . ."[10]

As a result of these incredible meetings, the organization was renamed *Gakudo-dojo*, and a four-point statement of guiding principles was written. The name was derived from a work by the great Zen master Dogen (1200–1253). *"Do,"* meaning the "Way," indicates the fundamental Awakening to reality. *"Gaku,"* meaning "learning," indicates both study and practice toward the realization of this fundamental Awakening. And *"dojo"* indicates a "place" where such study and practice can happen. So, on April 8, 1944, "A Place for Study and Practice of the Way" was founded. And its "Statement of Guiding Principles for Attaining Awakening" was set forth. Each member vowed first to study and practice thoroughly to attain Awakening to the Great Way in order to contribute to the honored work of creating a renewal of the world. This connection between personal spiritual transformation and working for social transformation was central to the new organization's vision of its mission in the world. This vision grew out of the ideas of Hisamatsu, as we shall see later, as well as the war situation facing the students. The particular practice they chose to help them in this quest for Awakening for the good of humankind was *zazen*, or Zen meditation.

The second vow of the new organization was to not follow narrow religious convention, but to penetrate to the depths of Reality in order to realize a free mode of living that will respond "wondrously" to all needs. Again we see here a connection between contemplation and action. The students felt that the Great Way was not something that existed in some organization or set of religious conventions. Organizational or conventional *ways* of being were not the Great Way. Rather, the Great Way was to be experienced personally by each person with the totality of his or her being. And this would lead to a living of the Great Way that would respond freely to all needs and answer all problems in daily life.

Third, they vowed "to guard against the impotence of one-sided academic study and the blindness of one-sided struggling practice. Thus, with study and practice as one, we will directly proceed into the Great Way."[11] Here we see the influence of Hisamatsu's "eternal task" mentioned above, namely, the development of both a philosophy *and* a religion of Awakening. Hisamatsu and his followers knew that one can attain Awakening without confronting contemporary ideas and issues. However, they understood that in order to work to renew the world, they had to confront the ideas and issues of the times. In fact, Abe points out that the philosophies such as Marxism, nihilism and existentialism, and such social issues as war and peace, the economy and poverty, were "inside" them.[12] They had to be addressed for the good of their own existential self-understanding as well as for social transformation. Finally, the group vowed to maintain a steady determination to achieve Awakening and to make that Awakening flourish for the good of all humankind.

After the war, those members of the organization who had been sent to the front returned and, fortunately, none had been killed. However, everyone, those who were in the military and those who were left behind, was wounded by the dehumanized conditions of war. So the question that the new organization faced together was the problem of human living: What does it mean to be a human being, to live as a true human being? And connected to this question was the question of what the world should be: What kind of world should be built in the future? Abe says that both of these questions haunted their youthful minds: "We could not consider the problem of the world apart from the problem of the self."[13] These were the problems facing many Japanese people after the war. Soon the organization gained members and eventually opened itself to students of other universities and laypersons in general. It had come to understand itself as a lay organization, and as a result Shin Buddhists, Christians and even Communists joined them. They were, as Abe puts it, "all one" in studying and practicing to attain the Great Way. While they held different views, they were "all one" in this spiritual quest and the desire to use it for the social transformation of the world.

The members of the organization realized that, on the one hand, there were persons addressing the social and political issues of the day without any spiritual foundation. They also saw, on the other hand, persons addressing the issue of individual salvation without any concern for the affairs of the world. Therefore, again following Hisamatsu's inspiration, they sought a "standpoint" where religious problems and social problems were held together. And so in response to the Korean War, in 1951 they composed and pronounced in public their famous "Vow of Humankind":

> Calm and composed, let us awaken to our true self, become fully compassionate humans, make full use of our abilities according to our respective vocations in life, discern the agony both individual and social and its source, and recognize the right direction in which history should proceed; joining hands as kin, free from discrimination of any kind, let us, with com-

passion, vow to bring to realization humankind's deep desire for emancipation, and construct a world in which everyone can live truly and fully.[14]

In this Vow of Humankind, and even in the original Guiding Principles, one can find three interconnected issues, namely, self, world and history. Questions as to what constitutes authentic selfhood, what is the real way of being a true person, and what is the True Self can only be answered adequately in terms of the world context in which the questioner finds himself or herself. This leads to questions about what makes the world to be as it is, and what would a true world of peace be like. And these questions lead in turn to the question of how history can be affected so as to bring this true world of peace into existence. Hisamatsu and his followers felt that this true world of peace can become a historical reality through the efforts of persons who are awakening to their True Self and compassionately choose to work on the basis of that Awakening, for the liberation of all humankind.

This three-part idea was clarified for Hisamatsu during his travels to various parts of the world during 1957–58. Also during that time, the membership of the organization had become much more international. So, upon Hisamatsu's return to Japan in 1958, the name of the organization was changed to "The F.A.S. Society." "F," standing for "Formless Self," means to seek spiritual Awakening to the Formless Self. "A," standing for "All Humankind," means to seek answers to all human problems from the perspective of all humankind and not the perspective of one class, group, nation or race. "S," standing for "Creating history supra-historically," means, on the basis of the transhistorical experience of the Formless Self, to actually move history toward the realization of a new age of peace. And until today, the F.A.S. Society has sought to cooperate with those persons throughout the world who also recognize the interconnection of the problems of spiritual realization, pressing social concerns and the need to affect history for the ultimate good of humankind.

The F.A.S. Society, as it is still known today, was seen by Hisamatsu in the 1970s to be what he called "a post-modernist movement."[15] What he means by "post-modernist" will become clearer when we look at Hisamatsu's philosophy. But for now it is perhaps enough to say that Hisamatsu saw history as coming to the end of the modern age with its basis in autonomous critical reason. He felt that a new post-modern age is about to emerge. And he believed that the F.A.S. way of living was a "post-modern way of being."[16] F.A.S., for Hisamatsu, represents the new spirit of the post-modern way of being embodied in their Vow of Humankind.

By following this Vow, the F.A.S. Society seeks to awaken to the Formless Self, to overcome all forms of egoism (for example, nationalism, racism, etc.) that divide all humankind, and to work together to create a new and united world at peace. In this way, it contributes to the creating of a post-modern age. Illumined with this vision, Hisamatsu lived and worked for this ideal until he died in 1980.

With this sketch of Hisamatsu's life in mind, we can now go on to explore his philosophy and spirituality. Again, what strikes one in reading Hisamatsu's writings is how they are developed from his existential experience. For example, Hisamatsu took his personal crisis, having to do with sin and death, into the Great Doubt. This crisis was brought about by his rejection of Shin Buddhist faith in favor of rational philosophy, and then his realization of the limited ability of reason to solve his existential questions about sin and death. The crisis was resolved in his Awakening to his True Self through Zen practice. In this Awakening, Hisamatsu realized not only the answer to his personal crisis, but also saw in the steps leading to the crisis and its ultimate resolution the basis for a philosophy of the history of humankind. It seemed to him that his own movement from a faith in traditional religion to a faith in reason reflected humankind's movement from medieval faith in the divine to the modern faith in the human. Medieval theistic faith found its ultimate standpoint in the divine. But in modern times humankind has turned to a humanistic faith on the standpoint of "autonomous reason."[17] However, just as Hisamatsu did personally, humankind has reached a point or "moment" where it is realizing the limits of modern life based on the standpoint of autonomous reason.

The experience of sin and death provided the "moment" in which Hisamatsu realized that reason cannot provide an adequate standpoint for true living. Sin and death revealed to him something negative about the nature of human existence that cannot be overcome by reason. In reflecting on this philosophically, Hisamatsu understood that human existence is characterized by a fundamental "antinomy" between the rational and the irrational.[18] This antinomy cannot be solved by the pure affirmation of one of its sides. Irrationality, and therefore sin, cannot be overcome by reason. There is a basic irrationality in human existence that limits reason and until the whole antinomy is overcome, sin and evil cannot be escaped. Hisamatsu also came to believe that sin and death expose another fundamental antinomy of human existence, namely, between life and death. Again one side cannot negate the other, life cannot overcome death because life is limited by death. As with good and evil, the whole antinomy of life and death must be overcome or life cannot be truly lived and death resolved. Finally, for Hisamatsu, these two cases of fundamental antinomy are inseparable. So, while modern persons cling to reason and life, they are plagued with the irrationality of sin and the ultimate fate of death. And to understand this is to be faced with the ultimate limits of reason, limits that make modern autonomous reason an inadequate standpoint for humanity's true way of being.

Hisamatsu's personal solution to this fundamental problem of human existence was its negation, or kenosis, in the Great Doubt: "Such a basic 'great doubting-mass' is itself the ultimate antinomy."[19] Out of this "ultimate" negation came the "ultimate affirmation" of Awakening to the True Self or Absolute Nothingness in which doubt and antinomy were resolved. This resolution was not theoretical but existential. In that resolution, Hisamatsu discovered that the limited way of being can be replaced with a true way of being: "This Nothingness is no mere logical negation but the way of being of the Self that comes breaking out through the bottom of ultimate antinomy."[20] In other words, Hisamatsu's *modern standpoint of autonomous reason* was replaced with the *postmodern standpoint of the True Self.* And on this new standpoint, he found that one is "emancipated from the ultimate antinomy of sin and death" and discovers a true way of being, a freedom in the midst of an antinomous world of good and evil, life and death. With this freedom, based on the standpoint of the True Self, the liberated person can live a universal "love of humankind" forming history with a compassionate motivation.

Realizing this Awakening personally, Hisamatsu understood that this is now the task of humankind as a whole. Humanity must face the antinomy of evil and death in itself and admit the limits of reason to deal with this antinomy. After the Renaissance, which looked backward to the classical age, the modern age looked forward to the future. Modernism has a future-oriented faith that autonomous reason will someday create a purely rational society by solving humanity's problems one by one. But for Hisamatsu this is not a real possibility given the fundamental antinomy of human existence. The problems of sin and death cannot be solved by reason alone. Therefore, humankind must negate or empty out this modern standpoint of autonomous reason in a kind of communal kenosis that achieves Awakening as the basis of a new post-modern mode of human living. This would move human history into a "post-modern age" wherein a true mode of human living can be found.

To the above analysis, I must quickly add that Hisamatsu does not reject reason as such, but only its being made the ultimate standpoint of human living.[21] He says that humanity should certainly proceed in the direction of resolving the problems of life through the use of reason. But he feels that it is impossible to completely resolve them by going just in that direction. Humankind must also go in a *depth* direction to discover something else that can provide a standpoint from which to exercise reason. This something else is the Awakening to the True Self. Masao Abe presents Hisamatsu's rationale for why this something else, this Awakening, is needed for the solution to humankind's problems today.[22] He points out that for Hisamatsu, autonomous reason is based on a Cartesian notion of the individual self as an independent and rational being. The radical individualism of this notion of the self cannot provide an adequate standpoint to aid humanity as it enters a new age that demands the building of a global community, of a new and more united humanity. To build this unity, persons must see themselves in a new way. They must see humankind as "a community with a single destiny—one living self-aware entity."[23] The present crises in the world, the ceaseless conflicts and disputes mean that humanity needs to realize what Abe calls "self-negation."[24] In this communal kenosis, humankind must negate the narrow modern standpoint of independent, rational selfhood and find a broader standpoint that sees the self as part of all humanity.

This view of the self as a being aware of itself as all humankind, as "a single, living, self-aware entity," demands something more than the Cartesian notion of selfhood. For Hisamatsu it demands the notion of the self discovered in Awakening to the True Self. And this boundless expanse of Awakening, this Absolute Nothingness that embraces all humanity as one reality, can provide a broad enough standpoint for the building of a new and united human community: "It is precisely humankind [understood] as a self-aware entity which can develop a unified, cooperative human community in the complete sense of the term."[25] For Hisamatsu, to move humankind from the modern paradigm of self-understanding to this post-modern paradigm is the philosophical and religious task of today. This was his "eternal task" because in his realization he found that Awakening is not a point of arrival but a point of departure to build a post-modern age: "We must proceed to build a solidarity of Self-awakening which includes humankind in the broadest sense. We must build a cooperative society of humankind within the universe. Herein lies the practical task of all humankind today."[26]

Awakening to the True Self involves an absolute negation, an absolute kenosis, of the autonomous rational self: "Awakening to the True Self is inseparable from this negating and stripping away of autonomous reason."[27] For Hisamatsu, and today for the members of his F.A.S. Society, this Awakening is sought through the practice of *zazen* and *koan* study. In this way, one can probe below the rational self-awareness to an Awakening to the Formless Self ("F"). This provides a "depth" dimension to the true post-modern way of living. Awakening thereby to the "width" dimension of humanity, that is, going beyond the ego or individual rational self, one can identify with all humankind ("A"). And with this new and broader standpoint as a foundation for living, one can develop the "length" dimension of humanity by creating together with others a movement of humanity toward an awakened or supra-historical history in the future ("S").

This activity implied in the "A.S." aspect of F.A.S. is based on the Awakening of the Formless Self ("F"). This is not brought about by the "self-as-being," but by the very manifesting of the True Self itself.[28] For Hisamatsu, Emptiness just is the emptying out or kenosis of the self in the disclosure of the True Self. This is the act of Awakening. That is, Emptiness as Awakening is that which discloses the True Self which just is Emptiness. Emptiness as Awakening is not something apart from oneself, it just is the Awakening of one's True Self. And in that Awakening, Emptiness is realized, actualized and manifested. In this view of Emptiness, Awakening is the functioning of Emptiness, not the result of human willfulness. And in the awakened locus of Emptiness, one discovers the True Self as the "boundless expanse of Self-Awakening" that embraces all things. All things are included in this locus and are experienced in their original True Self as fully realized in a "totally awakened absolute present." The world is seen in its suchness where "mountains are just mountains, and rivers are just rivers." In this locus of the absolute awakened present, one finds a deep unity with all humanity and indeed all creation. And this Formless Self becomes the standpoint that can unite all humankind and transform history into a true living of this Locus of unity.

In the above, one can certainly see the influence of Nishida's philosophy of place. So at this point, it may be helpful to discuss Hisamatsu's own notion of Emptiness. Then we can go on to examine how Hisamatsu feels that an Awakening of this Emptiness in personal and communal realization can provide a basis for creating a post-modern world. Hisamatsu says that Emptiness is "the core of Buddhism, and, moreover, the essence of Zen. Further, it is the living experience of Self-realization which constitutes the concrete base of my own religion and philosophy."[29] This Emptiness is not a non-being that is relative to being, but it is called by Hisamatsu a "true, concrete, living Nothingness" that is the "Source" of both being and non-being. And as the Formless Self, it is the Source of our experience of being and non-being, and ultimately our experience of the Formless Self itself. As Hisamatsu puts it, it is "Subject-Nothingness" so that seeing our true empty nature is itself a seeing by this ultimate Subject, the Formless Self. And since this Awareness is the functioning of the Formless Self, or Emptiness, then it is an Awareness in which subject and object are one. It is Emptiness knowing itself, itself as Formless Self: "In this sense, in its being aware of Itself by Itself, it must be said that Oriental Nothingness knows Itself."[30] This Formless Self is empty of the ego-self which is attached to things, clinging to life and fearful of death, seeking good and falling into sin. It is always pure and clear, always free and unattached. So the "dust" of the world cannot affect it. And as Awareness, it provides a solution to the fundamental antinomy of human existence.

Emptiness, Hisamatsu notes, is referred to in Buddhism as being "like empty space" in that it is the formless and uncreated locus of all things and is bounded by nothing beyond itself. It is in itself pure and undefiled and yet embraces all things, be they pure or impure. It clings to nothing and casts out nothing, thus it is absolute compassion and "absolute poverty."[31] In Buddhism, Emptiness is also said to be "like Mind" in that, unlike empty space which is inanimate, Emptiness is Life and Awareness itself. It is Awareness unbounded by ego-awareness and thereby sin. And it is Life unbounded by ego-self and thereby death. Again, it is in the Awakening to this Formless Self that one overcomes the fundamental antinomy of human existence. In this way, one attains Buddhahood because this Mind, or Formless Self, is itself Buddha. Here Buddha is not an Other-power of faith and worship, but it is the absolute Subject itself, the Formless Self.

With this Subject as the basis of one's actions, one can create a Buddha Land here in this world. This is possible because the Formless Self, like Mind, is creative. Hisamatsu quotes the Buddhist expression that says that "All is created by Alone-Mind."[32] And he uses the Buddhist analogy of water and waves to illustrate the creative power of Emptiness and to explain how it can be lived more purely through Awakening. It is as though we are waves formed on a formless ocean of water. Emptiness, like water, is the essence of our forms, like waves. One can say that the Formless Self is the true Subject of our ego-selves like the water is the true essence of the waves. However, without an awareness of this fact, one can be caught in the snares of the ego form, including sin and death. On the other hand, if one "returns to the Source" and discovers True Life therein, then one can reemerge from such an Awakening as the living of the True Self. And this can become the standpoint for building a new world that gives social form to the creative freedom, compassionate embracement, and unity of Emptiness.

Hisamatsu refers to this "reemergence" as "resurrection."[33] From the kenosis of the self into Emptiness or Formless Self, one is resurrected. However, this resurrection is not a denial of the ordinary self, but its absolute reaffirmation. What has changed is the way of being of the self. It now lives its true way of being in the world. In other words, it is no longer enslaved to things and it is not living for its own self-centered purposes. Rather, it now experiences a new freedom and lives for the good of others. Hisamatsu says that such a person living this resurrected life no longer takes the rational self as the fundamental subject of living. Rather, he takes the Awakened Self as the fundamental Subject of living. And yet while transcending limited reason, the person "freely lives the rational life. . . ."[34] Therefore, the person can freely use reason to create history, but always from the transcendent standpoint of the Formless Self that embraces all humankind. This is what Hisamatsu means by "F.A.S." That is, Awakening to the Formless Self, one finds a transcendent standpoint that embraces all humankind and enables one to create history from that supra-historical standpoint. This is to create history supra-historically such that history can more purely reflect the freedom, compassion, peace and true creativity of Emptiness. In Hisamatsu's words, Awakening to the Formless Self enables one to stand "on the perspective of brotherly love for all humanity" while "living the life of history while transcending history."[35]

Hisamatsu feels that this new creation of history is important today because modern civilization has become extremely complicated. And the problems that face modern humanity are interconnected and worldwide. Humankind has lost the moral reasoning to deal with this complexity because it continues to think on the basis of autonomous reason. As mentioned above, such a standpoint cannot embrace all humankind in a manner that can unite it and overcome its problems. So, now humankind is faced with a world that is beyond its control. The modern era is in crisis. Hisamatsu feels that civilization should continue to develop its scientific and technological forces to deal with modern problems. However, he also feels that there must be a corresponding development of spiritual Awareness and thereby of moral awareness. Spiritual Awareness can provide humanity a new and broader standpoint from which to find moral guidance to solve its problems. This standpoint on the Formless Self ("F") would provide the depth needed to give form to a true living of peace and unity. And this standpoint, including all humankind ("A"), would provide an adequate scope to solve the interrelated and worldwide problems. And finally, this standpoint could ground the creation of a post-modern age in which autonomous reason is replaced by Awareness as the standpoint for forming history supra-historically ("S").

Hisamatsu hoped that the F.A.S. Society could put his ideas into practice and make this kind of contribution to the building of a post-modern era. He criticized those conservative religious movements that react to the problems of modernity by trying to return to what he considered "pre-modern" forms of religious life. And he also criticized liberal movements that give "a mere theological interpretation [of events] based on modern humanism. . . ."[36] Also, his view of the ecumenical movement was that it, too, would fail unless its unity is based on the emergence of "post modernity." Hisamatsu saw this "emergence" of the post-modern spirit at the basis of the unity of the F.A.S. Society. The members are not only to be united in the mutual commitment to live F.A.S. as expressed in their Vow of Humankind, but they should also become united in the actual emergence of the spirit of post-modernism. United in this spirit, they can contribute to the creation of a new history for humanity.

Because of the importance of living together the spirit of One Humanity, Masao Abe has recently called for "more harmony, more unity" within the F.A.S. Society.[37] The Society should manifest the unity for which it works. Abe points out that even though the members may hold different views, there should be a "dynamic unity," for that "is the original idea of F.A.S."[38] One must remember the unity of Hisamatsu and Shozan Roshi at the moment of Hisamatsu's Awakening, and the unity of Hisamatsu and the students at the beginning of the Society. Abe sees the importance of such unity among Society members today in the pursuit of Awakening because the ideal of F.A.S. is a collective ideal of a new and "united, cooperative human community" based on the Awakening of a new humankind "as a single, living, self-aware entity." This must be a vision lived by the Society itself through its own unity in its communal spirituality. Hisamatsu himself emphasizes this communal spiritual search for Awakening: "Shakyamuni awakened to the Way as an individual. In our organization, however, awakening is not an individual awakening, but rather is the awakening of the whole group. It is realized through the mutual diligence of numerous members of the F.A.S. Society."[39]

What is involved in this "mutual diligence" in communal spirituality needed to achieve the collective Awakening that Hisamatsu envisioned? Here we arrive at the question of practice in F.A.S. spirituality. Hisamatsu's practice was formed in the tradition of Rinzai Zen. However, in the formation of the F.A.S. Society as a lay organization, he made some changes in the traditional practice. Rinzai Zen uses *koan* practice with *zazen*, and traditionally this means that the layperson must work with a Zen teacher in a master-disciple relationship. However, for the lay members of the Society, Hisamatsu developed another system. Instead of working on a number of *koans* with a teacher, he recommended one "fundamental *koan*" which he felt expresses the essence of all of them. This *koan* is the following: "Right here and now whatever you do will not do; what do you do?" Hisamatsu believed that in the practice of this *koan*, one will be brought face-to-face with the ultimate antinomy or contradiction of human existence. At the extremity of practice, the True Self can awaken itself from the root of this antinomy exposed in this *koan* practice. The members of the Society practice this *koan* in every aspect of their lives as laypersons working in the world. Also, the membership gathers weekly to practice *zazen* together and discuss issues. And twice a year there is a week-long retreat that also includes "mutual inquiry" whereby members discuss their practice in pairs and as equals. This replaces *sanzen*, or the master-disciple structure, used in traditional Rinzai Zen retreats. Again, these changes were implemented because of the lay nature of the Society. However, it is also the case that by all persons practicing the same *koan*, and also by working together as equals in mutual inquiry, the "dynamic unity" of the Society can be strengthened.

As we have seen, this communal dimension is quite important in F.A.S. spirituality. The personal kenotic practice, or what Hisamatsu calls "becoming nothing," of the individual members leads from the "limited 'I' " to the "unlimited 'I' " of the Formless Self.[40] And the communal kenotic practice by the members practicing together leads from what Hisamatsu calls the "limited 'we' " to the "unlimited 'we' " of true oneness. This true oneness in which there is "unity in multiplicity and multiplicity in unity" is then the basis of true human relations. And this "dynamic unity," as Abe calls it, is manifested in the communal practice of the Society. For Hisamatsu, a prime ingredient in the generation of this dynamic unity in communal practice is compassion or love. So I would like to conclude this first half of the chapter with a look at the connection between love and unity in Hisamatsu's thought.

In reflecting on the Zen-based philosophies of the Kyoto School mentioned in the chapters above, one could conclude that compassion comes *after* one's practice is complete, that is, "Emptiness empties out as compassion." However, Hisamatsu stresses that compassion should be lived "right from the start" in Zen practice.[41] This compassion should be manifest in the very desire to practice not for oneself, but for the benefit of all sentient beings. Hisamatsu says that "when this kind of spirit exists in a society it makes the society a truly warm one. This kind of love is crucial in religion."[42] It is interesting that even though he sees Christianity as a medieval form of religion, Hisamatsu says that he finds this kind of love, this kind of "warm heart" in the Christian God who carries the burden of all the sins of humanity onto the cross. His hope is that this "essential" love will be lived in the F.A.S. Society: "With [compassionate] hearts, members of our organization *link together* and gather here for each other's sake. This is essential."[43]

The result of practicing this love is not only unity between the

members of the Society, but also its effect on others. Hisamatsu says that
by living this communal spirituality together:

> F.A.S. will become warm and congenial. If we spread this
> warmth externally, in the same way a charcoal fire lights in one
> spot and spreads, everyone in this room will become warm.
> When each of us becomes a charcoal fire, this warmth can ex-
> tend to those around us, the places we find ourselves, and the
> places to which we go.[44]

This process of generating a fire of love by living compassion in
community and then carrying that fire to enkindle others is of crucial
importance in building a united humankind. Hisamatsu says that "the
present world can be called a world without love." It is a "cold and
self-centered" world that needs "a little more love to emerge in human
hearts."[45] Humankind needs to be warmed by the fire of love. F.A.S.
members can help to transform the world by bringing it this love from its
community and the result will be a more "harmonious" world.

Hisamatsu distinguishes between a passive love, where one feels
love, and an active love, whereby one actively attempts to overcome the
ego and actively care for the needs of others. He sees Amida Buddha as a
model for active love. The F.A.S. members are encouraged to practice
this active love in all situations from the very beginning. He or she should
function in this true Way of being in the home, at work, everywhere. In
this manner, he or she can help to "establish one world in a living,
integrated way."[46] One does not need to wait for Awakening to begin to
live the true and original Way of being human. From the very beginning,
one can live for others in a selfless manner. Hisamatsu says that this
practice may be "difficult," but it is possible. And the kenosis of this
practice can help one to progress toward Awakening and at the same
time contribute to enkindling a communal "fire" that can warm humanity and transform history.

Finally, when this transformation is ultimately based on Awakening,
it has as its Subject, the Formless Self. And this Subject "can make
history into the wondrous form of the root-source fundamental subject,
and lend the living in history its wondrous activity."[47] This Subject, as
Buddha, will make of this world a Buddha Land. This Buddha Land will
be the supra-historical creation of one humanity to which the fire of love
even now can contribute. Hisamatsu says that today humankind is only
"a mere aggregate of individuals," and that "humankind as one whole
does not exist now."[48] This unity of humankind will only take shape in
the creation of a post-modern era. Then in the history of a new human-

kind, there will be a realization of true living as one united whole based
on the fundamental unity of the Formless Self, or on what Hisamatsu
calls "the ultimate unity which is original to history."[49] For Hisamatsu,
this unity means a concrete transcendence of egoistic and nationalistic
structures resulting in a "sharing of all wealth . . . all material and spiritual wealth" in a kind of "communalism" as the active functioning of the
compassionate unity of Emptiness.[50] In the end, it is for such a communal and social transformation with particular goals like these, and not
just for personal transformation, that the F.A.S. Society was established
based on Hisamatsu's philosophy and religion of Awakening.

◆   ◆   ◆

Chiara Lubich was born in 1920 into a devout Catholic family in
Trent, Italy. She was given the name "Silvia" which, as we shall see, she
later changed to "Chiara." As a young girl, she went to school in Trent
and decided to become a schoolteacher. She, like Hisamatsu, was especially attracted to the study of philosophy. She had a strong desire to
understand the truth; and, like Hisamatsu, she also saw truth as something to be lived, as the basis of a true way of living. At the age of
eighteen, she was appointed to her first teaching assignment, a school at
Castello in the region of Trent. Records of her life in Castello show a
young woman who was deeply religious and yet quite human so that "the
whole village grew to love her and respect her."[51]

In 1939, after her year of teaching in Castello where she was a leader
of the local Catholic Action group, Lubich was invited to attend a student convention of Catholic Action in Loreto, Italy. She was poor, but
because her way was paid, she was able to go. This was at a time when she
had not yet found her vocation in life. Little is known about her religious
experiences before Loreto, but the particular experience she had at that
convention has been described in some detail because of its importance
for Lubich's discovery of her vocation. Lubich says:

> I was greatly moved when I first entered the little house at
> Loreto [thought to be the house where Jesus, Mary and Joseph
> lived in Nazareth and brought there many centuries ago]. . . .
> There was certainly no time for me to wonder whether this was
> historically the house where the Holy Family had lived. I felt all
> along immersed in that great mystery, and though it was un-
> usual for me, I wept almost continuously as I thought of all that
> might have happened there. . . . I would not let a day pass with-
> out rushing into the house. There I would always experi-

ence the same deep emotion, as if I were embraced by a particular grace of God, almost overwhelmed by a divine atmosphere.
This was contemplation, prayer and, in a way, simply life together with the three. It was unforgettable. The conclusion of
the course was held right there in the church, crowded with
people and mainly with girls wearing white veils. . . . Suddenly I
understood. I had found my way, which would be followed by
many, many others.[52]

After this mystical experience, Lubich returned home and told a
priest that she had discovered her vocation, or "way," in Loreto. For the
priest, this meant one of three things: to become a nun, to get married or
to dedicate oneself to a celibate life as a layperson in the world. But
Lubich said that she had found a "fourth way." It would be something
new, but with elements of the other three ways. Based on the model of
the family of Nazareth, of Mary and Joseph living consecrated lives as
laypersons with Jesus in their midst, it would include something of the
vowed life of a nun, of the family life of marriage, and of the lay life in the
world of the dedicated person. However, what this meant concretely,
Lubich did not know. So, she went off to teach in another school at
Varollo di Livo, again in the region of Trent. At the end of that year, she
was able to attend the University of Venice to continue her study of
philosophy. But soon, war came to Italy and she had to return to Trent
where she earned money for her family tutoring students in the city.

During this time in Trent, Lubich and a small group of her friends
began to share together a new spiritual experience of life. These young
women ranged in age from 15 to 25, and because of her deep spiritual
life, Lubich became the person to whom all the members of the group
turned for spiritual guidance. One of these girls was Dori Zamboni,
whom Lubich tutored in philosophy. One day in 1943, they were discussing the philosophy of Kant. During the discussion, Lubich was struck
by the fact that Kant's philosophy, indeed all philosophy, could not explain the deep mysteries of God and the ultimate meaning of life. It is
interesting that Lubich was struggling with Kant's philosophy at the same
time that Nishida was finalizing his own critique of Kant's ideas. Lubich
says that she felt urged from within to set aside philosophy based purely
on reason and to affirm her Catholic faith and its basis in the experience
of God.[53] In that moment she felt her mind illumined by what she calls "a
light which comes from above, an understanding which is not a fruit of
our intelligence, but which comes from God."[54] In that light, Lubich
understood certain Christian doctrines that were incompatible with

Kant's philosophy, and she was able to communicate this understanding to Zamboni.

Later, Lubich asked Zamboni: "What should we call this light which comes from above?" And, answering her own question, she said: "The Ideal!" This Ideal is, for Lubich, ultimately God whose light she says "enlightens the intellect and motivates the will."[55] The Ideal she experienced was God and, at the same time, it was a charism given to Lubich when she made God the "standpoint," to use Hisamatsu's term, of her life. Also, like Hisamatsu, Lubich saw that reason was limited in its ability to fully comprehend the truth as an existential reality. Hisamatsu understood this in terms of the fundamental antinomy of sin and death, while Lubich understood it in terms of reason's inadequacy to explain with completeness the truths of her faith. In fact, it may be the case that this is why she called God, "the Ideal." Because Kant, whose philosophy she had just been discussing, himself referred to God as "the Ideal" in that one may theoretically assume the existence of God as an ideal of pure reason in order to fully explain the order of the universe. For Lubich, thinking more existentially than theoretically, God as the Ideal was necessary to give her a full comprehension of reality.

Later Lubich shared this discovery with her other friends and they all experienced that through Chiara they, too, received this charism of the Ideal. And so, they also made God their Ideal, the new standpoint of their life. Before this, they had all been pursuing other ideals—even Lubich had been pursuing the study of philosophy. They now understood that all these ideals which they had *created* were partial and limited; they could not give them the fullness of truth and life that they were seeking. And also, all of these ideals were being destroyed by the war. So it was in God that they *discovered* the Ideal that was an eternal standpoint for their life, one that even the war could not destroy.

Making God the Ideal of her life, as the formative and ultimate standpoint of her life, in December of 1943 Lubich was doing an act of charity for her family. While passing a shrine to the White Madonna, she experienced God calling her to consecrate her life to him.[56] So on December 7, 1943, Lubich consecrated her life to God. This event is considered the birth of the Focolare Movement. And it is interesting to note that this "birth" of the Focolare took place during the same month that Hisamatsu was meeting for the first time with the Japanese Buddhist students in Kyoto in order to form what would become the F.A.S. Society. To mark the consecration of her life to God, Lubich took a new name: "It was when Silvia became Chiara and the forest fire of the Focolare [meaning "hearth," or "fireside"] started in a young girl's heart."[57] Lubich, when later talking about St. Chiara (or St. Clare), said that when St. Francis asked St. Chiara what she wanted when she had run away from home at the age of eighteen to join him, she replied "God."[58] God was all that Lubich longed for as a new Chiara living only for this Ideal. A few days later, her group of young women companions joined her and began to be inflamed by the charism of this fire that burned in Lubich's heart. And as Abe says about his early days with Hisamatsu, which were taking place at the same time across the world, soon they became "all one."

Meanwhile, Trent came under heavy bombing by the Americans. On May 13, 1944, there was a particularly devastating bombardment. So, the Lubich family left their home and spent the night on a hill overlooking the city that was being destroyed by the bombs. Lubich's parents had decided to leave Trent, but she felt that God was asking her not to abandon her friends and the special "oneness" in the Ideal they had chosen. She was greatly torn and stayed up all night weeping. She calls that night "the night of stars and tears." During that night, Virgil's words came to her mind: "Love conquers all." At dawn her family discovered that their house was in ruins and this confirmed their decision to leave Trent. Lubich told her father that she had to stay in the city for she now belonged to God and that there were others who were following her. Somehow, he understood and gave her his blessing; and so she parted from her family. A few moments later, Lubich learned a profound lesson about spiritual kenosis:

> I went back towards the town. The destruction was total. . . .
> Tears came to my eyes and I let them flow. Suddenly a woman appeared at the corner of a street, grabbed hold of me and began to shout in a frenzy: "They are dead, all four of them! Do you understand, all four of them!" I comforted her and realized that I must silence my own grief in order to take on that of others.[59]

Lubich went on into the city and found all of her friends alive. From that day, they continued to meet together in the bomb shelters in Trent, sometimes as much as eleven times each day. They would take only the gospels with them and read together with the light of the Ideal to illumine the meaning of the scripture for their lives. In this way, which was quite radical for Catholics at that time, they began to develop a new form of spirituality. It is interesting that this was taking place in a similar situation and during the same time that Hisamatsu and his students were meeting in Japan. As the group of young Japanese Buddhists were developing their Guiding Principles and deciding on a new name for their organization, this group of young Italian Christians were forming their own spirituality and accepting a new name for their group as well. In fact the name, "Focolare," was not chosen by them. Rather, it was given to them by others who found that being near them was like being near a "focolare," or "family fireside." People experienced the warmth and light of the Ideal, of God, when they were near these young women. Going to be with them, they would often say, "I am going to the Focolare." One remembers here what Hisamatsu says about experiencing the "warmth" of the "fire" of authentic spiritual life.

After Lubich had lived for a short time by herself, she and her friends moved into an apartment together at Piazza Cappuccini. This became the first Focolare Center. It is also interesting to note that when they moved in together, they spontaneously began to live the "communion of goods" that Hisamatsu saw as so important in building a new and united humankind. They put all their belongings in one room and took from the pile what they needed and gave the rest to the poor: "Love led us to put in common what we had: material and spiritual goods."[60]

What are the basic elements of this new "collective" spirituality that came into existence by the light of the Ideal during those months in 1944? In giving an answer to this question, and later in this section when I give a more sustained analysis of Lubich's spirituality, I will be using terminology from the Kyoto School as I have in previous chapters. For example, I will speak of the "self-determination of God" or the "self-determination of the unity of God itself." In so doing, I do not intend to imply that what is taking place in Lubich's spirituality is the *same* as what is happening in Buddhist spirituality. As we shall see, I do find *similarities* between Lubich's spirituality and Zen and Shin spiritualities, but I also find differences. For instance, in terms of the above example, it is important to always remember that for Lubich, unity opens into a depth dimension in which one experiences intimacy with God, with the persons of the Trinity. The question of how similar or how different these Christian and Buddhist spiritual phenomena really are is a matter that requires further research. With these remarks in mind, let us then look at some of the basic elements of Lubich's new spirituality.

In the choice of God as their Ideal, Chiara Lubich and her companions discovered that this God is Love: "For us, from the very first instant, God was synonymous with love; he was Love itself. And scripture told us, 'God is love' (1 John 4.8)."[61] For them, this was not an intellectual conclusion but an overwhelming mystical experience that transformed their lives. Their hearts were inflamed by this "infinite fire" of God-Love. And as their minds were opened by its light, they began to see God as the Source of all, as the ground of being, and as present in a special way in themselves and in others. And so, they, as Lubich says, "learned to recognize and love Christ in each person."[62] That is, they realized that God is not a reality to be just contemplated, but as Love, God can be lived. One can "be Love" for others as God is Love for us. As we have seen, the members of the Kyoto School also emphasize the *living* of ultimate reality. And for Lubich, this meant that one should live Love, to "be" this Love or Fire in each present moment for the good of others.

In living this way, the young women realized that the present moment was all they had. The past was being destroyed by the bombs and the future, given the war, may never come. So, they focused on loving, or, as they said, "being Love" for the person next to them in each present moment as if that were all they had to do in their whole life. In this way of loving, this way of being God-Love for others, lived on the standpoint of God-Love itself, they discovered a new way of being, what they considered the true human way of living. They emptied themselves before their neighbors in order to "make themselves one" with their neighbors. This phrase, "to make oneself one" with the other, is used by Lubich as well as Nishitani. For Lubich it means to live as true images of God, selflessly imaging God-Love in serving each neighbor. One might say, using Nishitani's language, that they found that they could become a self-determination of God-Love itself for the good of others. And through this kenotic love, Lubich found that their own union with God increased, they passed through their neighbor into a deeper union with God at the Center of their being: "The more we loved Christ in everyone, empty of ourselves, the more our hearts were filled with God."[63]

So, this way of constant compassionate action "emptied" their egoselves and enabled them to pass more deeply into their inner Center to discover a greater union with God. But by loving in this way, they made another discovery as well. Namely, when their love became mutual, they found another kind of union with God. This union was with the presence of God at the communal Center of their community. About this communal presence of God among them, Lubich says:

> Our mutual love was the powerful means of rendering him [Christ] present. We used to say: "If we crossed some logs on top of a mountain and ignited them at night, the fire would be seen all over the valley. . . . But if we unite our hearts by loving one another as he loved us, we shall have Love—who is Fire itself—burning in our midst, and we will be able to be God's instruments for many others."[64]

This image is certainly similar to Hisamatsu's image of a "charcoal fire" for the love that "links" people together and warms everyone. Also,

Hisamatsu says that one must "become the fire" so that one can take it to warm others. Lubich says something similar. And the name for those persons who live in the Focolare is "Focolarini," or "carriers of fire." For Lubich, becoming fire means to be kenotically transformed into God: "He could destroy our ego and transform us into himself."[65] This transformation into God is carried out between two fires, the fire of God within oneself at the Center of one's being, and the fire of God in the midst of the community at the Center of the Focolare. By loving, the ego is emptied and the inner fire is fueled so that one finds oneself transformed into a deeper union *with* God. By mutual love, egos are emptied and the collective fire is fueled so that all find themselves transformed into a deeper unity *in* God. To use terms from the Kyoto School, they found themselves "merged," "gathered together as one," *by* and *in* God.

This discovery, and many others, came through Lubich and her friends reading of the gospels illumined, or Awakened, by the Ideal and then putting into practice that which they came to understand as the will of God for them. For example, they were struck by the two passages: "Not those who cry 'Lord, Lord,' will enter the kingdom of God, but only those who do the will of my Father in heaven" (Matthew 7.21); and "I give you a new commandment: love one another; just as I have loved you, you also must love one another" (John 13.34). This meant for them that being a fulfilled Christian requires more than just belief, it requires a way of living. It requires living the kenotic love that Jesus lived. Jesus loved to the point of dying for humankind. So, Lubich felt impelled by the Ideal within her to love in this kenotic way by giving her life, her time and energy, for others, with Jesus forsaken as her model of what love ought to be.

Another passage that the Ideal illumined was: "Where two or three are gathered in my name, there am I in their midst" (Matthew 18.20). When their kenosis of love became a mutual kenosis in mutual love, they discovered, as I said above, this transforming presence of the Ideal at the Center of their community. Lubich says: "we felt as if we were in heaven, as if paradise were in our midst. Christ, in whom we were sisters and brothers, now came among us spiritually . . . he enkindled in our hearts a flame that the world did not know. . . ."[66] Again, using Nishitani's terminology, one can see this collective mystical phenomenon as the self-determination of the trinitarian unity of God itself. In this experience of God as a communal trinitarian Center, the members of the community found themselves living together the self-determination of the unity of God which is the very life of paradise. And they found themselves inflamed by the flame of God burning away divisions and making them "all one."

As others were warmed by this fire, Lubich had over five hundred people united in following her in just a few months. These people were from all divisions of Italian society, from the very poor to the aristocracy. And for the first time, they found themselves united by the fire of the Focolare. They became so transformed by that fire of unity that they lived the communion of material and spiritual goods with Lubich and her young companions. In this way, the poor and those wounded by the war in Trent were soon taken care of so that no one went without. Each day, Lubich and her followers would go into the poor or bombed-out sections of the city searching for those in need. United in this cause with all types of persons, Lubich and her friends read, illumined by the Ideal, the priestly prayer of Jesus: "May they all be one" (John 17.21). They realized that by living in the way that was being revealed to them, there was a self-determination of God among them as a communal transforming Center that could unite humankind: "It became more and more evident that God was urging us to seek his reign, not only within us, but among us."[67] Lubich understood this reign in terms of the very love and unity of the Trinity: "We had the impression that the Lord was opening our eyes and hearts to the kingdom of God in our midst, to the Trinity dwelling in this small cell of the mystical body."[68]

As her community developed in 1944, Lubich realized that this Focolare was, in fact, the "fourth way" that she had glimpsed in Loreto in 1939. It was a way of life for laypeople like herself that had a depth of spiritual dedication as well as the warmth of a lay family, living as Mary and Joseph with Jesus in their midst. And as she saw more and more people united by this Ideal lived by her community, she also realized that the Focolare was a work of God that could contribute to the realization of Jesus' last prayer, that all humankind "be one." In this way, Lubich was not just founding a religious community, but was laying the basis for a new social transformation. Lubich says that: "Mutual love is a reflection of the life of the Trinity such that people can live it."[69] And by living it, she understood that a "New Humanity" can be created united on this standpoint of living God-Love, the trinitarian life of love and unity on earth. Although she does not use the words "post-modern age," the meaning of what she calls a "New Humanity" is similar. It is a new civilization of love created on the supra-historical standpoint of God-Love that embraces all humankind in unity and peace.

As a Buddhist, Hisamatsu says that loving in a way that generates unity is "difficult." Lubich says that for the Christian, "Unity has to be earned; it demands death to oneself, not only mortification, but being 'dead' so that Jesus can live in us."[70] This kenosis of self that is implied in kenotic love for others is necessary for unity and certainly involves a difficult kind of asceticism. But Lubich found what she calls a "key" to unlock this kenotic dynamic of death and new life. The key is what she calls "Jesus forsaken." We have already seen something of what this means for Lubich in Chapter Four above. And we will explore it in more detail later, but for now it is important to note that Lubich and her companions felt that their unity was not achieved by a kenosis derived from just their own effort. Rather, it came from their being united in their kenotic love with the kenosis of Christ's love on the cross. It is his cross that leads to the resurrection. So, by being one with Jesus forsaken in their own sufferings, and/or by making themselves one with Jesus forsaken in the sufferings of others, they experienced themselves passing through the cross with Christ into the resurrection life of trinitarian love and unity.

Thus, for Lubich and her friends, Jesus forsaken was the source of their kenotic love and the way to the resurrection life of unity that they lived together in their communal spirituality. In this way, their kenosis in love generating unity was not just an asceticism, but a mystical participation in the cross of Christ and, through that cross, in the resurrection life of love and unity. Lubich says: "We too . . . have experienced that in embracing the cross one does not find only suffering. On the contrary, one finds love, the Love that is the life of God himself within us."[71] Therefore, Lubich says, they discovered the "divine alchemy" by which their suffering was transmuted into a love that, when mutual, generated a unity that was the self-determination of the life of the Trinity lived on earth.

Chiara Lubich and her friends continued to live this communal spirituality of unity in the city of Trent during the years after the war. Some men joined them and opened a men's Focolare in Trent in 1948. Then in 1949, the Bishop of Trent advised them to rest for awhile during the summer in the Dolomites. Those weeks were what Lubich calls "the time of enlightenment in our history."[72] It was during those days together that they all shared in the mystical experiences received by Lubich and came to understand many things about God and his plans for their little community. Based on that experience, the Focolare has held summer retreats as part of its spiritual formation. Each of these retreats is called a "Mariapolis," or "City of Mary." Just as Mary gave birth to Christ in the midst of the world, the people at the Mariapolis try to live the Ideal so that Christ can be "born" spiritually in the midst of the community. With this communal Center, the members of the Mariapolis share in the light and warmth of the Focolare and thereby often experience a certain degree of "enlightenment," or Christian "awakening," that nurtures and guides their spiritual growth. It is interesting that the

F.A.S. Society also developed a yearly retreat for their spiritual development. The first such Zen retreat was held in 1947, two years prior to the
first Mariapolis.

In 1950, Focolares opened in Rome, Florence and Milan. Also in
that year, Lubich moved the central Focolare to Rome. Over the next
few years, Focolares opened in other European cities. And as the Focolare Movement spread, it met some resistance.[73] Some felt that it seemed
too "Protestant" and others that it seemed too "Communist." Indeed, it
is true that little was said about "love" in the Catholic Church in those
days; to read and live the gospel under direct inspiration seemed unusual
for Catholics. No one was talking about unity and the communion of
goods except the Communists and, after all, they were women. However,
Pope Pius XII personally defended the Focolare from the opposition it
experienced in the particular Italian Catholic milieu of that time. And by
so doing, he prepared the way for its future approval. That approval was
given by Pope John XXIII in 1962. It seems to me that Pope John XXIII
understood the Focolare Movement in light of his vision of the new
church to be born from Vatican II. And it is certainly the case that the
Focolare has become a true example of a post-Vatican II spirituality. Its
official name in the church is "the Work of Mary," because, as I said
above, it seeks to give birth spiritually to Christ in the midst of the world,
as Mary did physically almost 2000 years ago.

There have been many developments in the Focolare Movement
over the years, but I will only mention three. First is that in the same
decade that the *Gakudo-dojo* responded to the Korean War with their
Vow of Humankind, Lubich responded to the Hungarian Revolution
with an important foundation in the Focolare. She saw how many dedicated Communists there were who volunteered their lives for an ideal
without God. And she heard the urgent appeal of Pope Pius XII to make
the name of God "ring" again where it was no longer spoken. In response to that appeal, Lubich founded the "Volunteers for God" in
1956. These are persons in the Focolare Movement who do not live in
the men's or women's Focolares but, nurtured by the fire of the Focolare, volunteer their lives to bring this fire of unity into the world in
practical ways in order to help build what they call a "New Humanity."[74]
They do this in hospitals, schools, businesses, farms, etc. Using Hisamatsu terms, they try to bring the fire of love into the world to warm the
hearts of persons. They also work together to address concrete problems
and to change social structures if necessary. They do not force their
religious ideas on others, but try to foster a new global mentality or way
of thinking so that persons of all faiths, and even persons of no faith, can

work together for the good of all humankind in order to foster a New Humanity united by "active love." They, along with all the Focolare, like the F.A.S. Society, see the need to overcome the divisions in today's world, such as nationalism and racism, in order to create a new world civilization of one humankind. This is not the place to discuss the projects of this dimension of the Focolare Movement, but their work in South America, Asia and Africa is quite impressive.[75]

The second development of the Focolare that I should like to mention is in the field of ecumenism.[76] In 1960, Lubich met with some German Lutherans and opened Centro Uno, the Focolare office for ecumenism in Rome. Many Lutherans soon became members of the Focolare and, in 1966, a small village for ecumenical life called Ottmaring was founded near Augsburg, Germany. Today one hundred fifty persons, half of whom are Catholic and half of whom are Lutheran, live in Ottmaring united in practicing together the spirituality of the Focolare. The Focolare also spread among the members of the Swiss and Dutch Reform Churches. And there is now the beginnings of a Catholic and Reform community in Holland. Also, in 1961, Canon Bernard Pawley, the representative of the Church of England to Vatican II, met Lubich and saw in the Focolare a living out of the spirit of the council. Through his initiative, the Focolare soon spread among the Anglicans in England. In 1966, Michael Ramsey, then Archbishop of Canterbury, told Lubich: "I am very grateful for the hand of God in this work. There are many ways in which you can work with the Anglicans in this country and have a spiritual communion with them so that their hearts can be warmed by the Spirit."[77] In fact, in 1981, Lubich was honored with the Order of Saint Augustine of Canterbury for this work for the Anglican communion.

As the Focolare spread west, it entered the various Protestant churches of America. And as it spread east, numerous Orthodox and Coptic Christians joined the Movement. In 1967, Lubich had the first of many audiences with Ecumenical Patriarch Athenagoras I in Istanbul. Because of her close relationship with Pope Paul VI, Lubich soon became a means of unofficial contact between Athenagoras and Paul VI, facilitating their eventual meeting.[78] Before he died, Athenagoras referred to himself as a member of the Focolare. In 1984, Demetrius I, who followed Athenagoras as Ecumenical Patriarch, awarded Lubich a special Byzantine cross as a "sign of unity" with the Orthodox churches. So in these events, one can see the Focolare's charism of unity at work on the ecumenical level. I should add that Lubich's ecumenical vision sees a new unity among Christian churches that does not deny the present multiplicity of ecclesial forms. She says that "the Holy Spirit will preserve numerous traditions that we have, many customs, rites of the different Churches, but there will be unity. . . . There will be unity in charity and in faith."[79]

Finally, the third dimension of the Focolare that I want to mention has more fully developed since the 1970s.[80] This is the development of interreligious relations. As the Focolare communities spread around the world, they came in contact with persons of other religions. In the West, they met Muslims and Jews. This began an interfaith collaboration and sharing that led to a greater mutual understanding and respect. Today, in North Africa, the Middle East and Europe, Muslims participate in Focolare gatherings as do Jews in Israel, Europe and the United States. This interreligious dialogue results in the participants of all religions being inspired to deepen their *own* religious faith and practice, and to do so in a greater unity with those of other faiths. This in turn often leads to local interfaith collaboration to address particular social problems.

As the Focolare spread to Asia, this kind of "dialogue of life" began with Buddhists, Hindus and people of other Asian traditions. One important collaboration that resulted from the dialogue with Buddhism is with the Buddhist lay organization, the Rissho Kosei-kai.[81] In 1985 the two organizations sponsored an Asian Interreligious Youth Forum in Manila to address issues of development and peace in Asia from an interreligious standpoint. Also, the two organizations collaborate in an ongoing way for the World Conference of Religion and Peace. The Focolare also has a relationship with Dr. A. T. Ariyaratne, founder of the Sarvodaya Shramadana Movement in Sri Lanka. As the dialogue in Asia progressed, Lubich founded a school for dialogue at the Focolare Center in Tagaytay, the Philippines, in 1983. This school prepares Asian members of the Focolare for grass-roots dialogue with persons of Asian religions. Again, the goal of such schools of dialogue is to have a more enlightened love and charity in order to foster a greater unity between persons of different faiths in Asia. I might add that the Focolare also has a school for dialogue with Jews in New York City, and promotes a deeper understanding of Islam through lectures and programs among its members in the Middle East and Europe.

For her work in these and other areas, Chiara Lubich was awarded the Templeton Prize for Progress in Religion in 1977. At that event, Lubich met a number of representatives of different religions. She later said that this gave her a strong desire to move the Focolare even more clearly in the direction of interreligious dialogue. She enjoys learning about other religions and, in fact, she mentions the teachings of Judaism,

Islam, Hinduism and Buddhism in a book she wrote in 1979 on loving God through serving the poor.[82] Chiara Lubich continues to live in Rome and guide the Focolare which now counts 1.5 million adherents.

One question that many laypeople ask today is how they can journey to their spiritual Center in order to be transformed in the mystical life and yet remain living as laypersons in the world. How can the spiritual treasures of the monastery be found in the home or workplace in a way that has an impact on family life and work and can contribute to social as well as individual transformation in today's world? In the above description of the development of Lubich's spirituality of unity, we have seen that it makes the riches of the Christian spiritual life available to everyone from priests, monastics and ministers, to laypersons, families and children, persons of other religions and even non-religious persons of good will. In the Focolare spirituality, a mystical Center is found in the midst of ordinary laypeople. And through their communal participation in that mystical Center among them, they find themselves entering a unique spiritual journey of sanctification. Since this is a collective sanctification they also find that they are being made one not only with God but with each other in a way that affects their family life as well as their life at work. And by living this unity with others, they find they can contribute to social change in concrete and practical ways. Given the broad scope of Focolare membership and activities, I feel that it is truly a radical development in Christian spirituality. And to appreciate this development, we need to look more in depth at Lubich's spiritual theology. In so doing, I will focus on what it teaches us about communal spirituality and the place of kenosis in such a collective spiritual life. And as we shall see, although Lubich and Hisamatsu have a similar vision of the future of humankind, the actual practice of the Focolare spirituality is different in a number of ways from Hisamatsu's more Rinzai-inspired Zen spirituality.

It seems to me that the goal in Lubich's spirituality of unity is not only to realize the reign of love within oneself, at one's inner mystical Center, but to live in such a manner that this Center is realized among people: in relationships, families and communities. In this way, the Focolare seeks to be a leaven for bringing the reign of love into the larger world community. In other words, such a spiritual community lives united by Christ in their midst such that their unity is a self-determination of the unity of God itself. By their participation in this divine unity, they are made one, they are sanctified into the oneness of God's trinitarian life. And they manifest this life in a communal imaging of God. Thus, using John of the Cross' terms, the community is "transformed" into the image of the triune God and "manifests" the trinitarian nature of God in and to the world. Through this communal *transformation* and *manifesta-*

tion, the community can aid in restoring humanity to its original dynamic interrelatedness with God and all creation. Therefore, I find here something more than the individual transformation by, and manifestation of, God from the inner mystical Center as called for by John of the Cross. Rather, I also find a communal sanctification that enables humanity as a whole, by participation in the transforming presence of the communal mystical Center, to manifest God. Here is a communal manifesting of the Trinity on earth that builds the reign of God in the midst of ordinary people making them one as the persons of the Trinity are one. In this way, it seems to me, the Focolare seeks to be an answer to the last prayer of Jesus: "That all may be one."

To contribute to creating a New Humanity that is the image of divinity, Chiara Lubich's spirituality of unity has, it seems to me, both an ascetic as well as a mystical dimension. While personal prayer has an important place in Lubich's spirituality, the emphasis of her asceticism is found in the kenotic love of neighbor.[83] Indeed, kenotic love of neighbor is her way to a deeper participation in God. In her initial care for the poor, Lubich put into practice the words of scripture: "Whatever you have done to the least of these my brethren, you did it to me" (Matthew 25.40). And so she discovered the presence of Christ in everyone she met, in all human beings. She realized that in loving her neighbor in each present moment of her life, she was loving God and therefore deepening her union with God who is Love. As she sacrificed herself in loving her neighbors, the life of God was developing within her: "We have passed out of death into life, because we love our neighbors" (1 John 3.14).

This asceticism involves kenosis, but not the type that is associated with contemplative prayer. And here we find what I see as Lubich's second radical development in Christian spirituality. Kenosis in prayer involves the *stilling* of the faculties in order to be open to the sanctifying action of the Holy Spirit that moves one into the inner mystical Center. The kenosis of love involves an active *use* of the faculties in serving others. That active love requires the silence or emptying of one's ego before the other. In this kenosis, one empties the self in the active use of the faculties for the good of others that facilitates the growth of one's True Self.[84] It is precisely in the love of others that one lives one's True Self, that one images God who is Love. Through kenotic love, one loves God in one's neighbor and finds God in that neighbor. And in this love, God fills one's kenosis with himself. So, active kenotic love of neighbor does not hinder the contemplative kenotic love of God but increases it since God is found in all neighbors. Even John of the Cross points out that: "When one's love for a creature is purely spiritual and founded in God alone, then in the measure that it grows, love for God grows in one's soul as well. Then, the more the heart is aware of the neighbor, the more it is also aware of God. . . ."[85]

In this way of love, one need not be in a monastery to find a deeper union with God. Being with others as a layperson in the world becomes, through the practice of kenotic love, a way to union with God. However, for Lubich this love of neighbor is not just an asceticism of the will. Rather, it seems to me that there is a mystical dimension as well. Lubich understood that for a Christian a spiritual kenosis of love is really a participation in Christ's divine kenosis of love. In a manner that is similar to Shinran's understanding of the primacy of Other-power, Lubich says that while we may make the choice to love in a particular present moment, that choice is in fact the decision to allow Christ to love in us: "He himself could love in us, with his love: Charity. We were loving Christ in the other person, but it was also Christ in us who had to love."[86]

For Lubich, as a Christian, it is by being united mystically with Christ crucified and forsaken that she discovers the Spirit of love poured into her by which she can truly love others. This Holy Spirit pours from the side of Jesus forsaken and therefore from that divine kenosis of the cross, "God's love has been poured into our hearts through the Holy Spirit which has been given to us" (Romans 5.5). Therefore, it seems to me that this kind of participation in the kenosis of Christ on the cross adds a mystical dimension of depth to the kenotic love in Lubich's spirituality. Christian charity is characterized by an unselfish loving service to everyone. It seems spontaneous and always new. It takes the initiative in loving without expectation of return. It may involve sacrifice and suffering, and sometimes takes one beyond one's natural limits to love even one's enemies. And to use Tanabe's terms, this is possible only through the "Great Action" of the Other-power. For the Christian, this possibility is realized by the Holy Spirit of love poured forth from the cross of Christ that makes one's kenotic love a self-determination of the kenosis of Love itself.

As I have said, in Jesus forsaken, heaven and earth meet and are united. So the love that one receives from being united to Jesus forsaken is a divine love that generates spiritual unity. This "religious love," to use Nishitani's terms, is a trinitarian love that unites persons in a mutual love that is a self-determination of the very unity of the Trinity itself. In a very practical sense, Lubich says that it involves self-emptying so that we can "make ourselves one" with our neighbor. That is, one can selflessly share one's neighbor's life and allow that neighbor to pour their life into one's own empty heart. And it is when this type of love is reciprocal, when it is a mutual love, that another mystical dimension of this spirituality of unity takes place. When two or more persons' mutual love flows from the kenosis of Jesus forsaken within them, unity is produced. Lubich says that in this type of mutual love, it is Christ loving Christ that generates the unity that flows between them and makes them one. To explain this she uses the image of electricity:

> Light is actually produced in an electric bulb only when the two poles make contact, and current flows between them. In a similar way, when mutual love was flowing between us, uniting our hearts, it caused us to experience something new: we felt we were experiencing the meaning of the words, "Where two or three are gathered in my name, there am I in their midst" (Matthew 18.20).[87]

It is my view that this flowing of mutual love produces something new, a unity wherein persons are outside themselves in an ecstatic mutual indwelling that is a self-determination of the very circuminsessional unity of God. To use Lubich's fire image, the fires within persons ignite a fire among them that produces a mystical cautery that unites them together in God. And in this fire, both persons are outside of themselves in mutual love so that there is an *ekstasis* of mutual indwelling. The presence of Christ in each person establishes a mutual indwelling that participates in the divine mutual indwelling of God. This is possible not through the willfulness of the persons, but through the grace of the Other-power of Christ within them. This is true spiritual unity, the self-determination of the unity of the Trinity itself. And here we find what I see as a "depth" standpoint to Lubich's communal spirituality of unity. This is not just an individual spirituality of personal prayer, but a communal living of the Trinity on earth that can be followed by all types of people who live in the midst of the world. This is what I see as a third aspect of the radical ascetic and mystical development of Christian spiritual life in Chiara Lubich's communal spirituality of unity.

I would interpret living in this unity as an experience of contemplation in the following way. The contemplative dimension is produced by the very love and unity of the Holy Spirit and is experienced as light. This is the divine reality that Lubich calls the Ideal. It is a light that illumines the darkness within so that one can find God within oneself. This light also illumines the darkness in one's neighbors so that one can see Christ within them as well. And it illumines the presence of God in the midst of the community. In fact, in the light of the Ideal, Lubich and her companions found God in all things as a "golden thread," as it were, linking everything in the trinitarian structure of God-Love. Furthermore, besides being a contemplative light, this Ideal of unity is also a source of contemplative *ekstasis* or joy.[88] In unity with God within oneself, among the community, and within others in a mutual indwelling of love, one can contemplatively experience a taste of paradise, the Trinity on earth. And in this way, humankind can not only contemplatively "discover" the Trinity, but it can actually "recover" the Trinity as the true way of being human. That is, humanity can live the Trinity together so as to recover its original way of living love and unity in the communal image of the Trinity which it was created to be. Therefore, this unity has the contemplative effect of healing and purifying so that individuals grow in union with God and unity with each other in community. In this way, humankind is transformed and united so that it manifests what it was created to be, namely, a communal image of the trinitarian life of love and unity. This to me is a true form of Christian contemplation in action.

In this transformation process in the life of unity, I find a fourth radical development of Christian spiritual life in Lubich's spirituality of unity. At this point, it may seem that one must follow an ascetic path of kenotic love for many years until one finds the mystical Center of the "external castle" and the unity of the Ideal. However, this is to read the above presentation with traditional contemplative spirituality in mind. In fact, Lubich did not find that one must follow an arduous, kenotic, ascetic ascent leading to this mystical communal Center. Rather, by living the Ideal together, she and her companions were drawn into a mystical communal participation in the life of God, in the love and unity of the Trinity, *from the very beginning*. They experienced Jesus in the midst at the *beginning* of their religious life, not just at the end. And, as I have said, they found that the unity of this mystical communal life was based on another kind of union with God, namely, a mystical union with Jesus forsaken from which their unity was derived as the resurrection life coming from the cross. This union with Jesus forsaken also came near the beginning of their life together.

Now, what Lubich went on to discover was that after being drawn into this mystical life, she and her companions were then refined and purified by that life of unity. That is, *first* there was the mystical life and *then* there was the ascetic life. This is the reverse of the traditional contemplative life where one *first* practices asceticism, although in response to a prior grace as the Pure Land Buddhist tradition reminds us, and *then* one is led into the mystical life. In the Focolare spirituality, first there is a certain degree of mystical participation in the circulation of divine kenotic love in the circuminsessional interpenetration of the Trinity at the Center of the community. And then the development of the virtues of Christian living such as humility, long-suffering, patience, etc., takes place within this mystical life of unity. This ascetic development is not a series of steps leading to the mystical life, but a process of conforming the person to the life of God he or she has already received. Again, one is first drawn by the Holy Spirit, flowing from Jesus forsaken, into the mystical life of unity. And then one is transformed by this Ideal to conform with more constancy and depth to the new life he or she has received. This is similar to baptism where one first receives a life of grace and then must learn to conform his or her life to that grace already received.

How is this conforming accomplished? It seems to me that for Lubich it is certainly achieved by the "Great Action" of the Holy Spirit, to use Tanabe's terms. But it also seems that it is achieved in the context of trying to live mutual love. To maintain unity, one must empty oneself before the others in order for the life of God-Love to flow between them. This is living in the image of the Father and the Son, who in this way generate the flowing of the Holy Spirit of Love between them. For humans to live in this "between," to use Ueda's term, takes humility, patience and all the virtues of Christian living. This is difficult to do, and takes a certain asceticism, a kenosis of self. But again, this kenosis is not done to progress from the ascetic to the mystical, but to ascetically deepen and make more constant the mystical life of unity that one has already received as a charism of the Ideal. And, when a person refuses to live in this way in the Focolare (or in a natural family for that matter), the unity is broken, a real purgation is experienced and steps must be taken to restore unity by starting again in mutual love. It is in this way that the persons in the Focolare are sanctified together in their communal living of the mystical life of unity.

Given this explanation of the Focolare's radical development of Christian spirituality, I want to say a few more words about what I see as the cause of this ascetic transformation based on the mystical presence of God as the Center of the community. It seems to me that Lubich's understanding of this cause is perhaps more similar to Tanabe's view than to Hisamatsu's. Tanabe talks of the "Great Action" of "Other-power" that makes persons "empty beings" through the process of "death-and-resurrection." The result of this "negation-affirmation" is a "new life" of freedom, joy and compassion. This results not from the efforts of the persons, but does demand their "cooperation" with the metanoetic action of Other-power. And Tanabe's logic of species goes on to posit that the "communion of Buddhas" can, through the spirit of Amida, be lived by the human Buddhist community. This communal spirit of "unity" can produce a transformation of the community and its members so that there is a "social solidarity" that overcomes the divisions of humankind and builds the "kingdom of God" on earth. This communal transformation also demands "cooperation" on the part of the members of the community, a cooperation that involves what Tanabe calls "reciprocal negation" and "compassion."

Lubich also says that the mystical depth of unity is a result of God, not just human willfulness, and that it also demands human cooperation. I read Lubich as saying that unity is from God in that the kenosis of Jesus on the cross poured out his Spirit, the Spirit of Love that united him to the Father. So in that moment, he felt abandoned by God because the Spirit that bound him to God was poured out. He suffered this privation in order to give that Spirit to humankind so that humanity could be united to God and to each other by the very Spirit that bound himself and the Father. Bowing his head "he gave up his spirit" (John 19.30). That same Holy Spirit also made Jesus the risen Christ so that to receive the Holy Spirit is to receive the risen Christ and to share in the resurrection life of God. This is the mystical presence of Jesus the risen Christ in the midst that comes from the mutual embracement of Jesus forsaken in mutual love. To become one with Jesus forsaken is to receive the Holy Spirit and to find the risen Christ within oneself and among those who live the kenosis of "reciprocal negation" in mutual love.

Since the risen Christ brings his Holy Spirit, it is my view that the unity of God that is experienced as fire in the Focolare is the Holy Spirit transforming those who share together in that fire. This requires a "cooperation," which for Lubich means to continue to embrace Jesus forsaken as the source of unity and to continue to live mutual love. Here again I see a mysticism that leads to asceticism rather than the other way around, as is the case in more traditional forms of spirituality. And I also conclude that the fundamental effect of this transforming power of the Holy Spirit is, as Tanabe says, "death-and-resurrection." This Spirit from the risen one among them enables them to die to themselves out of love for the others and be regenerated in the new life of the resurrection in which they share. In this "negation-affirmation," as Tanabe puts it, it seems that God is demolishing and building up at the same time. As John of the Cross puts it, in a "sweet cautery" the fire touches the soul which becomes "altogether wounded and altogether healthy."[89] It seems to me that the Holy Spirit is the fire in the midst of the Focolare that produces the divine alchemy that transforms suffering into love, darkness into light, death into resurrection. The mystical presence of God as the ground of the unity in the Focolare works on the hearts of its members bringing them to sanctification, but doing so in such a way that on the kenosis of their mutual love, they are made more and more one in the life of the Trinity. In this mystical atmosphere, little by little, defects disappear and the Christian virtues are developed through the power of the

Holy Spirit and the ascetic cooperation of the members living mutual love.

This interpretation of the mystical and ascetic elements of Lubich's spirituality of unity explains another aspect of that spiritual life. Above, I mentioned that Lubich seemed to have received a special light to understand the things of God. Now one could conclude that this light, which she called the Ideal, is *Claritas*, or the Holy Spirit as light. It is God and a charism of God as the illumination of the Holy Spirit. Today, this *Claritas* is experienced in the atmosphere of the Focolare as a light given by the fire of the Ideal at the Center of the community, by the risen Christ among them so that they can realize an "awareness" of a deeper oneness with God and each other, and can see how to live better this life of unity.[90] This mystical fire also warms their hearts so that they can better practice ascetic kenotic love, conformed to the will of God in each present moment. In this way, it seems to me that the mystical self-determination of the Trinity forms the ascetic life of the community in such a way that eventually the community reflects the Trinity's own image in love and unity.

In my study of Lubich's spirituality, I must conclude that this dynamic of spiritual growth is not always consoling. Rather, it would seem that this process can be painful at times because the light of the Ideal can reveal aspects of one's life that need to be healed. This self-knowledge, and realization of one's negative kenosis, is necessary for spiritual growth in the life of unity. This painful self-realization, as Shinran saw, is necessary; and it is the communal presence of God in the midst of the community that illumines this situation so that it can be purified and transformed in order that the members of the community, who are already united to some degree in that mystical Center, can grow in sanctity. Again, one may feel broken down, confused, angry, and at the same time be aware that one is being affected by a compassionate reality that is rebuilding oneself. One's true and dynamic self, interrelated with others and all creation, is being realized in the very process of the emptying out of one's false and static self isolated from others and the world. This is an emptying out of the negative kenosis of humankind into a true form of living united in a trinitarian structure with God, others and all creation. Again, this is the experience of death and resurrection, of kenosis and new life. What is taking place here is similar to what Teresa of Avila describes as a purgation of the soul as it enters more deeply into the interior castle. So, too, as one enters more deeply into the exterior castle of the Focolare, one is also purified and transformed.

The light of the Ideal, the *Claritas*, can be so intense, as John of the

Cross puts it, that the person can be overwhelmed and experience a profound taste of Jesus forsaken, even to the degree of the dark night. In the case of the dark night, it would seem that most persons in the Focolare experience "portions" of this experience, as Catherine of Siena would say. And they often seem consoled by the presence of Jesus in the midst in a manner that modifies the more painful aspects of the dark night. Perhaps God works in them in this way because most of these people are laypersons working in the world. In any case, these are moments of participation in the cross of Jesus forsaken. These portions are like digging caverns in the heart that are later filled with light. In this way, kenosis and new life alternate. At times when someone recognizes Jesus forsaken in his or her suffering, immediately that cavern is filled with light and peace, and joy returns, often to the great surprise of the person. These tastes of the cross and the growth through them into a deeper union with God and unity with others in God are again part of the fundamental process of death and resurrection. And the result is always a more pure spiritual detachment and love. Therefore, we can see here that while the Focolare communal spirituality may begin with a mystical experience of unity, the asceticism that follows has the important effect of making that unity deeper and more constant.

It is also the case that the more mature members of the Focolare develop a deeper and more constant *awareness* of God at the Center of themselves, others, the community and all creation.[91] This, along with the life of virtue, always in the will of God, is the "transforming union" with God that is the highest contemplative state in Christian mysticism. Again, Lubich's spirituality is a radical development of the Christian spiritual tradition in that this form of personal sanctity is generated in a communal life fully open to laypersons. God is the mystical Center that makes these persons not only individual saints, but makes them saints together so that in the end they are "all one" as the Trinity is one. Here there is a mystical "transformation" and "manifestation" of not only persons but of community. All members of the community, if they cooperate with grace by living the "reciprocal negation" of mutual love, become what they receive, namely, the image of the Trinity, or the collective imaging of God which humankind was created to reflect in its original nature. And in this way the community can become a leaven for the ultimate transformation of all humankind into a new and more united humanity in the "post-modern" future.

Before going on to give some final comparative comments about Lubich's spirituality and the Kyoto School, I want to make the following two qualifications to what I have presented so far. First, in this section on Lubich's spirituality, I am stressing its kenotic dimensions. I do so because that is the topic of this book. However, there are many more dimensions to her spirituality. For example, being love for others in the present moment is practiced in such a way that one takes into consideration one's own condition in making choices as to what one can and cannot do. Kenosis is an aspect of the Focolare spirituality which is balanced by other aspects that insure a healthy spiritual, psychological and physical life. Second, I have also been stressing the communal aspect of the Focolare spirituality because that is the topic of this chapter. However, there are also other aspects to Lubich's own mystical life and her spirituality than those associated with the exterior castle. A study of those other aspects, like personal prayer and meditation, would help one to appreciate the inner as well as the interpersonal, and the vertical as well as the horizontal, dimensions to Lubich's mystical life and the spiritual life of the Focolare. However, that would take us beyond the task of this book.

On the other hand, with what I have presented of Lubich's spirituality it should now be clear that it is, as I have claimed above, a radical development of traditional Christian spirituality in the spirit of Vatican II. And it is similar in some ways to the F.A.S. Zen philosophy and religion of Hisamatsu. Yet, given its clear emphasis on what Buddhism would call Other-power, and on the far-side reality of God, it is also dissimilar in other ways to Hisamatsu's thought and practice. I find that Lubich confirms the traditional Christian understanding of God in her own mystical writings and in her standpoint for world transformation. In so doing, she does not reject the other religions but accepts them as bearers of truth. She seeks through dialogue to build bridges of mutual understanding and respect between all religions in order to lay the groundwork for mutual collaboration in creating a New Humanity where all people, cultures and traditions will be respected in a new age of love and peace.

Also for Lubich, the Ideal gives a light to see the presence of Jesus forsaken in the sufferings of humanity. And so it engenders a warmth that moves one to compassionate action to respond to the cry of Christ in the poor and oppressed. It enkindles a desire to liberate all the crucified parts of humanity so that all may share in a new and more just society. And it impels one to dialogue with persons of other faiths to seek ways to achieve this goal of building a New Humanity. It seems to me that Lubich feels, like Hisamatsu, that this project must be based on a religious standpoint because only in that way can humankind find the depth, width and length it needs to transcend its individualistic limitations and achieve true oneness in the future. She also seems to feel that such a religious foundation is important in serving the poor because among the poorest in the world are those who are poor in spiritual life. This is the case both in the materialistic West and the atheistic East.

So it would seem that true interreligious dialogue must seek a way of living united together in progressing as fellow pilgrims into the truth, and at the same time facing the untruth of the world in order to liberate a suffering humanity and build a new world of compassion and peace. If persons of different religions can practice the "dialogue of life" suggested by Lubich, there can be a greater "reciprocal negation," a mutual kenotic love that generates interreligious unity so that there can be a deeper communion of persons committed to the healing of a broken, wounded, divided and suffering humanity. In this way, there can be an interreligious collaboration for the creation of a supra-historical self-determination of unity that can embrace all humankind.

Finally, the spiritual genius of Hisamatsu is found, in part, in his ability to see in his spiritual Awakening a philosophical and religious standpoint for the F.A.S. approach to Awakening and to creating the unity of humankind in the future. When I reflect on Hisamatsu's life, writings and activities, I must conclude that his experience of Emptiness, the Formless Self, is most profound. It should lead the Christian to a silent awe before the overwhelming mystery of Buddhist Emptiness. And when I reflect on the life, writings and activities of Chiara Lubich, I must conclude that in the light of the Ideal, of God, she must also have had a profound mystical experience. For her, it was being drawn into the inner trinitarian kenosis of God. She seems to have experienced the mutual kenosis of the persons of the Trinity and found therein the circuminsessional interpenetration of unity which that kenosis involves. And what is surprising in Lubich's case is that this Ideal not only gave her a light to penetrate beyond the mystical Void into an intimacy with the persons of the Trinity, but it gifted her with a charism that enabled her to share that penetration with others so that together they are enabled to live that trinitarian life of mutual kenotic love and circuminsessional unity here on earth. No wonder she often speaks of her life in Focolare as a "taste of paradise." Here too, one is led to silence this time before the overwhelming mystery of God.

So to conclude this important chapter, it is valuable to remember that throughout this book, I have stressed that spirituality today must seek not only the personal transformation of the individual, but also the social transformation of humankind. From the Buddhist side, besides this emphasis in Hisamatsu's F.A.S. philosophy and religion, we saw that Nishida believes that through the "casting aside of the self," one could pass beyond the "vanishing point" of the ego into a "matrix of Emptiness" which has a "trinitarian structure." In that "place," one can find a "merging with the other" in a way that "mirrors the absolute" and brings unity and compassion into true "I-thou relations." Nishitani also speaks of "overturning" the "field of self-centeredness" in order to realize our original "home-ground" that is characterized by "circuminsessional interpenetration." Through this "making oneself empty," one lives on a field of *agape* where one finds oneself "gathered into one," into a self-determination of the original "unity" of our home-ground itself. Here, there is true "religious love" and "absolute harmony reigns." Abe, too, writes of the "kenosis of self" as "self-emptying love" in the image of God who is Love. Through this kenosis, one can realize a "true self-awakening" to, and "realization" of, the original unity of humankind as a "corporate entity," as a "single, living, self-aware entity." And Ueda, again from a Zen point of view, also sees the need for more than personal transformation. He, too, recognizes the possibility of the "selfless dynamic" of Emptiness as being the unifying "between" of true I-thou relations.

For Tanabe, on the Pure Land side of the Kyoto School, unity requires a "metanoesis" by "Other-power" which makes us "empty beings" full of compassion in order to be "co-workers" in building the "kingdom of God." This "communion," or "mutuality" or "solidarity" is achieved by the "true individual and mutual reconciliation" of persons that mediates a divine communion among humankind and brings "the joy of social harmony." Takeuchi also sees the "ad-venting" of Other-power as producing a unity of humankind with divinity and all creation that "mirrors" the Pure Land here on earth. In some ways, Lubich seems to share this view that the grace for both personal and social transformation comes from a far-side reality. It "ad-vents" from the Center of one's being as the Ideal that sanctifies the person and also provides a communal Center that in turn can be a standpoint of depth, width and length, to use Hisamatsu's words, for the social transformation of humankind. In other ways, Lubich seems to share many of the insights of the Zen tradition about the negative kenosis of the human person, the need for a positive kenosis, the trinitarian ground and structure of existence, and the possibility for a self-determination of the unity of that ground as a "fire" for the transformation of humankind. In other words, she presents a Christian spiritual theology with similarities to and differences from the various philosophies of the Kyoto School. But her spirituality seeks the kind of social transformation of humankind that is the common ideal of all members of the Kyoto School. So now I would like to conclude this dialogical exploration of Emptiness and kenosis by looking at two persons, one Buddhist and one Christian, who provide us with models for living this ideal in contemporary spirituality.

Chapter Seven

Mary: A Model of Kenosis

In the previous chapter, I tried to develop in some detail a line of thinking that has been running throughout this book. That is, I presented two forms of contemporary spirituality, one Buddhist and the other Christian, that combine a concern for personal transformation with a concern for social transformation. On the Buddhist side, we saw that Hisamatsu combines new forms of Zen practice with working for the creation of a post-modern age in which humankind can be united on a spiritual standpoint. And on the Christian side, we saw that Lubich combines a new and communal spirituality with actively building a New Humanity that images its trinitarian standpoint so that "All may be one." Since I see the future of spirituality East and West as developing in this direction, I would like to continue that line of thought in this final chapter.

One of the most fascinating Buddhist-Christian comparisons to be made by one of Hisamatsu's followers is the comparison between Maya, mother of Gautama Buddha, and Mary, mother of Jesus Christ. This comparative work is presently being done by Gishin Tokiwa, who is one of the leaders of the F.A.S. Society. His existential interpretation of the spiritual meaning of these two historical persons provides Buddhist and Christian models for living kenotic spirituality. However, before looking directly at Tokiwa's comparison, I would like first to examine a fundamental aspect of Hisamatsu's thought that I believe will help us better understand Tokiwa's work. This particular dimension of Hisamatsu's philosophy of religion is explored in a lecture Tokiwa once gave to the F.A.S. Society.[1]

In this lecture on "The Emancipation of History," Tokiwa states that religion must lead to the emancipation of history itself, and that an important objective of being a religious person today should be to "help" history to "awaken" to itself. In other words, for history to become emancipated, it must awaken to something that "constitutes the

182

content of the True Self of history."[2] Tokiwa understands this return of history to its True Self as the "ideal" taught by Hisamatsu. Here, we clearly see that Hisamatsu saw Awakening in its fullest realization as something more than an individual matter. It involves the Awakening of all humankind in a social-historical realization. But for Hisamatsu, this cannot happen in the "ordinary" course of history. History takes place in an ordinary manner that follows the ordinary course of unawakened human existence. That is, in ordinary history, as in a person's ordinary life, certain problems arise and are addressed, certain crises happen and are overcome, certain stages begin, develop and come to an end only to be replaced by other stages.[3]

Being caught in this process (*samsara*), the process itself is not questioned either by the individuals living historically or by history itself. Thus, neither individual Awakening nor the Awakening of history itself happens. Instead, ordinary life and history advance and their true basis is never questioned. If there are criticisms of history, they are always *within* the historical process and the critique never reaches the depths of the entire historical process itself. This is because the individual persons and social organizations, which might make a critique of the process, are ordinarily part of history. Self, society and world share the structure of history, and so the questioner finds no standpoint from which to criticize history as such. He, she or they can criticize some aspect of history but not the basis of history itself. The individual person or social group have no standpoint from which to make this kind of radical critique. This, Tokiwa believes, is why Hisamatsu says that history itself must come to criticize itself.[4] For this to happen, it must be led to the ultimate critique of its own historical process, its ordinary historical mode of becoming. And this is not a task *within* history, it is the task *of* history. History must be led to realize what it "ordinarily" is and awaken to its True Self, namely, to what it "originally" is and thus can truly become.

Tokiwa says that: "This is a supra-historical task which history is unable to elucidate in history."[5] By "elucidate," Tokiwa means to "cast off" the ordinary mode of history. And this can only be done by the ultimate Awakening of history itself that casts off its ordinary functioning and creates a new supra-historical functioning on the basis of this Awakening. Again, we see that this Awakening of history is not just an individual matter but must be achieved by all humankind. It is all humankind on a supra-historical standpoint, for Hisamatsu the standpoint of the Formless Self, that can lead history into this supra-historical task of casting off ordinary history and creating Awakened history. But, Tokiwa laments, humankind is far from being awakened, so it sometimes seems that history "must go on endlessly trying to solve its problems."[6] However, here we come to Hisamatsu's paradoxical Zen mode of reflection on this situation. For Hisamatsu and for Tokiwa, it is the case that history has always been awakened to its True Self. Behind the contradictions and resolutions of ordinary history is a deeper original "unity," as Tokiwa also calls it. And this original unity is none other than the very contradictions and resolutions of ordinary history. This is the Buddhist paradoxical identity of Nirvana and *samsara*: identified with the dissatisfactory samsaric process of history is a nirvanic unity as the True Self of history. Therefore, Tokiwa says, "History has never been astray. History has always been awakened to its True Self. We need only be awakened to this."[7] In this way, we can realize the true face of history itself and thereby "this awakened self of history can promote history itself. . . ."[8]

This, according to Tokiwa and following Hisamatsu's philosophy, is the true direction of history that should form the life of the religious individual. The religious person must learn to live the true way of history so as to lead history in the direction of its Awakening to this true way: "Religion must be the true way of being of history."[9] In other words, if religion can realize its supra-historical standpoint, it can find that "place" from which it can criticize history as such and help cast off the ordinary way of history and realize the true way of historical being that has always been at the root of history waiting to be realized by humankind. For Tokiwa and Hisamatsu, this root of true history is the Formless Self which is the original way of history, the "true face" of history. And for both Tokiwa and Hisamatsu this true face of history is at once all humankind and all the universe.[10] Therefore, the task of history, of humankind, and of the universe is to realize this one true face, this true way of being. The ordinary way of being must be emptied out in order to realize the true original way of being. Again, this realization is not just an individual achievement, but is the realization of a supra-historical history, of a united humankind, and an awakened universe.

In an analysis of the Four Noble Truths that were taught by Gautama Buddha, Tokiwa develops this distinction between an "ordinary way of being" and an "original way of being." The Buddha, on the standpoint of his Awakening, taught the truths of suffering, its cause, its cessation, and the way leading to this cessation. Tokiwa says that the common subject referred to by these truths is the totality of the world including humankind.[11] However, he also says that the first two statements, which claim that there is suffering and its cause is ignorance and selfish desire, refer to a subject that exists in a particular way that causes this suffering. It is the world, and therefore humankind, that exists as subject in a particular way that causes suffering. Tokiwa goes on to claim that the last two statements, which state that this suffering can be brought to an end and give the way that leads to this cessation, refer to a Subject that realizes the true nature of suffering and its cause. In this Awakening, the true Subject is the Formless Self which realizes the cessation of suffering and the way that leads to this cessation.[12] In other words, as ordinary persons, or as ordinary humankind, or as ordinary history, or as the ordinary universe, particular subjects follow an "ordinary way of being" that causes the suffering of existence. However, as original persons, or as original humankind, or as original history, or as the original universe, there is a realization of an Awakened Subject that follows an "original way of being" that creates an end to the suffering of existence.

So we are led to the question: "What is this original way of being that liberates individual persons, all humankind, history and the universe from the suffering of existence?" Tokiwa says that "the ultimate cause of suffering . . . is my way of being and the way of being of the world which constitutes my way of being, and this is 'ignorance.' "[13] In Awakening, one realizes that this ignorance has no root in one's True Self. And so one can say with Tokiwa: "I realize that freedom from, and the cessation of, suffering is my true way of being. . . . I am Self without any form. Hence THIS, Formless Self, is the cessation of suffering."[14] Therefore, for Tokiwa, the original way of being that is the cessation of suffering is the way of the Formless Self realizing itself in Awakening. Now, to see how we can understand this original way of the Formless Self as freedom from suffering, it is important to note that the True Self implies Emptiness that is essentially empty of suffering. However, for Tokiwa, "Emptiness as the True Self can, does, and will suffer."[15] Here again we find the identity of Nirvana and *samsara*, of Emptiness and form. That is, the person emancipated from suffering can truly understand what suffering is: "It is the emancipated who can say and go through what suffering is."[16] What this means, we will discuss in more detail later. But for now it is enough to note that the one who is awakened to the True Self liberated from suffering (Nirvana), can truly live the suffering of his or her existence (*samsara*) in an authentic manner, namely, in order to liberate others from their suffering. This is to live Emptiness in a form that empties out Emptiness as compassion for the sake of all sentient beings.

It is in this kenotic dynamic of compassion that one can, according to Buddhism, *see* what one's "original way of being" truly is. And Tokiwa *sees* humankind's original way of being as represented in Maya, mother of the Buddha, and in Mary, mother of the Christ. I believe that it is this vision of their ways of being as representative of our original way of being that is behind Tokiwa's comparative study of the existential meaning of these two historical figures. So with this in mind, we can go on to explore Tokiwa's existential interpretation of the meaning of Maya and his comparative comments about Mary.

Tokiwa points out that in certain forms of Buddhism, Maya is called the *tathagata-garbha*, or the "womb of the Buddha." In this kind of Buddhist thinking, Maya represents all humankind in that every person is originally a *tathagata-garbha*. For Tokiwa, the *tathagata*, or Buddha, in the ultimate sense is "the true oneness or unity of all beings—the original, true formless Self of all of us."[17] When one is empty of self, like a "womb" (*garbha*), this True Self can manifest itself within one's kenosis so that one can be transformed by it. One can realize the same "Buddha-nature" of the True Self. That is, when one is empty of self, and is "womb" of the Buddha, the true original way of being of this True Self becomes one's own way of being: "That One Person manifests as the human issue of a human womb, so that the mother also comes to be of the same nature, that is, the original, true Formless Self of all beings."[18] By becoming womb, one becomes Buddha; or better, by being womb, One is realized as Buddha in one's own way of being.

For Tokiwa, *tathagata-garbha* not only represents the essential nature and existential potential of individual persons, but of all humankind. When humankind can become empty of individual selfhood, and realize within its "womb" the "unity of all beings," as Tokiwa puts it, then it can be transformed by that unity. Humankind can be made *one* humankind. But this realization is not achieved by its own effort alone. It can only be fully realized by the True Subject of humankind and history itself. Therefore, humankind as the "womb of the *tathagata*," which is the true way of being that brings a cessation of suffering, can awaken to this original way of being and live it in a manner that liberates human history and the universe. Humankind as just *garbha*, or womb, "ordinarily" generates a suffering existence. But, humankind as *tathagata-garbha*, can "give birth" to the original way of being which is a source of emancipation for itself, its history and the universe. Tokiwa says: "In my understanding, *tathagata-garbha* represents humanity awakened to its original, true Formless Self (*dharmakaya*). It is the womb—which stands for ordinary, unawakened beings—returned to its original, true way of being, the womb that gives birth to tathagatas."[19]

This last quotation is quite important in understanding Tokiwa's notion of *tathagata-garbha*. That is, it is not the case that humanity is a passive "holder" of the Buddha. Rather, the word *garbha* can also mean "embryo." So, this implies that the person, or humankind, that is empty of self like a womb does not just passively contain the Buddha, but it is transformed into the Buddha. As Tokiwa puts it, the womb is returned to the True Life that it contains. Being empty as a womb is not just to be empty in a negative sense, but to be the embryo of True Life. The mother does not just contain in a passive manner the inner life as something different from herself, but the mother lives the new life as her very own life. In other words, by emptying oneself of one's ordinary way of being, one can in that womb-like emptiness realize one's original, true way of being—not as something different from oneself, but as one's True Self. As Tokiwa says, the original way of being, contained *by* the womb, is the original way of being *of* the womb, of all humankind.[20]

Tokiwa points out that in the early Buddhist text, the *Lalitavistara*, it is said that Maya is so influenced by the *tathagata* within her that she says:

Of me there is nothing defective or deficient;
There is no rage, not even the delusion of mind.
I am full of the comfort of being in dhyana;
And know that my mind is free from passion.[21]

Dhyana, or meditation, is not only enjoyed by Maya, but in the Mahayana tradition it is understood as clearing the delusion of her mind so that she is identified with wisdom (*prajna*). This wisdom is not just a contemplation of Emptiness, but a living of Emptiness. Maya is empty of ordinary self-centered and ignorant personhood, and in this kenosis, lives Emptiness. And as we know from all the members of the Kyoto School, lived Emptiness, or to be an "empty being," is the life of compassion. Therefore, the "way of being" of Maya, the *tathagata-garbha*, is one of contemplative wisdom expressing itself as active compassion. And for Tokiwa, this is the "original way of being" of humankind to be realized in Awakening.

Another interesting point that Tokiwa makes about compassion is that in a Mahayana text, the *Gandavyuha*, Maya "proclaims herself not only to be the mother of Gautama Sakyamuni but to enjoy being the mother of all the tathagatas," "the eternal womb for all the tathagatas."[22] That is, she proclaims herself to be the functioning of the eternal and boundless womb of Awakening for all times: "She announces herself to be the mother of all the tathagatas of the past, present, and future."[23] This, Maya says, is the profound truth of the "Great Womb of Compassion" (*mahakaruna-garbha*). One might take this to mean that in Maya one can find Emptiness emptying out as the Great Compassion in a manner that is fundamental to Awakening in all times and places. Some Buddhists take this to refer symbolically to a feminine principle of compassion found in Maya and necessary in all cases of Awakening. Tokiwa gives these statements by Maya a more existential interpretation. For him, humanity is originally the *tathagata-garbha*; and to realize Awakening, one must realize this original way of being empty of self, being selfless (*anatman*) in order to give birth to True Life. Tokiwa says: "Lady Maya, the mother of Sakyamuni, exemplifies in her own being how ordinary human beings could be the tathagata's womb."[24] And this is to be "empty of that which prevents itself from emancipation."

At this point, I would like to return to the issue raised earlier, namely, that the person who has found this emancipation from suffering is the person who can truly suffer, and who in fact does suffer. We now see that the Formless Self (Emptiness/Nirvana) is that which is free from suffering and yet is that which goes through suffering as the ordinary self (form/*samsara*). When one lives the *tathagata-garbha*, one lives the Formless Self precisely because the womb and the embryo are one. This womb, this lived Emptiness, is our original way of being of contemplative wisdom and active compassion. Therefore, one lives what one understands as Emptiness through wisdom in active forms of compassion for the sake of others. In this life of compassion, one suffers with and for others. And in this suffering, one comes to understand more deeply that the Formless Self, which is Emptiness free from suffering, is the Great Compassion that just *is* suffering in ordinary history for the good of all sentient beings. Again the paradox is that with wisdom, one is, as Formless Self, free from suffering (Nirvana). And at the same time with compassion, one is an ordinary being that "goes through suffering" (*samsara*) for the sake of others. This is truly living the Bodhisattva Ideal as an "empty being." It is the True Life of the Formless Self born from the *tathagata's* womb, full of the compassion of that womb, for the benefit of all sentient beings.

Tokiwa relates this life of the Bodhisattva Ideal to Christianity when he quotes the five vows that Hisamatsu made while under the Bodhi tree in 1958. This is the tree in India under which the Buddha gained enlightenment. The first four have to do with following in the footsteps of the Buddha in order to gain Awakening for the good of all humankind. However, Hisamatsu's fifth vow has to do with Jesus Christ: "Let us respectfully follow in the fragrant footsteps of the Great Sage Jesus Christ, and bear the cross on ourselves, for our fellow beings' sake."[25] In reflecting on Hisamatsu's fifth vow, Tokiwa sees in the cross of Christ the Buddhist ideal of going through suffering for the sake of others. Tokiwa sees Christ as one of those sages "who left their fragrant footsteps behind, by taking the suffering of the world as their own, and by exemplifying the way for emancipation from suffering in their own way of being."[26] Tokiwa follows this reflection with another quotation from Hisamatsu:

In this world in our present life,
How nobly exalted these are:
The Golgothan hole for the cross
And the Bodhi tree of Gaya.[27]

Could it be that the "Golgothan hole" is the emptiness in which the cross can be lived? The *tathagata-garbha* is the womb of our original way of being that is compassionate living for the benefit of others. The Golgothan hole is perhaps the empty way of being that is necessary for planting this cross in order to give one's life for the benefit of others. This poetic image provides us with a rich source for meditation on the relation of Buddhist Emptiness to Christian kenosis. For the Buddhist, the womb is not an end in itself but the place to find the Buddha. For the Christian, the emptiness of the Golgothan hole is not an end in itself, but rather is a "place" in which one can find the cross. More, it is a place wherein one can find Jesus forsaken who is the true source, for the Christian, of living and dying for the sake of others, for the sake of the unity of all humankind. In this regard, it is interesting to note that Chiara Lubich also wrote a meditation on her experience of seeing this Golgothan hole during a visit to Jerusalem in 1955. In reflecting on how this "first cross" gives a name and a meaning to all the "crosses" in the "sea of anguish" that touches the lives of all of us, Lubich prays: "Here Jesus I want to plant once more my cross, our crosses, the crosses of those who know you and of those who do not know you."[28]

Finally, it should be no surprise that, given Tokiwa's notion of *tathagata-garbha*, he is quite taken by the Christian concept of the "Mother of God" (*Theotokos*). Tokiwa comments:

When I have a chance to see Christian paintings called *pieta*, I am deeply moved by the eternal truth of humanity: the mother of God embracing and watching and finally collapsing at the sight of the son, who died bearing the cross of all beings. In fact, in St. Mary I see what Buddhists call the Buddha's womb (*tathagata-garbha*).[29]

In the context of a Buddhist-Christian dialogue, Tokiwa gives his existential interpretation of how this mystery of Mary can be lived:

In my interpretation, when Mary was pregnant with the Son of God as a virgin, that means that Mary was the mother of the Son of God. The point . . . indicates a real truth about human beings, I think. And Mary stands forth. Mary is not just a woman, is not just a specific person, but Mary stands for all human beings, all humanity. All humanity can be the mother of God, that is my view. The same humanity always gives rise to this suffering and causes suffering, but the same humanity can be the mother of the Son of God, this is my point of view.[30]

In a letter to me, Tokiwa says that a photograph of a particular statue of Mary that I had sent to him is an excellent representation of humankind "at once in agony and in peace."[31] Here, we see Tokiwa's Zen thinking about Mary's representation of humankind as living *samsara* (agony) and Nirvana (peace) at the same time. For Tokiwa, the womb (*garbha*) as such "is samsara itself."[32] This is the ordinary history of humankind itself, humankind's ordinary way of being represented by the agony on the face of Mary. On the other hand, when the cause of *samsara* ceases, then this very *samsara* realizes its original way of being not as just a womb as such, but as the womb of tathagatas (*tathagata-garbha*), represented by the peace on the face of Mary. And when humankind lives this original way of peace sharing in the agony of the world for the sake of others, "it begins to exercise the productive nature of the womb of tathagatas."[33] And it seems to me that from the Christian point of view, in the hole of Golgotha, one can find the "productive" cross, the love poured forth from the love of God. This production can transform history into supra-history in which all humankind is made one on the basis of living together its original way of being. Humankind can become awakened in this original way of being both lived and represented by Maya and Mary. In this way, this original way of being, so beautifully seen in Maya and Mary, can give birth to itself in a new history of peace, wisdom and love.

◆   ◆   ◆

Gishin Tokiwa is certainly not the only Buddhist actively involved in the Buddhist-Christian dialogue who is interested in the Christian understanding of Mary. Often in dialogues, Buddhists will ask about Mary. They know that many Christians see Mary as a human person who has realized the fullness of the spiritual life. Therefore, Buddhists often are interested in this life of perfection realized by Mary. I personally feel that Buddhists can see in Mary the reflection of spiritual fulfillment, a model for the spiritual life and a source of spiritual maternity. It is this vision of Mary that I want to explore in the final section of this inquiry into the notion of Christian kenosis in relation to the philosophy of the Kyoto

School. And I would like to do so by responding to Tokiwa's study of Maya and the Buddhist notion of the *tathagata-garbha*. I will focus on the writings of two persons who base their reflections about Mary on personal spiritual experience. These persons are Maximilian Kolbe and Chiara Lubich. First, I will examine Kolbe's trinitarian understanding of Mary that I feel is an extension of my own trinitarian view of God. Then, in order to continue the central line of thought concerning communal spirituality and the transformation of humankind developed in the previous chapter, I will again turn to Lubich, this time for her existential interpretation of the life of Mary.

Kolbe, who today is recognized by the Catholic Church as a Franciscan saint, lived in Japan in the 1930s. After returning to Poland, he was arrested for the first time by the Nazis in 1939, about the time that Chiara Lubich was in Loreto. In 1941, he was arrested again and sent to Auschwitz where he died during that same year in the starvation bunker, taking the place of an unknown fellow-prisoner who had been condemned to death in reprisal for the escape of another prisoner. A few hours before his second and final arrest, Kolbe had time to put down on paper his thoughts about Mary. In these lines, one can find a certain understanding of Mary that had evolved over a period of twenty-five years. During those years, Kolbe had pondered the mysterious name Mary had given herself when speaking to Bernadette at Lourdes in 1858. She told Bernadette: "I am the Immaculate Conception." One would think she would say that she was conceived immaculate. How could she *be* her own Immaculate Conception?

For Kolbe, this question became his *koan*, so to speak, and it formed his life and his death. He would continually ask himself: "Who then are you, O Immaculate Conception?"[34] As with a Zen *koan*, the answer is not found apart from one's own existence. Rather, to gain an answer that goes to the ground of one's existence, one must become what one questions. So, too, for Kolbe who said that in answering this question, one must "learn to live according to it."[35] And for him this meant to be "Marianized" or "immaculatized" so as to *be* the question and to thereby be able to *be* the answer to this question. As a Christian, this meant that one must "resemble her [Mary] . . . and be changed into her."[36] So, what did Kolbe learn about Mary as the Immaculate Conception by living this existential Marianization? When we look at the last letter he wrote on February 17, 1941, we can see that the answer to his question had to do with his experience of the Trinity. And in reading this letter, one wonders if Kolbe was so Marianized that he experienced the life of the Trinity as it was the basis of Mary's conception, and in this way, answered his life's question.

In that final letter, Kolbe says that the "Father begets; the Son is begotten; the Spirit is the 'conception' that springs from their love."[37] This "conception," that is not *of* the Holy Spirit but that just *is* itself the Holy Spirit, Kolbe calls the "eternal Immaculate Conception." So for Kolbe, the Holy Spirit is an eternal and divine Immaculate Conception within God-Love. As one theologian puts it, for Kolbe, the Holy Spirit is "a divine motherhood of Love which unites Son to the Father."[38] This love and unity is for Kolbe the life of the Trinity: "God is Love; that is the Holy Trinity. The ebbing and flowing of love is what constitutes the life found in the bosom of the Trinity."[39] In my view, the mutual kenosis of the Father and the Son "conceives" the Holy Spirit, not as a something separate from themselves, but as the very kenotic love and unity that make them one. And it is this divine "mothering" of God's love and unity, as a creative Conception, that pours this Life from the womb of God forth in creation, redemption and sanctification as the three functions of the kenosis of God. Therefore, this spiritual mothering of the Holy Spirit is experienced in nature, in the new birth of redemption and the process of spiritual nurture in sanctification.

Kolbe believes, in good Franciscan fashion, that this spiritual mothering of the Holy Spirit as the eternal Immaculate Conception within the Trinity is also at the ground of all creation giving it a trinitarian structure. And he believes that the creature most filled with this eternal Immaculate Conception of Love is Mary. She is thereby the fulfillment of creation, the creature most perfect, and therefore the model for humankind in living Love, in "imaging" God as a person. Mary is such a model because, while we are all images of God, we image God in distorted ways in our "ordinary way of being." Mary, on the other hand, always imaged God in the "original way of being" that all humankind is intended to live. This she was able to do from the beginning of her life because of a special kenosis of the Holy Spirit. The eternal Immaculate Conception was in her from the moment of her human conception: "This eternal 'Immaculate Conception' (which is the Holy Spirit) produces in an immaculate manner divine life itself in the womb (or depths) of Mary's soul making her the Immaculate Conception, the human Immaculate Conception."[40] And for Kolbe, this is what Mary meant at Lourdes when she said, "I am the Immaculate Conception." She was made so by the eternal Immaculate Conception itself.

For Kolbe, Mary is the "personification of the mercy of God" in all its beauty.[41] Her person is empty of the self-centeredness that is at the basis of humankind's "ordinary way of being" which is so dissatisfactory. Thus, she personifies the compassionate love for others that is the kind of love that defines God as Trinity and which humankind was created to image. In her emptiness of self, she images Love as the original way of being of humankind. And in this emptiness of self, the life of God within her, the Immaculate Conception of the Holy Spirit, is a "productive" force that forms Christ within her womb. One can say that like Maya, Mary is the Great Womb of Compassion. By living this compassion she gives birth, by the grace of what she bore, to Christ. Also Maya is said to be transformed by the light of wisdom that radiates from what she carries in her womb. Mary bears within her the Holy Spirit which is the Wisdom of God. So, she is not only full of love and compassion, but is called the "seat of Wisdom." Here it is important to stress that from this Christian perspective, Mary was *made* the Immaculate Conception and the Mother of God by the grace of the Holy Spirit within her.

When Mary gives birth to a New Humanity, and a new history of humankind and the entire universe, she fulfills a particular historical task. In this task given to her by God, Mary is unique. But in another sense, she is also a model for all humankind. The life within her generated Christ in her womb that made her the unique person she was created to be, Mary the Mother of God. In a similar manner, when a person is empty of self, there begins, as the Buddhists note, the living of the "embryo" of new life. For the Christian, this means that when one begins to live the kenosis of self, that kenosis of love just is the embryo of living the trinitarian life within him or her. He or she becomes a womb of the Christ who can transform that person into the true person he or she was created to be. In this way of death-and-resurrection, he or she can then become the mediation of Christ for the creation of a new humankind.

There is another dimension to Mary that is very important to Kolbe. Mary is seen by him to be much more than a model for spiritual living. Her spiritual maternity enables her to be an instrument of the Holy Spirit for the sanctification of humankind. Kolbe felt, and the Catholic Church teaches, that Mary is the spiritual mother of all humankind. Where there is a realization of God's grace, she is present with her spiritual maternity, since it is a personification of the spiritual maternity of the Holy Spirit from whose kenosis all graces flow. Again, one is reminded here of Maya's claim that wherever there is the birth of a Buddha, she is present as the Great Womb of Compassion. For Kolbe, the spiritual maternity of Mary is the personification of the spiritual maternity of the Holy Spirit which makes her a "handmaid" for the sanctification of humankind.

Kolbe and his followers participate in this Marian task. Lubich and her followers also see themselves as participating in this task for world transformation. In fact, the official name given to the Focolare by the Catholic Church is "The Work of Mary." The members of the Focolare "live Mary" in order to give birth spiritually to Christ in the midst of the world in order to generate a New Humanity. As we conclude this examination of Kolbe's ideas about Mary and turn to Lubich's, I think it is interesting that Kolbe, Lubich and Hisamatsu all use the same image of fire for the life that unites humankind. Kolbe says that those who are being immaculatized "wish to burn with a love so powerful that it will set fire to everything in their milieu, and cause as many other souls as possible to burn with the same flame."[42] So now I want to go on to explore how this fire is brought about in Lubich's spirituality, for both personal and social transformation, as expressed in her understanding of the way of Mary.

Let me begin this section on the ideas of Chiara Lubich with a quotation from one of her meditations that echoes Kolbe's ideas that we have been considering. Here Lubich is meditating on the monastic life:

> She is the Mother of her Son, and through Him, the Mother of humankind. For the virgin that follows Mary's way her convent takes on the dimension of the world. Like a fountain of clear water, she is full of maternity toward souls, because she is a pure, shining, living image of God, who is Love. She is almost an incarnation of love, the outstretched arms of Providence serving humankind, drying people's tears healing their wounds and pointing out God to them.[43]

Now it is important to recognize that Lubich is not talking just about Mary here, but about a person who "lives Mary." That is, Mary's "way of being" is something that can be lived. And by living this way, one can be "immaculatized." For Lubich, this idea of living Mary was clarified in an experience she had while praying in a church. Prompted, she says, by the Holy Spirit, she asked Jesus why he had remained on earth, in every part of the world, through the eucharist, and yet had not found a way for his mother to remain on earth to help persons in their journey through life. Lubich says that from the tabernacle, in silence, Jesus seemed to be saying:

> I did not leave her because I want to see her again in you (in all of you). Even though you are not immaculate, my love will purify you, it will virginize you. You will open your arms and hearts as mothers to humanity, which as then, is thirsty for God and for His mother. Now it is up to you to soothe the sufferings, to heal the wounds, to dry the tears. Sing the litanies and try to reflect them.[44]

Therefore, the life of Mary has existential meaning for Lubich. This meaning is found in the formation by and of Jesus in the life of the person who lives Mary. To use Tokiwa's terms, by emptying out one's "ordinary way of being" (the negative kenosis of humankind) and living an "original way of being" (Mary), one is living the original image of God (Christ) in which one is created. By living Mary, one gives birth to Christ, one finds the formation of Christ as the source of one's True Life. And as Lubich says, this process is accomplished by Jesus. By living Mary, one finds oneself being lived by Christ. In Lubich's words:

> How then can I live as Mary? How can I let her characteristics harmonize my life? By silencing the creature in me, and letting the Spirit of the Lord speak out with this silence as a background. In this way I will live Mary and Jesus. I will live Jesus with the background of Mary. I will live Jesus by living Mary.[45]

How does one live Mary's way of being, this kenosis of silence as our original way of being such that in this "womb," one is immaculatized by the True Life that is formed and lived for the sake of all humankind? This leads us to Lubich's own explanation of the way of Mary. In her explanation, it is clear that Lubich saw this way of Mary in the events of Mary's life described in the Christian scriptures. And she saw that these events have existential meaning for persons today, in that each event represents a possible stage in the Christian spiritual life.[46] Lubich came to a special appreciation of this meaning by reflecting on the writings of Teresa of Avila. Lubich recognized that members of her own community were passing through stages of spiritual development similar to those described by Teresa. However, Teresa's "way" was written for persons in the monastic life while Lubich and her followers were mainly laypersons. So, she found in the events of Mary's life a particular way of sanctification that can especially apply to the life of laypersons. In Lubich's discussion of these events, and their corresponding stages of existential Christian growth, I find the kenosis of a model Christian. Therefore, I believe that these episodes in Mary's life can help us to understand the spiritual stages involved in the growth of a kenosis of love that contributes to the unity for which Paul was pleading in his letter to the Philippians.

Lubich chooses to focus on Mary as portrayed in Christian scripture, so she does not begin with the Immaculate Conception, but with the annunciation.[47] In this event, the angel Gabriel announces to Mary what God has in mind for her. Mary says: "Behold the handmaid of the Lord; be it done to me according to thy word" (Luke 1.38). Thereafter, the new life of Christ begins to grow within her womb. The redemptive kenosis of Christ, of which Paul spoke in his letter to the Philippians, began in the womb of Mary. In a similar way, at the beginning of the spiritual life, one experiences the inner growth of divine love. For the Christian, this is a making more fully present of the reality of baptism. As a person says his or her own "Yes," the new Christ reality begins to form within, the Word becomes more "flesh," as it were, within the "womb" of one's spirit. But for this to happen, a person must be empty of his or her plans, as Mary was, and be willing to enter a divine adventure of further kenosis and love, of death-and-resurrection. As one is more empty of self, then like a womb, one can experience the spiritual growth of new life within, the redemptive kenosis of Christ that physically grew in the womb of Mary. And as this life grows, one is *transformed* into what one has received and can *manifest* it in one's way of being. In this way of being, one can be transformed further into the image of Christ and *discover* and *recover* one's original and True Self as an undistorted image of God.

This new life within not only brings love and compassion but also "light" (*Claritas*). In that light, one can see God, one's life and the world in a different way. One finds a "seed" or "embryo" of enlightenment by which one can discover God-Love in all things. And in that Love, all the events of one's life, indeed of all forms of life, are seen to have a meaningful connection. In this interrelatedness of all in God-Love, it seems that one was born only for this new life that one is now experiencing. It seems that the whole universe from the beginning of time is taking form, in this moment, in the spiritual generation of new life within one's soul. Finally, in this light a person also finds a source of illumination that leads and guides one into the future.

In Mary's case, this enlightenment is seen in the second event, the visitation of Mary to Elizabeth.[48] Mary goes to help Elizabeth who is much older than Mary and further along in her own pregnancy. Mary does not go to tell about what was happening to her, but just to help Elizabeth, out of compassion and loving kindness. In kenotic self-forgetfulness, Mary lives the love of the new life within her and "makes herself one" with Elizabeth. Elizabeth returns that love which then becomes mutual. In that unity of love, there is also a unity in the light, in the truth. And Mary is able to express what she had understood by the enlightenment from the new life within her. In her song of joy, her Magnificat, she, like a clear and empty mirror, reflects and magnifies God: "My soul magnifies the Lord" (Luke 1.46). Upon her own nothingness she "images" the greatness of God. She sings forth from her original and true way of being in the world, a way of selfless love that images God-Love and is the way that all humankind was created to image.

Mary goes on to express the truth not only about herself but also about God and humankind. She tells how what is happening to her is connected to events in her people's history. And she tells how her place in these events will be regarded in the future. Mary also tells the truth about how God sees these events. She emphasizes that these events have to do with the salvation of the world which will liberate the humble and the poor, and will "pull down" the mighty and the rich. Here, the Magnificat is a prophetic call by the Word of God within Mary to work in the world for the liberation of humankind. I want to emphasize this point. Mary is *not* a model for a kind of *distorted kenosis* where one allows oneself to be dominated by others. To be empty of self, in the authentic sense, means to be empowered by God in freedom and openness in one's choice to give compassionate care *to* others, and also to be humble enough to accept the compassionate care *from* others when necessary. So Mary is a model of a kenotic love that seeks to aid and liberate *all* who are in need. Thus, in this second stage of spiritual growth, Lubich says that a person must translate his or her "Yes" into love. To say "Yes" to God-Love is to live that Love by being empty of self in order to go out of oneself to people in need, as Mary did. In this way, one can "make oneself one" with them in sharing their sufferings and needs. One can thereby echo Mary's Magnificat if one follows her example and lives the love and light of Christ within one's own nothingness. The new life within will express itself in deeds of compassion and words of truth that seek the liberation of humanity.

The next event is the birth of Jesus.[49] Here Mary offers the new life within her to the world. From the womb of Mary, in the midst of suffering, is born the Christian source of help and happiness for all sentient beings. When persons live this new life together in the mutual kenosis of mutual love, then God within them is born among them: "Where two or three are gathered in my name, there am I in the midst of them" (Matthew 18.20). This is a special presence of Christ in the midst of humanity. It is a mystical incarnation of Jesus in the midst of people that further unites them in the trinitarian life on earth. Here again we see the way of Mary not from an individualistic point of view but from Lubich's communal point of view. This is part of the spiritual genius of Lubich's thought and spirituality. It is not just that a person can *be* Mary, but persons together in mutual love can *be* Mary as a "communal womb" that gives birth to Christ among them. The inner Center is "born" as the communal Center. In this way, people living love and unity can relive together, spiritually and collectively, the birth of Jesus to Mary. And they can offer the world what is in one's spiritual womb, a new life of light and love that can unite humankind and make it one as the triune God is one.

Persons so united can offer the world this sacrament of unity for the liberation of humankind, the reign of Love.

In a spiritual sense, the kenosis of Mary is the womb, the horizon of nothingness, in which there is the self-determination of the Image itself. Through the kenosis of the Holy Spirit, the new life of Christ is within her and she becomes a "new creature." By living Mary in this spiritual sense, one can grow in the image of God, the original way of being until that inner presence develops to the point that it can be born, through a graced mutual kenosis of love, into the midst of persons. Here, Christ becomes a mystical communal Center that can unite persons and make them one in a collective reflection of the Trinity. This reflection of the likeness of the love and unity of the Trinity is possible upon the collective nothingness of the community. This incarnation among persons of what they carry in the spiritual womb at the inner Center of their being is the incarnation or the self-determination of the unity itself. And it is precisely this that makes humankind truly what it collectively should be. On the collective nothingness of humankind's communal nature, it can reflect the unity of God and become truly one humanity reflecting divinity.

The next event is the presentation of Jesus at the temple in Jerusalem.[50] This is an important moment in the spiritual life of Mary. Simeon confirms for Mary who Jesus is; but he also gives her an intuition of the cross. And he tells Mary that she, too, will participate in that painful event: "A sword will pierce through your own soul also" (Luke 2.35). Scripture says that the Holy Spirit spoke through Simeon. Lubich says that it is as though Mary is being asked to say her "Yes" for a second time. But this time it is a "Yes" to the cross. In a similar way, one can be drawn into a certain religious enthusiasm by the light, joy and splendor of God when Christ is born among us. It seems that he liberates one from suffering and is a constant source of joyful contemplation. But then through some word one hears, or something one reads or sees, a person realizes that this new life is not just for one's own consolation. Rather, it is for the liberation and unity of all humankind and the cosmos. And this ideal entails sacrifice and suffering, and ultimately the kenosis of the cross. So, as happened with Mary, there comes a time when one realizes who one has chosen and what one has chosen, namely, Jesus abandoned and forsaken. In this solemn moment, one is asked for his or her "Yes" a second time. And if one is to continue to be a "womb" that gives Jesus to the world as Mary did, to follow the "way of Mary," one must learn to say "Yes" again, indeed, again and again.

Next, we have the flight of Mary, Joseph and Jesus into Egypt.[51] Here, Mary makes her "Yes" concrete by fleeing Herod and leaving her home and her country for the sake of her child. In Herod's slaying of the innocent children, Mary experiences the suffering of the poor and oppressed at the hands of the rich and powerful. She sees how the evils of persecution and injustice lead to violence, pain and the death of innocent persons. She realizes why the cross is inevitable in the holy journey toward the liberation of humanity. That to which she had given birth is in conflict with the blind self-will that rules the world. Jesus is a sign of contradiction that inflames the wrath of those motivated in the world by blind self-will. So, Lubich says, a person who lives the new way of being of mutual love, united in the communal Center of God with others, will also encounter this type of opposition and will need to protect this new life as Mary did. Of course, when one is more mature he or she finds the strength and discernment to face and challenge the powers of oppression, or finds oneself used as an instrument of liberation by the presence of God within oneself and among the community.

While the flight into Egypt represents a situation where others are trying to destroy one's spiritual life, in the next event it seems that God himself is destroying that life. When Jesus is twelve years old, Mary loses him in the temple.[52] After searching for him for three days (symbolizing the three days between Jesus' death and resurrection), she and Joseph finally find him. Then Mary asks: "Son, why have you treated us so? Behold, your father and I have been looking for you anxiously" (Luke 2.48). To this "Why," that seems to prefigure his own "Why" on the cross, Jesus answers that he has been doing his Father's will. In a similar way, as one's spiritual life grows, a person knows times when God seems to abandon him or her. In these times, one experiences a taste of the abandonment of Jesus forsaken, of the kenosis of the crucified one. Lubich sees this as the dark night of the senses. In it, one is empty of joy and consolation. Everything bothers one, old temptations return along with impatience, anger, impurity and a desire to return to the old "ordinary way of being." One is empty of enthusiasm, lacks charity, and complains all the time. One is anxious about everything, and especially, like Mary, one is anxious about the kenosis of God he or she is experiencing in what seems such a negative manner.

This spiritual anxiety leads one to seek Jesus more and more until he is found again. And then one finds that, as Jesus told Mary, he was indeed in the temple doing the will of his Father. We are the temple of God, and throughout the dark night he was effecting an inner transformation hidden by the darkness of the night through which one was passing. After this night, out of its kenosis, one realizes that new life is not a product of one's own willfulness but a gift of God's grace. This realization gives one a deep sense of gratitude and thankfulness for this gift, and for all things. One also finds that the transformation of the night has led to a deeper union with God: out of the great darkness comes a greater light. And in this union, one goes on to live a hidden and intimate life with God as Mary did for many years after finding Jesus in the temple.[53] This is a time of sublime contemplation and communication from God about the things of heaven and the things of the earth. Christ within one grows more and more with his love, light and joy. And one is able to live more purely the new life with others in mutual love that keeps Jesus in the midst, as he was with Mary and Joseph as the source of their contemplation.

The next event in Mary's life that Lubich considers is the wedding feast in Cana of Galilee.[54] According to John, this is when Jesus performed his first miracle. It begins with Mary drawing Jesus' attention to a concrete need of the people: they need more wine. At first Jesus hesitates but Mary has the courage to again encourage him to act by telling the servants to do whatever Jesus tells them. So, Jesus goes ahead and changes water into wine. Mary had physically given birth to Jesus and is now giving birth, as it were, to his ministry. Mary had been living with Jesus in a life that was full of divine contemplation. But now she is moving from contemplation to action. Mary does not retreat from a problem of human need to simply be with Jesus, but asks Jesus to do a concrete action to solve the problem. So, Mary is not passive in her compassionate concern for human needs. As with Elizabeth, she sees a need and out of selfless compassion seeks to do something about it. Through her kenosis, she becomes less and less, and Christ becomes more and more, until she becomes an instrument of Christ's ministry. It is no longer she who acts but Christ who acts.

In a similar way, one's more hidden contemplative life with God at a certain point must emerge into a public active life with God for the sake, not only of oneself, but of all humankind. Through the kenosis of self, Christ grows within and among persons transforming them into the image and likeness of God. As one lives with others the mutual love and unity that images the Trinity, one develops more and more a universal concern for the needs of all humankind. One wants to see all humankind united as one humanity on the standpoint of spiritual love and unity. But more than this, one also finds that the growing presence of God within oneself and among oneself and others makes both oneself and the community a source of help and happiness for all in need. One not only has a greater altruistic aspiration to free everyone from suffering and join them to happiness, as Buddhists would put it, but one has a greater ability to do so. Through spiritual kenosis, the negative kenosis of ego-centeredness becomes less and less and Christ-centeredness becomes more and more until it is no longer the person or persons who act but

Christ within and among them who acts. Not only the person, but, from a communal point of view, the community with God as its communal Center becomes an instrument of God acting in the world. Through a mutual kenosis, the ministry of Christ can be born from the womb of the community for the liberation of the world. In this way the community lives Mary collectively as it gives birth to a self-determination of the unity of God for the unity of humankind.

This ministry of unity ultimately culminates in the crucifixion, for as was pointed out in the previous chapter, the key to unity is the cross. And here we find the most painful event in Mary's way of kenosis.[55] As Simeon had predicted, Mary finds that beside the cross, a "sword" pierces her soul with pain as she is spiritually one with her son in the pain of his dying. Lubich says that as Mary desolate, Mary adds her pain to that of Jesus forsaken. Faithful to him to the end, she is united in his passion. And her suffering and loss take on a redemptive meaning in this mystical union with Jesus forsaken. But for Mary, this is certainly the most diffi- cult moment for her faith. It is the moment Catholic's pray for in the liturgy for the sick: "May all who suffer pain, illness, or disease realize that they are chosen to be saints, and know that they are joined to Christ in his suffering for the salvation of the world."

There is a second aspect to the suffering kenosis of Mary. Because when Jesus sees Mary standing by the cross with John, he says to her: "Woman, behold your son!" And to John he says: "Behold your mother!" (John 19.26–27). So, Mary loses her son and her God, and Jesus is replaced as her son by John. Mary must renounce her son to embrace John. Mary had emptied herself of all things to have only Christ as her son. But now she must empty herself of even this most sacred reality to be a mother to John. She must be empty of everything to be love for this person who stands beside her.[56] But, it is precisely through this painful loss that Mary becomes mother of all humankind, repre- sented by John. And when, in a complete kenosis, she gives up her em- bracement of everything, in John she embraces all of humanity as her sons and daughters. Chiara Lubich says that in a similar way when St. Francis of Assisi lost his religious order toward the end of his life, his heart embraced many more people than just those in his order. Because of this, his spiritual maternity has over the centuries embraced many people of many faiths throughout the world.

Finally, there is a third aspect to Mary's kenosis at the cross of her son. In the first place, Mary desolate is united with Jesus forsaken in his redemptive kenosis on the cross. Second, Mary loses Jesus as her son. And then Jesus dies in the completion of his kenosis. In this third mo- ment, Mary's kenosis is also complete. She is plunged into the absolute annihilation of the cross. In this absolute annihilation, her kenosis and the kenosis of Jesus become identified. Mary, who had become less and less so that Jesus could become more and more, now becomes nothing. And Jesus, who had become more and more, becomes, through his own kenosis, nothing. The nothingness of Mary, once filled like a womb with Christ, becomes a nothingness filled with nothing. This spiritual and total annihilation is the great agony of Mary at the foot of the cross. It is an agony that is identified with the cross.

The kenosis of Mary is completed in the kenosis of Christ. By Mary's participation in the kenosis of Christ, her nothingness becomes complete. And thereby the duality between the kenosis of her soul and that of God is transcended into what might be called one "Kenosis-Mass." Mary and Christ are no longer two. Mary is transformed into Christ by this mystical participation in Christ. Jesus, at the moment of absolute kenosis when he dies on the cross, reaches the peak of his glory. When he is absolute negation, he has redeemed everything. As absolute kenosis, there is not one thing that separates him from all things. He has recovered everything into his absolute emptiness. His nothingness contains all things so that when his absolute negation is negated in the affirmation of the resurrection, the Holy Spirit fills that nothingness with the resurrection life. So all creation shines with new life. Christ in his kenotic union with all things brings them eternal life. Mary, in her union with Christ's death and resurrection, finds her son now in all humankind and all creation as well. Thus, she becomes the mother of all humankind who, as Kolbe also saw, "mothers" with the maternity of the Holy Spirit giving new life to all creation.

Mary, in her kenosis at one with the kenosis of Christ also sums up all creatures that are in that absolute kenosis of Christ. So by her participation in the kenosis of Christ, she too is filled by the grace of the Holy Spirit with the resurrection life. She is the model "new creature" and can say, again with Paul, "It is no longer I who live, but Christ within me who lives." And out of her own nothingness, in the absolute nothingness of God, also comes an affirmation of all things in the absolute affirmation of God. In this affirmation, as a negation of the negation in death-and-resurrection, she affirms all humankind as their spiritual mother and finds in all humanity, and nature as well, her son that she had lost. It is this grace, that comes from sharing in the absolute redemptive kenosis of Christ, that enables Mary to be the mother of humanity that Jesus asked her to be by giving her to John.

Lubich points out that in this way, Mary is a Christian model for one's own existential participation in the cross. One may encounter the cross in one's sufferings on the holy journey. When a person does this, he or she can unite himself or herself in that suffering with Jesus forsaken. In that unity with Jesus forsaken one "lives" Mary desolate. And one's own sufferings gain a redemptive meaning. However, in a particular time of desolation, it may be that one loses Jesus' consoling presence not just as Mary did at the temple, but as she did next to the cross. This is not a matter of the anxiety of the dark night of the senses, but of the agony of the dark night of the spirit. In this suffering, one's kenosis of self is merged into the redemptive kenosis of God. Yet, in this absolute kenosis, one's life is transformed so that one's heart is enlarged with God's own divine love and compassion that embraces all humanity and the cosmos. One can love with God's love and develop in that love, following the model of Mary, a universal spiritual maternity that embraces everyone.

And from that kenosis, one's mind is also illumined so that one can find the Son that was lost, in all things. One loves what one sees in all things, and one sees what one loves in all things. Therefore, by living Mary desolate, united to Jesus forsaken, one can existentially move from the cross to the resurrection, and participate in the maternity of Mary flowing from the Holy Spirit. As Lubich says, by living Mary, one lives Jesus. So by living Mary desolate, one lives Jesus forsaken. One's kenosis is one with the kenosis of the cross and so one finds, in a way similar to Mary, that through the purification of the cross, one's heart and mind embrace all humankind as a mother loves and cares for her children. In this way, one can live the maternity of Mary and become a mother of many souls. Again this is possible, not by the effort of one's own will, but because it is no longer oneself who lives but Christ within. And, from the communal point of view, this can be said of a community that lives Mary desolate together so that they can also live together the spiritual maternity of Mary for the sake of all humankind.

After the crucifixion, Mary goes to live with John: "From that hour, that disciple took her to his own home" (John 19.27). Again, when John refers to himself as "the disciple whom Jesus loved," he is asking the reader to identify with him. In fact, Mary is in the spiritual home, or home-ground, of all humankind. Her universal spiritual maternity embraces everyone. And as the bearer of Christ, she seeks to give birth to his love, light and life more fully in the hearts of all persons. It is not uncommon for one to first experience the new life of Christ and then after some time, if it is the will of God, come to experience the holy gift of a relationship with Mary. It is like Jesus giving Mary to John as his mother. Then one, like John, may find in his or her spiritual "home" the presence of Mary and thereby realize the part that she played, by the grace of the Holy Spirit, in Christ's birth in his or her life. But in any case, one can find in Mary a model that impels one to be a bearer of Christ for all humankind. Therefore, one can be encouraged by this example to expand one's heart to include all humanity, to be a maternal source of both spiritual and material help and happiness for everyone.

This leads us to the last episode in Mary's life that we will consider. Mary, while living individually with John, is found in the Upper Room united in prayer with the other disciples of Jesus.[57] She, at this last stage can say *fully:* "It is no longer I who live, but Christ who lives in me." She is here a model for transforming union with God—the final stage in Christian spiritual growth. And Mary, in her perfection, is a model for what every Christian should be, namely, another Christ with the particular personhood that God has given him or her. Lubich says that Mary is thus "all Word of God." She is the particular word of God that God has "spoken" her to be and *fully* reflects in this uniqueness the Word by which she is spoken by God. Therefore, in a special way, she is in the Upper Room in the center of the community as a spiritual mother bearing Christ among them. So, one finds Mary at the inner Center (John's home) and the communal Center (the Upper Room). In regard to the latter, earlier I spoke of three related events: the new presence of Christ within Mary, her giving birth to that presence in the world and her giving birth to his ministry. Now Mary is present in the community at the birth of the church, sharing the presence of what God has made her for the edification of all. She also adds her maternal presence to the mystical body of Christ, the church, that is filled with the resurrection life by the Holy Spirit at Pentecost. This is a special gift for Christians because she is the mother of the Christ that makes Christians the church. So, in this sense, Mary is the Mother of the Church as well as of all humankind. Mary is present as a spiritual mother in the spiritual home-ground of all persons. And she is also present as a spiritual mother in a special way in the church. While she is at the service of all humankind, she is in a particular way at the service of the church so that it, too, can be more fully a servant, or handmaid, for the sake of all humanity.

In this last episode of the way of Mary, one sees a model Christian. Living Mary is to live a spiritual maternity in the midst of community, living in mutual kenotic love with others so that Christ can be present in the midst. This presence is a source of the love and unity of the Trinity that unites the members of the community, makes them one, makes them the church. From Lubich's communal perspective, the community can be a collective Mary that lives this life together so that it becomes more fully the church, the presence of what it carries in its collective womb. Thereby the embryo can transform the womb into itself. The collective womb can give birth to its True Self, a communal imaging of the Trinity on earth. Mary demonstrates how, not only persons but the church, can become a fuller "spiritual womb" of the love and unity of the Trinity that embraces all humankind. In this way of Mary, the church, too, can become a more perfect sacrament of trinitarian love and unity.

In conclusion, we can now see that Mary's life presents the Christian with a model for a positive way of spiritual kenosis that can empty out the negative kenosis of our ordinary way of being. In living Mary, one can realize our true home-ground in God-Love and our original way of being in that trinitarian home-ground. And when persons live this Marian way in a communal kenosis of mutual love and unity, the dynamic kenosis of this trinitarian life can, by its self-determination among persons, realize the "merging" of these persons in that unity, gathering them together and making them one. Mary gives us a Christian model for the existential realization of a lived kenosis whereby one can discover this original and true way of being and contribute to a new and more united world. By realizing this True Life, Christians can give birth to the self-determination of unity itself for the benefit of all humanity. And they can thereby create a new history based on this spiritual standpoint for the liberation of all humankind, for the reign of Love on earth.

Notes

INTRODUCTION

1. The essay that Abe presented at the conference in Hawaii is published under the title: "Kenosis and Emptiness," in Roger Corless and Paul F. Knitter, eds., *Buddhist Emptiness and Christian Trinity*. New York: Paulist Press, 1990, pp. 5–25.

2. Donald W. Mitchell, "The 'Place' of the Self in Christian Spirituality: A Response to the Buddhist-Christian Dialogue," *Japanese Religions* (Vol. 13, No. 3: December, 1984), pp. 2–26.

3. This group was originally known as "the Abe-Cobb group," and is now the International Buddhist-Christian Theological Encounter Group.

4. Donald W. Mitchell, "Responses To Masao Abe," *Buddhist-Christian Studies* (Vol. 7, 1987), pp. 25–30.

5. This was especially the case at the third meeting of the Abe-Cobb group here at Purdue University, October 10–12, 1986. The topic of that meeting was "Notions of Ultimate Reality in Buddhism and Christianity." The proceedings of the dialogue are published in *Buddhist-Christian Studies* (Vol. 8, 1988, pp. 45–168; and Vol. 9, 1989, pp. 123–229). In emphasizing the importance of a sustained response to Abe's work from the point of view of Christian spirituality, I also recognize the importance of the kinds of sustained philosophical-theological responses being worked out by persons like Robert C. Neville and Steve Odin.

6. Donald W. Mitchell, "Compassionate Endurance: Mary and the Buddha, A Dialogue with Keiji Nishitani," *Bulletin of the Vatican Secretariat for Non-Christians* (Vol. XXI, No. 3, 1986), pp. 296–300; and "A Dialogue with Kobori Nanrei Sohaku," *Japanese Religions* (Vol. 20, No. 2: July, 1986), pp. 19–32.

7. Donald W. Mitchell, "Zen Meditation and Christian Prayer," *Zen Culture* (Vol. 124: April, 1987), pp. 121–130 [in Japanese].

8. Donald W. Mitchell, "Unity and Dialogue: A Christian Response to Shin'ichi Hisamatsu's Notion of F.A.S.," *F.A.S. Society Journal* (Spring, 1986), pp. 6–9.

9. Donald W. Mitchell, "Christian Mysticism and Shinran's Religious Philosophy," *The Shinshugaku Journal of Studies in Shin Buddhism* (Vol. 74: June, 1986), pp. 27–45 [in Japanese]; an English version of this paper is "Shinran's Religious Thought and Christian Mysticism," *Pacific World: Journal of the Institute of Buddhist Studies* (No. 4: Fall, 1988), pp. 15–22.

10. John B. Cobb, Jr. and Christopher Ives, eds., *The Emptying God: A Buddhist-Jewish-Christian Conversation.* Maryknoll, N.Y.: Orbis Books, 1990, hereafter referred to as *EG*.

11. Ibid., back cover. See Kung's own response to Abe's thesis in his "God's Self-Renunciation and Buddhist Emptiness: A Christian Response to Masao Abe," *Buddhist Emptiness and Christian Trinity*, pp. 26–43.

12. Ibid., pp. 142–143. Tracy attempts to do just this in his response to Abe by an examination of Eckhart and Ruuysbroec.

CHAPTER ONE

1. This view is perhaps most clearly developed in Masao Abe's "Kenotic God and Dynamic Sunyata," *EG*, pp. 3–65.

2. Lucien J. Richard, *A Kenotic Christology: In the Humanity of Jesus the Christ, the Compassion of Our God.* New York: University Press of America, 1982, p. 268.

3. Keiji Nishitani, *Religion and Nothingness.* Berkeley: University of California Press, 1982, p. 59, hereafter referred to as *RN*.

4. Richard, p. 261.

5. For an exposition of Nishida's concept of "pure experience" see his *A Study of Good.* Tokyo: Japanese Government Printing Bureau, 1960, hereafter referred to as *SG*.

6. Ibid., pp. 1–4.

7. Ibid., p. 36.

8. For an exposition of Nishida's concept of the logic of "place" (*basho*) see his *Intelligibility and the Philosophy of Nothingness.* Honolulu: East-West Center Press, 1958, hereafter referred to as *IPN*; also see his *Fundamental Problems of Philosophy.* Tokyo: Sophia University Press, 1970, hereafter referred to as *FPP*; and *Last Writings: Nothingness and the Religious Worldview.* Honolulu: University of Hawaii Press, 1987, hereafter referred to as *LW*. Also for a study of Nishida's work on this topic see:

Robert J. J. Wargo, *The Logic of Basho and the Concept of Nothingness in the Philosophy of Nishida Kitaro*. Ann Arbor: University Microfilms International, 1972.

   9. *IPN*, p. 136.
   10. Ibid., p. 134–135.
   11. Ibid., p. 137.
   12. *LW*.
   13. Ibid., p. 56.
   14. Ibid., p. 54.
   15. Ibid., p. 68.
   16. Ibid., p. 70.
   17. Ibid., p. 100.
   18. Ibid., pp. 86–87.
   19. Ibid., p. 111.
   20. Ibid., p. lll.
   21. *SG*, p. 186.
   22. Ibid.
   23. Ibid., p. 187.
   24. *FPP*, p. 106.
   25. *LW*, p. 104.
   26. Ibid.
   27. Ibid., p. 105.
   28. Ibid., p. 74.
   29. Ibid., p. 73.
   30. For a reference to Nishitani's use of "home-ground" see *RN*, p. 311.
   31. For an explanation of this idea in Dogen's view of Buddha-nature, see Masao Abe, *Zen and Western Thought*. Honolulu: University of Hawaii Press, 1985, p. 27, hereafter referred to as *ZWT*.
   32. See the *Heart Sutra* of the Prajnaparamita tradition of Mahayana Buddhism: E. Conze, *Buddhist Wisdom Books*. London: George Allen and Unwin Ltd., 1956.
   33. *RN*, p. 294.
   34. *EG*, p. 27.
   35. *EG*, p. 29.
   36. Hans Waldenfels, *Absolute Nothingness: Foundations for a Buddhist-Christian Dialogue*. New York: Paulist Press, 1980, p. 73, hereafter referred to as *AN*.
   37. *RN*, p. 99.
   38. Ibid.
   39. Ibid., p. 58.
   40. Ibid., p. 59.

41. Ibid., pp. 279–280.

42. Donald W. Mitchell, "Compassionate Endurance: Mary and the Buddha, A Dialogue with Keiji Nishitani," *Bulletin of the Vatican Secretariat for Non-Christians* (XXI: 3, 1986), p. 298.

43. Ibid.

44. *Summa Theologica*, I, Q VIII.

45. Ibid.

46. Kitaro Nishida says that Absolute Nothingness "lines" (*urazukeru*) all forms of existence. See *IPN*, p. 248.

47. *The Soul's Journey into God*, I, 14.

48. Ibid, II, 1.

49. Chiara Lubich, *When Did We See You, Lord?* New York: New City Press, 1979, p. 17.

50. Thomas Merton, *The New Man*. New York: Mentor-Omega Books, 1961, p. 89.

51. *The Living Flame of Love*, 1.11.

52. Ibid.

53. The Japanese Catholic theologian, Masaaki Honda, has treated this paradox of the identity of opposites in his work, yet unpublished in English, on ascending and descending transcendence. When one passes the vanishing point of the ego descending into oneself through meditation, one finds the Absolute Subject which is the same God one also finds when one passes the vanishing point of the ego in ascending through prayer to God in heaven. The former path is more Eastern while the latter is more Western.

54. Buddhists also recognize this unique potential in human beings.

55. St. Teresa of Avila, *Interior Castle*. New York: Doubleday, 1961, p. 207, hereafter referred to as *IC*.

56. Again Masaaki Honda points out in his work on descending transcendence, that in the East this Ground-God is understood more as Mother than Father.

57. I use here a term from the philosophy of Keiji Nishitani. See his use of "*moto*" in *RN*.

58. This identity of opposites (*soku*) is a topic of much debate in Japan today. See Seiichi Yagi, "Japanese Christian Theology in Encounter with Buddhism," *Buddhist-Christian Studies* (Vol. 2, 1982), pp. 131–135; and Masaaki Honda, "The Encounter of Christianity with the Buddhist Logic of *Soku*: An Essay in Topological Theology," in Paul O. Ingram and Frederick J. Streng, eds., *Buddhist-Christian Dialogue: Mutual Renewal and Transformation*. Honolulu: University of Hawaii Press, 1986, pp. 217–230.

59. Shizuteru Ueda, "Emptiness and Fullness: Sunyata in Mahayana

Buddhism," *The Eastern Buddhist* (Vol. XV, No. 1, Spring, 1982), p. 26. In his analysis of the Ten Oxherding Pictures, Ueda shows how it is that the experience of the fullness of nature (picture nine) follows after the experience of Emptiness (picture eight).

60. Ibid., p. 9.

61. Ibid., p. 19.

62. Chwen Jiuan A. Lee and Thomas G. Hand, *A Taste of Water: Christianity Through Taoist-Christian Eyes*. New York: Paulist Press, 1990, Chapter 9.

63. Ibid., p. 98.

64. Ibid., p. 157.

65. For this understanding of Absolute Nothingness, I am indebted to Professor Eiko Kawamura of Hanazono University in Kyoto, Japan.

66. *EG*, p. 27.

67. Shoto Hase, "The Structure of Faith: Nothingness-qua-Love," in Taitetsu Unno and James W. Heisig, eds., *The Religious Philosophy of Tanabe Hajime*. Berkeley: Asian Humanities Press, 1990, pp. 89–116.

68. Simone Weil, *Waiting for God*. New York: Harper and Row, 1973, p. 145.

69. Hase, p. 104.

70. Weil, p. 158.

71. Ibid., p. 126.

72. Ibid., p. 127.

73. My point here was also made by Hans Urs von Balthasar in his own reflections on the Kyoto School and the Buddhist-Christian dialogue. He rejects the view that sees "perfection in the 'one' and failure in the 'two.' " See his editorial, "Buddhism—An Approach to Dialogue," *International Catholic Review* (Winter, 1988).

CHAPTER TWO

1. *AN*, pp. 49–63.

2. *RN*, p. 85.

3. *AN*, p. 56.

4. *RN*, p. 89.

5. Frederick Franck, ed., *The Buddha Eye: An Anthology of the Kyoto School*. New York: Crossroad, 1982, p. 115, hereafter referred to as *BE*.

6. *RN*, see Chapter Three for a discussion of nihility.

7. *RN*, p. 235.

8. Ibid., 235.

9. Ibid., p. 3.
10. Ibid.
11. Ibid., p. 263.
12. Ibid., p. 141.
13. Ibid., p. 145.
14. Ibid., p. 143.
15. Ibid., p. 146.
16. Ibid., p. 144.
17. Ibid., p. 145.
18. Ibid., p. 146.
19. Ibid.
20. Ibid., p. 147.
21. *BE*, 122.
22. Ibid.
23. *RN*, p. 21.
24. Ibid.
25. Ibid., p. 18.
26. Ibid., p. 19.
27. *BE*, p. 126.
28. Ibid., p. 128.
29. *RN*, p. 145.
30. Ibid., p. 107.
31. Ibid., p. 150.
32. Ibid., p. 70.
33. Ibid., p. 58.
34. *BE*, p. 56.
35. *RN*, p. 74.
36. Ibid., p. 72.
37. *BE*, p. 57.
38. Ibid., p. 30.
39. *RN*, p. 264.
40. Ibid., p. 261.
41. Here, and throughout this book, my use of "dissatisfactory" to characterize existence as ordinarily lived is taken from David Kalupahana's translation of *dukkha*. See David Kalupahana, *Buddhist Philosophy: A Historical Analysis*. Honolulu: University of Hawaii Press, 1976, p. 57.
42. Thomas Merton, *Zen and the Birds of Appetite*. New York: New Directions Books, 1968, pp. 15–32.
43. Ibid., p. 22.
44. Ibid., p. 23.
45. Ibid., p. 24.
46. Ibid.

47. Ibid.

48. See Thomas Merton's dialogue with D.T. Suzuki about innocence and purity of heart in Ibid., pp. 99–138, especially p. 117.

49. Ibid., p. 127.

50. *The City of God*, XII.

51. Merton, p. 120.

52. See Masao Abe, "Transformation in Buddhism," and Donald W. Mitchell, "Personal and Social Transformation in Christian Spirituality: A Response to Masao Abe," *Buddhist-Christian Studies* (Vol. 7, 1987), pp. 5–30.

53. Merton, p. 120.

54. Ibid., p. 132.

55. See B. McGinn and J. Meyendorff, eds., *Christian Spirituality: Origins to the Twelfth Century.* New York: Crossroad Publishing Co., 1988, pp. 297–299.

56. *BE*, pp. 55, 56.

57. Ibid., p. 57.

58. Ibid., p. 60

59. See Robert Slesinski, *Pavel Florensky: A Metaphysics of Love.* New York: St. Vladimir's Seminary Press, 1984, pp. 134–138.

60. Ibid., p. 158.

61. See *ZWT*, pp. 231–240.

62. Compare with *ZWT*, p. 250

CHAPTER THREE

1. See: Roger Corless and Paul F. Knitter, eds., *Buddhist Emptiness and Christian Trinity.* New York: Paulist Press, 1990; and *EG*.

2. *EG*, p. 3.

3. Ibid., p. 4.

4. Ibid., p. 27.

5. Ibid.

6. Ibid., p. 28.

7. Ibid.

8. *ZWT*, p. 226.

9. Ibid., p. 227.

10. *EG*, p. 29.

11. Ibid., p. 31.

12. Ibid., p. 32.

13. Ibid.

14. Ibid., p. 33.

15. Ibid., p. 50.

16. Ibid., p. 33.

17. Ibid., p. 28.

18. Masao Abe, "Siddhartha Gautama and Jesus the Nazarene," unpublished manuscript, p. 7, hereafter referred to as SGJN.

19. *Samyutta-nikaya,* 22.87.

20. *EG,* p. 45.

21. *SGJN,* p. 5.

22. Philippians 2.4–8; I quote here the passage as given in *EG,* p. 9.

23. *EG,* pp. 9–10.

24. Ibid., pp. 10, 10–11.

25. Ibid., p. 11.

26. Ibid., p. 14.

27. Ibid.

28. Ibid., p. 16.

29. Ibid., pp. 16–17.

30. Ibid., p. 4.

31. Hans Urs von Balthasar, "Buddhism—An Approach to Dialogue," *International Catholic Review* (Winter, 1988).

32. Again I refer the reader to the books by Orbis and Paulist Presses mentioned in footnote n.1 above.

33. *EG,* pp. 19–23.

34. J. Moltmann, *The Crucified God.* New York: Harper and Row, 1974, p. 244.

35. Ibid., p. 278.

36. *EG,* p. 26.

37. Ibid., p. 25.

38. Ibid., p. 18.

39. Katsumi Takizawa, "On the Primary and Secondary Contacts Between God and Man," *Buddhist-Christian Studies* (Vol. 3, 1983), pp. 123–127.

40. Seiichi Yagi and Leonard Swidler, *A Bridge to Buddhist-Christian Dialogue.* New York: Paulist Press, 1990.

41. Lucien Richard, *A Kenotic Christology: In The Humanity of Jesus The Christ, The Compassion Of God.* New York: University Press of America, 1982, pp. 133–134.

42. Ibid., p. 251.

43. This mutual identity is implied in the notion of *soku,* that is: "Emptiness *soku* form" and "form *soku* Emptiness." This identity involves mutual determination so that apart from forms there can be no Emptiness and apart from Emptiness there can be no forms. In Bud-

dhism, the *soku* relation of mutual determination means that there is a mutual reversibility between the Absolute and the forms of the world. This is not the case in Christianity.

44. Richard, p. 268.

45. Ibid., p. 253.

46. Ibid., p. 167.

47. For what follows, I rely on Chiara Lubich, *Unity and Jesus Forsaken*. New York: New City Press, 1985.

48. Ibid., p. 32.

49. *BE*, pp. 56, 60.

50. Richard, p. 190ff.

51. J. K. Kadowaki, S.J., relates this Christian experience to Zen in *Zen and the Bible: A Priest's Experience*. New York: Routledge and Kegan Paul, 1980, p. 159.

52. Lubich, p. 64.

53. See my "Dialogue with Kobori Nanrei Sohaku," *Japanese Religions* (Vol. 14, No. 2, July, 1986), pp. 26–29.

54. For an excellent discussion of the development of Bodhicitta in the Bodhisattva Path, see: His Holiness Tenzin Gyatso, The Fourteenth Dalai Lama, "The Practices of Bodhasattvas," in Donald S. Lopez, Jr. and Steven C. Rockefeller, eds., *The Christ and the Bodhisattva*. Albany: SUNY Press, 1987, pp. 217–227.

55. Chiara Lubich, *Meditations*. New York: New City Press, 1974, p. 35.

CHAPTER FOUR

1. In his *The Logic of the Place of Nothingness and the Religious Worldview*, Nishida, while never mentioning Tanabe by name, also criticizes Tanabe's views.

2. Hajime Tanabe, *Philosophy as Metanoetics*. Berkeley, CA: University of California Press, 1986, p. lii. Also see Ch. 1, ftn. 67 above.

3. Ibid., p. lx.

4. Ibid., p. xxxvii.

5. Ibid., p. 2.

6. Ibid., p. li. Note that the divine qualities referred to here and in the previous quotation are "absolute light" and "new life." Amida Buddha worshiped in Shin Buddhism as the personification of Otherpower is the Buddha of infinite light and life.

7. Ibid., p. 3.

8. Ibid., p. 172.
9. Ibid., p. 8.
10. Ibid., p. 68.
11. Ibid., p. 235.
12. Ibid., p. 121.
13. Ibid., p. 124.
14. Ibid., p. 19.
15. Ibid., p. 22.
16. Ibid.
17. Ibid., p. 81.
18. Ibid.
19. Ibid., p. 143.
20. Ibid., p. 194.
21. Ibid., p. 10.
22. Ibid., p. 4.
23. Ibid.
24. Ibid., p. 8.
25. Ibid., p. 158.
26. Ibid., p. 155.
27. Ibid., pp. 170–171.
28. Ibid., p. 95.
29. Ibid., p. 119.
30. Ibid., p. 6.
31. Ibid., p. 45.
32. Ibid., pp. 6–7.
33. Ibid., p. 123.
34. Ibid., p. 204.
35. Ibid., p. 80.
36. Ibid., pp. 128–129.
37. Ibid., pp. 172, 213.
38. Ibid., pp. 82–83.
39. Ibid., p. 81.
40. Ibid., pp. 50, 206.
41. Ibid., p. 183.
42. Ibid., p. 140.
43. Ibid., p. 215.
44. Ibid., p. 220.
45. Ibid., p. 264.
46. Ibid., p. 284.
47. Ibid., pp. 290–291.
48. Ibid., p. 292.
49. This is the opposite of our static identity in the condition of origi-

nal sin where we live clinging to ourselves through the blind will to be and to possess.

50. John P. Keenan develops this notion of the "Abba experience" in his own work in the Buddhist-Christian dialogue: *The Meaning of Christ: A Mahayana Theology.* Maryknoll, N.Y.: Orbis Books, 1989, pp. 243–251.

51. See Jean-Pierre de Caussade, *Abandonment to Divine Providence.* New York: Doubleday, 1975.

52. Ibid., pp. 25–26.

53. Ibid., p. 36.

54. Ibid., p. 37.

55. Ibid., p. 29.

56. Ibid., p. 110.

57. Ibid., p. 56.

58. *The Living Flame of Love,* 1.13.

59. Ibid.

60. Ibid.

61. I again refer to my Buddhist-Christian dialogue on this topic; see my dialogue with Kobori Nanrei Sohaku: "Dialogue with Kobori Nanrei Sohaku," *Japanese Religions* (Vol. 14, No. 2, July, 1986), pp. 19–32.

62. Masao Abe, *ZWT,* p. 250.

63. Chiara Lubich, *Unity and Jesus Forsaken.* New York: New City Press, 1985, p. 32.

64. Ibid., p. 31. This kenosis of self, this poverty of spirit, in living the other is one of the most difficult aspects of Lubich's spirituality, as I shall explain later. Lubich remarks, "It is no easy thing. We have to be empty in ourselves: chase our own ideas out of our heads, our own affections out of our hearts, everything out of our wills, to identify ourselves with the other person." (Ibid., p. 32) Therefore the grace of Other-power is needed as an enablement to live this kenosis.

65. The two fires metaphor is a common theme in Lubich's talks to the members of the Focolare Movement.

66. Here I am stating the position of the Roman Catholic Church. See the church's statement on "Mission and Dialogue," *Bulletin of the Vatican Secretariat for Non-Christians* (Vol. XIX, No. 2, 1984).

67. See Arnulf Camps, *Partners in Dialogue: Christianity and Other World Religions.* New York: Orbis Books, 1977.

68. Ibid., Part III. Also see Robert Schreiter, *Constructing Local Theologies.* New York: Orbis Books, 1985.

69. Revelation, 21.2.

70. See John B. Cobb, Jr., *Beyond Dialogue: Toward the Mutual Transformation of Christianity and Buddhism.* Philadelphia: Fortress Press, 1982.

CHAPTER FIVE

1. Takeuchi, Yoshinori, *The Heart of Buddhism: In Search of the Timeless Spirit of Primitive Buddhism*. New York: Crossroad Publishing Co., 1983, p. xix, hereafter referred to as *HB*.

2. Ibid., p. 4.

3. Ibid., p. 11.

4. Ibid., p. 18.

5. Ibid., p. 30.

6. Ibid., p. 24.

7. This *Sutta* is part of the *Digha-nikaya*. See tr. T. W. and C. A. F. Rhys Davids, *Dialogues of the Buddha*, 3 Vols., London: PTS, 1899–1921.

8. *HB*, p. 39.

9. Ibid., p. 38.

10. Ibid., p. 35.

11. Ibid., p. 39.

12. Ibid., p. 40.

13. Ibid., p. 36.

14. *The Spiritual Exercises*, 23.

15. *HB*, p. 42.

16. See the *Itivuttaka*, 38.

17. *HB*, p. 51. This view is based on early Buddhist eschatology which claims that there are three periods of the Dharma, or Teaching of the Buddha. We are in the last period where genuine and full religious experience in Buddhism is not found.

18. Ibid., p. 57.

19. Ibid.

20. Ibid., p. 133.

21. Ibid., p. 135.

22. Ibid., p. 142.

23. Ibid., p. 58.

24. Ibid., p. 52.

25. I have in mind here the recent works of the Jesuits at Sophia University in Tokyo: (1) H. M. E. Lassalle, *Zen Meditation for Christians*. La Salle, Ill.: Open Court, 1974; (2) William Johnston, *The Still Point: Reflections on Zen and Christian Mysticism*. New York: Fordham University Press, 1982; (3) J. K. Kadowaki, *Zen and the Bible: A Priest's Experience*. London: Routledge and Kegan Paul, 1980.

26. Johnston, p. 5.

27. Lassalle, p. 48.

28. Ibid., p. 142.

29. Johnston, p. 53.

30. For a presentation of the Ten Oxherding Pictures, see D. T. Suzuki, *Manual of Zen Buddhism*. New York: Grove Press, 1960, pp. 127–144. Ueda's analysis of the Zen spirituality involved in this ten-stage practice is given in the above referred-to essay, "Emptiness and Fullness: Sunyata in Mahayana Buddhism," *The Eastern Buddhist* (Vol. XV, No. 1, Spring, 1982).

31. Ueda, p. 13.

32. Ibid., p. 17.

33. Ibid., p. 19.

34. Ibid., p. 34.

35. Ibid., p. 35.

36. Thomas Merton, *The Ascent to Truth*. New York: Harcourt and Brace, 1951, p. 8.

37. Examples from the Catholic tradition are the Benedictines, Carmelites, Dominican, Franciscans, Jesuits, etc. For a good history of these and other spiritualities, see L. Bouyer, J. Leclercq, F. Vandenbroucke, and L. Cognet, *History of Christian Spirituality*, 3 Vols. New York: Seabury Press, 1982.

38. *IC*.

39. Ibid., p. 31.

40. Ibid., p. 37.

41. Ibid., p. 32.

42. Bloom, Alfred, *Shinran's Gospel of Pure Grace*. Tucson, Arizona: University of Arizona Press, 1965, p. 38.

43. *IC*, p. 34.

44. Bloom, p. 38.

45. Ibid., p. 16.

46. *The Ascent of Mount Carmel*, I, 13, 3–4.

47. *IC*, p. 51.

48. Ibid., p. 47.

49. Bloom, p. 29.

50. *IC*, p. 56.

51. Ibid., p. 80.

52. *The Book of Her Life*, 11, 9.

53. *IC*, pp. 59–69.

54. Ibid., p. 66.

55. *The Dark Night*, I, 1–7.

56. See my "Response to Masao Abe," *Buddhist-Christian Studies* (Vol. 7, 1987), pp. 25–30.

57. *IC*, pp. 81–82.

58. Ibid., p. 87.

59. Ibid., p. 76.

60. Ibid., p. 84.

61. *The Living Flame of Love*, 3, 37.

62. *IC*, p. 97.

63. Ibid., p. 99.

64. Ibid., p. 100.

65. Ibid., p. 117.

66. Ibid., p. 116.

67. Ibid., p. 123.

68. Shinran, *Notes on "Essentials of Faith Alone,"* ed. by Y. Ueda. Kyoto: Hongwanji International, 1979, pp. 6–8.

69. *IC*, p. 158.

70. Ibid., p. 153.

71. Ibid., p. 194.

72. *The Spiritual Canticle*, 13–15.

73. *IC*, p. 165.

74. Ibid., pp. 169–178.

75. Ibid., p. 178.

76. Ibid., pp. 198, 200.

77. *The Dark Night*, II.

78. *IC*, p. 202.

79. Ibid., pp. 214–215.

80. Ibid., p. 218.

81. Ibid.

82. Joseph Cardinal Ratzinger, "Letter to the Bishops of the Catholic Church on Some Aspects of Christian Meditation." Vatican City: Libreria Editrice Vaticana, 1989, p. 16.

83. Ibid., pp. 17–18.

84. This distinction seems to me to be similar to the one drawn in Zen Buddhism between "original enlightenment" (*honkaku*) and "acquired enlightenment" (*shikaku*). We all are originally enlightened but must acquire an awareness of that fact, the fact of our enlightened existence.

85. Thomas Merton, *The New Man*. New York: Mentor-Omega Books, 1961, p. 85.

86. Lassalle, p. 144.

87. *The Spiritual Canticle*, 22, 4.

88. Johnston, p. 167.

CHAPTER SIX

1. Shin'ichi Hisamatsu, "Memories of My Academic Life," *The Eastern Buddhist (New Series)* (Vol. XVIII, No. 1, 1985), p. 10.

2. Ibid., p. 20.

3. Ibid. One is reminded here of spiritual scruples in Christian spiritual life.

4. Ibid., p. 21.

5. Ibid., p. 26.

6. Ibid., pp. 26–27.

7. Masao Abe, "Hisamatsu's Philosophy of Awakening," *The Eastern Buddhist (New Series)*, (Vol. XIV, No. 1), p. 33.

8. Masao Abe, "A History of the F.A.S. Zen Society," *F.A.S. Society Journal* (Autumn, 1984), p. 2.

9. Ibid., p. 5.

10. Ibid.

11. Gishin Tokiwa,"The F.A.S. Society," *F.A.S. Society Journal* (Autumn, 1987), p. 18.

12. Abe, "A History of the F.A.S. Zen Society," p. 6.

13. Ibid., p. 9.

14. Tokiwa, "The F.A.S. Society," p. 19.

15. "An Interview with Shin'ichi Hisamatsu," *F.A.S. Society Journal* (Winter, 1986), p. 2.

16. Shin'ichi Hisamatsu, "After My Student Years," *F.A.S. Society Journal*, (Winter, 1985–86), p. 2.

17. Shin'ichi Hisamatsu, "Ultimate Crisis and Resurrection, Part I," *The Eastern Buddhist (New Series)*, (Vol. VIII, No. 1), pp. 15–18.

18. Ibid., pp. 20–22.

19. Ibid., p. 26.

20. Ibid., p. 29.

21. Shin'ichi Hisamatsu, "Ultimate Crisis and Resurrection, Part II," *The Eastern Buddhist (New Series)*, (Vol. VIII, No. 2), p. 48.

22. Abe, "Hisamatsu's Philosophy of Awakening," pp. 31–33.

23. *ZWT*, p. 249.

24. Ibid.

25. Ibid., p. 253.

26. Ibid., p. 260.

27. Abe, "Hisamatsu's Philosophy of Awakening," p. 37.

28. Ibid., p. 39.

29. Shin'ichi Hisamatsu, "The Characteristics of Oriental Nothingness," *Philosophical Studies of Japan* (Vol. 2, 1960), p. 65.

30. Ibid., p. 72.

31. Ibid., pp. 80–85.

32. Ibid., p. 95.

33. Hisamatsu, "Ultimate Crisis and Resurrection, Part II," p. 52.

34. Ibid.

35. Ibid., pp. 12–13.

36. Hisamatsu, "After My Student Years," p. 2.

37. "An Interview with Masao Abe," *F.A.S. Society Journal* (Winter, 1985–86), p. 8.

38. Ibid.

39. "The Vow of Humankind: Talks by Shin'ichi Hisamatsu: Part I," *F.A.S. Society Journal* (Spring, 1986), p. 2.

40. Ibid., p. 4.

41. "The Vow of Humankind: Talks by Shin'ichi Hisamatsu: Part IV," *F.A.S. Society Journal* (Winter, 1988), p. 8.

42. Ibid., p. 9.

43. Ibid., p. 12.

44. Ibid., p. 13.

45. Ibid., p. 12.

46. "The Vow of Humankind: Talks by Shin'ichi Hisamatsu: Part IV, Section 2," *F.A.S. Society Journal*, (Winter, 1989–90), p. 8.

47. Shin'ichi Hisamatsu, "Ordinary Mind," *The Eastern Buddhist (New Series)*, (Vol. XII, No. 1, 1979), pp. 28–29.

48. "An Interview with Shin'ichi Hisamatsu," pp. 3–4.

49. Hisamatsu, "Ordinary Mind," p. 28.

50. "An Interview with Shin'ichi Hisamatsu, p. 7.

51. Edwin Robertson, *Chiara*. Ireland: Christian Journals, 1978, p. 6, hereafter referred to as *C*.

52. Ibid., pp. 10–11.

53. William Proctor, *An Interview with Chiara Lubich*. New York: New City Press, 1983, pp. 27–28, hereafter referred to as *ICL*.

54. Ibid., p. 28.

55. Ibid., p. 29.

56. Michel Pochet, *Stars and Tears: A Conversation with Chiara Lubich*. London: New City, 1985, p. 19, hereafter referred to as *ST*.

57. *C*, p. 30.

58. Chiara Lubich, *May They All Be One*. New York: New City Press, 1984, p. 27, hereafter referred to as *MTABO*.

59. *ST*, p. 25.

60. *MTABO*, p. 14.

61. Ibid., p. 28.

62. Ibid., p. 31.

63. Ibid.

64. Ibid., p. 33.

65. Ibid.

66. Ibid., p. 32.

67. Ibid., p. 80.

68. Ibid., p. 52.

69. *ST*, p. 103.

70. Ibid., p. 29.

71. *MTABO*, p. 68.

72. *C*, p. 97.

73. *ICL*, p. 63.

74. S. Lorit and N. Grimaldi, *Focolare After 30 Years*. New York: New City Press, 1976, pp. 64–80.

75. *ST*, pp. 137–150.

76. *C*, pp. 33–43.

77. Ibid., p. 41.

78. *ICL*, pp. 46–47.

79. *ST*, p. 88.

80. Donald W. Mitchell, "The Focolare Movement and a Buddhist-Christian Dialogue of 'Deeds and Collaboration,'" *Buddhist-Christian Studies* (Vol. 5, 1985), pp. 195–202.

81. Agnes T. Briones, "Rissho Kosei-kai and the Focolare Movement: A Way of Buddhist-Christian Encounter," *Unitas*, Vol. 60, No. 4, 1987, pp. 439–512. Also see Donald W. Mitchell, "The Focolare Movement and the Rissho Kosei-kai," *The Catholic World*, Vol. 233, No. 1395, May/June, 1990, pp. 105–108.

82. Chiara Lubich, *When Did We See You, Lord?* New York: New City Press, 1979, pp. 69–99.

83. Chiara Lubich, *When Our Love is Charity*. New York: New City Press, 1972.

84. Lubich, *When Did We See You, Lord?* p. 12.

85. Ibid., pp. 106–107.

86. Ibid., p. 110.

87. *MTABO*, p. 80.

88. Compare this with what Nishitani says about *ekstasis* in his *RN*, p. 6. For him this event takes place as one goes from self to ground of self. What I am suggesting is that the *ekstasis* takes place as one moves out of a static identity into a dynamic identity in the circuminsessional unity of the trinitarian life as the ground of selves.

89. *The Living Flame of Love*, II, 2.6.

90. Chiara Lubich, *Jesus in the Midst*. New York: New City Press, 1976, p. 43.

91. I base this claim, in part on my own contact with such persons in the Focolare as Igino Giordani (1894–1980). For a biography of Giordani, see: Edwin Robertson, *The Fire of Love: A Life of Igino Giordani "Foco."* London: New City, 1989. Excerpts from Giordani's journal are published in Igino Giordani, *Diary of Fire*. New York: New City Press,

1982. Also, Lubich herself discusses how this level of sanctity is possible in her talks on the way of Mary which I will present in the next chapter. Finally, for an overview of the Focolare Movement as a whole, see: *Unity–Our Adventure*. New York: New City Press, 1989.

CHAPTER SEVEN

1. Gishin Tokiwa, "The Emancipation of History," *F.A.S. Society Journal*, (Spring, 1979), pp. 7–10.

2. Ibid., p. 7.

3. Ibid., p. 8.

4. Ibid.

5. Ibid.

6. Ibid.

7. Ibid.

8. Ibid., p. 9.

9. Ibid., p. 10.

10. Ibid.

11. Gishin Tokiwa, "The tathagata-garbha as the Fundamental Subject of the Four Satyas," *Journal of Indian and Buddhist Studies* (Vol. XXXIII, No. 1, December, 1984), p. 13.

12. Ibid., pp. 13–14.

13. Gishin Tokiwa, "Chan (Zen) View of Suffering," *Buddhist-Christian Studies* (Vol. 5, 1985), p. 103.

14. Ibid.

15. Ibid., p. 104.

16. Ibid., p. 107.

17. Ibid.

18. Ibid.

19. Ibid., p. 108

20. Ibid., p. 111.

21. Ibid., p. 110.

22. Tokiwa, "The tathagata-garbha as the Fundamental Subject of the Four Satyas," p. 15; and "Chan (Zen) View of Suffering," p. 110.

23. Tokiwa, "Chan (Zen) View of Suffering," p. 110.

24. Ibid., p. 114.

25. Ibid., p. 126.

26. Ibid.

27. Ibid.

28. Chiara Lubich, *Scritti Spirituali*. Rome: Citta Nuova, 1978, p. 180.

29. Ibid., p. 108.

30. Ibid., p. 148.

31. This letter, written on May 28, 1984, refers to a statue by the contemporary Italian artist, Ave, of Centro Ave in Loppianno, Italy.

32. Tokiwa, "The tathagata-garbha as the Fundamental Subject of the Four Satyas," p. 18.

33. Ibid.

34. H. M. Manteau-Bonamy, *Immaculate Conception and the Holy Spirit: The Marian Teachings of Father Kolbe*. Kenosha, Wi.: Franciscan Marytown Press, 1977, p. xxxiii.

35. Ibid., p. xxv.

36. Ibid., p. xxii.

37. Ibid., p. 3.

38. Ibid., p. 68.

39. Ibid., p. 30.

40. Ibid., p. 4, from Kolbe's letter of February 17, 1941.

41. Ibid., p. 96.

42. Ibid., p. 115.

43. Chiara Lubich, *Meditations*. New York: New City Press, 1974, p. 143.

44. Chiara Lubich, *L'attrativa del Tempo Moderno*. Rome: Citta Nuova Press, 1978, p. 58.

45. Lubich, *Meditations*, p. 20.

46. Chiara Lubich has spoken about her insights concerning Mary and the way of Mary in certain talks. A talk given on June 15, 1971, is summarized in *C*, pp. 84–99. What follows in this section of my last chapter is *my* interpretation of Lubich's ideas in comparison to the Buddhist ideas we have been considering. Tokiwa is familiar with Lubich and her writings on this topic, and in his letter to me dated May 28, 1984, he says: "This is a pinnacle in my approach to Mary. Here is a person (Chiara Lubich) who does live Mary."

47. Luke 1.26–38.

48. Ibid., 1.39–56.

49. Ibid., 2.1–20.

50. Matthew 2.13–23.

51. Luke 2.22–39.

52. Ibid., 2.41–51.

53. Ibid., 2.52.

54. John 2.1–10.

55. Ibid., 19.25–27.

56. One is reminded here of the Buddhist caution that in full enlightenment, one must empty out Emptiness, and this is true compassion for all sentient beings.

57. Acts, 1.14.